Complex Organizations
A Critical Essay / Second Edition

Complex Organizations
A Critical Essay / Second Edition

CHARLES PERROW
State University of New York at Stony Brook

Academic Consultants
Albert J. Reiss, Jr.
Harold L. Wilensky

Scott, Foresman and Company **Glenview, Illinois**
Dallas, Tex.   Oakland, N.J.   Palo Alto, Cal.
Tucker, Ga.   London, England

Cover: M. C. Escher, "Cubic Space Division," Escher Foundation-Haags Gemeente-museum-The Hague.

Library of Congress Cataloging in Publication Data

Perrow, Charles.
   Complex organizations.

   Bibliography: p. 248
   Includes index.
   1. Organization.   I. Title.
HM131.P382   1978   301.18'32   78-24300
ISBN 0-673-15205-7

1 2 3 4 5 6-GBC-84 83 82 81 80 79 78

Acknowledgements

From EXPLORATION IN MANAGEMENT by Wilfred Brown. Copyright © 1960 by Wilfred Brown. Reprinted by permission of John Wiley & Sons, Inc.

From "Introduction" by Talcott Parsons in Max Weber, THE THEORY OF SOCIAL AND ECONOMIC ORGANIZATIONS, translated by Talcott Parsons. Copyright 1947 by Talcott Parsons. Renewed 1975 by Talcott Parsons. Reprinted by permission of Macmillan Publishing Co., Inc.

From LAWRENCE AND OPPENHEIMER by Nuel Pharr David. Copyright © 1968 by Nuel Pharr David. Reprinted by permission of Simon & Schuster, a Division of Gulf & Western Corporation and The Sterling Lord Agency, Inc.

Reinhard Bendix. WORK AND AUTHORITY IN INDUSTRY: IDEOLOGIES OF MANAGEMENT IN THE COURSE OF INDUSTRIALIZATION. Berkeley: University of California Press, 1974, p. 254.

Rev. M. D. Babcock as quoted in A. W. Griswold, *The American Gospel of Success.* Cited in Reinhard Bendix, WORK AND AUTHORITY IN INDUSTRY: IDEOLOGIES OF MANAGEMENT IN THE COURSE OF INDUSTRIALIZATION. Berkeley: University of California Press, 1974, p. 257.

From C. R. Henderson, "Business Men and Social Theorists," *American Journal of Sociology*, Volume I (1896). Cited in Reinhard Bendix, WORK AND AUTHORITY IN INDUSTRY: IDEOLOGIES OF MANAGEMENT IN THE COURSE OF INDUS-TRIALIZATION. Berkeley: University of California Press, 1974, p. 257.

From N. C. Fowler, *The Boy, How to Help Him Succeed.* Cited in Reinhard Bendix, WORK AND AUTHORITY IN INDUSTRY: IDEOLOGIES OF MANAGEMENT IN THE COURSE OF INDUSTRIALIZATION. Berkeley: University of California Press, 1974, p. 259.

Elbert Hubbard, *A Message to Garcia.* Cited in Reinhard Bendix, WORK AND AUTHORITY IN INDUSTRY: IDEOLOGIES OF MANAGEMENT IN THE COURSE OF INDUSTRIALIZATION. Berkeley: University of California Press, 1974, pp. 264–265.

David M. Perry, *Proceedings of the National Association of Manufacturers*, 1903. Cited in Reinhard Bendix, WORK AND AUTHORITY IN INDUSTRY: IDEOLOGIES OF MANAGEMENT IN THE COURSE OF INDUSTRIALIZATION. Berkeley: University of California Press, 1974, p. 266.

A. W. Griswold, *The American Gospel of Success.* Cited in Reinhard Bendix, WORK AND AUTHORITY IN INDUSTRY: IDEOLOGIES OF MANAGEMENT IN THE COURSE OF INDUSTRIALIZATION. Berkeley: University of California Press, 1974, p. 267.

From *The Review*, October 1910. Cited in Reinhard Bendix, WORK AND AU-THORITY IN INDUSTRY: IDEOLOGIES OF MANAGEMENT IN THE COURSE OF INDUSTRIALIZATION. Berkeley: University of California Press, 1974, p. 271.

Frederick W. Taylor, as quoted in F. B. Copley, *Frederick W. Taylor.* Cited in Reinhard Bendix, WORK AND AUTHORITY IN INDUSTRY: IDEOLOGIES OF MANAGEMENT IN THE COURSE OF INDUSTRIALIZATION. Berkeley: University of California Press, 1974, p. 280.

From *The Management Review*, Volume XVII (February 1928). Cited in Reinhard Bendix, WORK AND AUTHORITY IN INDUSTRY: IDEOLOGIES OF MANAGE-MENT IN THE COURSE OF INDUSTRIALIZATION. Berkeley: University of California Press, 1974, p. 294.

From *The Management Review*, Volume XXIV (June 1935). Cited in Reinhard Bendix, WORK AND AUTHORITY IN INDUSTRY: IDEOLOGIES OF MANAGEMENT IN THE COURSE OF INDUSTRIALIZATION. Berkeley: University of California Press, 1974, p. 296.

Preface

to the First Edition

Many conceits go into the writing of books, and one of those found in textbooks is the hope that the effort will reward both the student and the specialist. I have such a hope. I have sought a casual style and a critical posture in order to hold the attention of the student and convince him of the importance and intrinsic interest of the subject matter. At the same time, I have attempted to provoke my fellow theorists to follow me through a discussion of the most critical problem our field faces—choosing from competing views about the nature of large, complex organizations.

Some critics may conclude that I have used the device of discussing the major perspectives on organizations in order to indulge a hostility toward them and the uses to which they put their power. Other critics, perhaps more charitable, may conclude that I have used a currently fashionable aversion to large organizations among college students as a means of enticing the students to learn something about the field. There is some truth in both charges. Organizational theory could benefit from a hostile perspective; it has been altogether too accommodating to organizations and their power. Students could benefit a great deal from more knowledge about both the necessity of organizations in our present social system and their inescapably authoritarian character. How else are we, students or teachers, to effectively guard against them or attempt to redirect their enormous power? Existing theories offer little hope; they provide fragmented, truncated, or romantic views of the nature of these beasts. I have, therefore, tried to bring about a realistic synthesis of worthwhile ideas in organizational theory; if successful, such a synthesis might influence both research on organizations and attempts to control their impact upon us.

Although this book criticizes some rather eminent people, it is a pleasure to say that each of those eminent people to whom I dared send drafts of my criticisms has enriched the final version. The most searching commentary came from my former teacher and mentor, Philip Selznick, who responded at length and to good effect to the first draft of the final chapter, where his views are extensively criticized. As an academic consultant, Harold Wilensky was responsible for reading the whole manuscript; he helped not only in many places neutral to his concerns, but also in those places where his own views were questioned. Peter Blau, who does not come in for much criticism, was gracious where he did, as was Herbert Simon.

George Strauss worked hard to keep me from going off the deep end in my analysis of the human relations movement, which he understands so well, and Larry Cummings registered perceptive, but fruitless, disagreement with the same chapter. Guenther Roth saved me from some awkward errors regarding Weber; Anthony Tillet put aside his admiration for Barnard to add some fuel to my fire, while William Form tried to cool it. Michael Savage and Richard Hamilton both contributed to the final chapter, and students in Pittsburgh, Madison, Berkeley, and Stony Brook helped me more than they knew as I struggled with my thoughts under the guise of teaching them.

One final conceit—that this is a book worthy of a dedication: To Edith.

Charles Perrow
Stony Brook, New York

Preface

to the Second Edition

I have done very little cutting of the first edition; there is no such thing as a loving scalpel, and I have an immodest affection for this book. There are additions to all chapters, some substantial. In particular, there is a discussion of new ideas at the micro level at the end of Chapter 3, the chapter on the human relations tradition, and some attention to the notion of organized anarchies and a further consideration of unobtrusive controls in Chapter 4. The most important addition is a new chapter considering very recent developments in conceptualizing the environment; for example, the striking consequences of examining networks of organizations rather than individual organizations. The first edition closed with a baleful hope, now excised, that somehow the institutional school and the neo-Weberian approach might inform one another. In the new chapter, I try to show how this hope is being realized with a burst of exciting work on networks, industries, and power by young theorists.

Some formal reviews of the first edition in the United States disappointed me because they ignored what I thought was the main thrust—the idea of organizations as powerful, though recalcitrant, tools in the hands of their masters, in contrast to system views, rational management theorist views, the human relations perspective, and the organization as the product of its environment. (European reviewers highlighted the tool view.) I have tried to sharpen this key point in several places. But at the same time I now see it as qualified by the notion of a *society of organizations*, wherein organizations are caught in a dense web of interdependencies such that they are also multipurpose tools for a variety of groups outside the organization as well as within it. Reconciling the obvious stability and power of large organizations—consistent with a tool view—with the notion of multipurpose usages and organized anarchies is a problem I have yet to solve, though it may be an example of the Marxism notion of contradiction. Thus, the reader may share with me some tension in the book between these two themes or realities.

I am grateful to Albert Reiss, Richard Hall, and John Meyer for their comments on the new chapter, and again to Harold Wilensky for an incisive critique of the whole volume.

Many readers have told me of their pleasure in reading the first edition, and more than anything else this has motivated me not to just update references and add a chapter, but to try again to produce a work worthy of a dedication—most of all again to Edith, and now in addition, to all those good people whose comments on the first edition put genuine excitement in my attempts to extend and improve this one.

Charles Perrow
Stony Brook, New York

Contents

Complex Organizations
A Critical Essay / Second Edition

1

Why Bureaucracy?

Tawas

Several miles from a medium-sized city near one of the Great Lakes there was a company which mined gypsum rock, crushed it, mixed it with bonding and foaming agents, spread it out on a wide sheet of paper, covered it with another sheet, let it set a bit, sliced it into large but inedible sandwiches, and then dried them. The resulting material was sold as wallboard, used for insulation and for dividing up rooms in buildings. Plants such as this were scattered about the country, some of them owned, as was this one, by "General Gypsum Corporation" (a pseudonym). A book by Alvin Gouldner, *Patterns of Industrial Bureaucracy*, described the plant and the surrounding communities as they existed in 1950.[1]

The towns around the plant were small and had been settled about a century before. The people in the area generally knew one another well and looked with lengthy misgivings upon strangers. They led a peaceful, semirural life, with an emphasis upon farming, hunting, and fishing. They were conservative in their outlook, straight-laced in their behavior, and, according to one member, "thrifty, religious, God-fearing, and anti-Semitic."[2]

The gypsum plant fitted comfortably into the style of life in the area. Most of the men working at the plant, some 225 including the miners, had worked there for many years. They knew one another well on the job and visited outside of the plant in the surrounding hamlets. Indeed, perhaps as many as one half of the workers were related to others employed in the plant. The personnel man who hired and fired people argued that it was good to learn something about a prospective employee by asking others in the plant or com-

---

[1]Alvin Gouldner, *Patterns of Industrial Bureaucracy* (New York: The Free Press, 1954).
[2]Ibid., p. 35.

munity about him and his family. He did not want hostile employees or troublemakers. He also preferred farm boys over city boys. The former worked harder, he thought, and took greater pride in their work. The personnel man had few other rules for hiring, firing, or other matters with which he had to deal, however. He disliked paper work and, as one employee said, "He regarded everything that happened as an exception to the rule." He had only an eighth-grade education, but since he relied so heavily upon the community norms and his own rule-of-thumb methods, not much education seemed to be required. Apparently, hardly anyone was ever fired from the plant. Even those who left during the war years to work in defense plants paying much higher wages were welcomed back when those plants closed. A city boy, however, or a stranger laid off by a defense plant in the city had a hard time getting a job from this man.

In the plant itself, the workers had considerable leeway. The men were able to try different jobs until they found one that they liked, as long as they did it within the general limits of their union regulations. Moreover, they stretched out their lunch hours, were allowed to arrive late as long as they had some excuse, and were not required to keep busy. As long as their work was done, their time was their own. Production records were kept informally. The trouble was that the company management felt that not enough work was being done.

Further, the rhythm of the plant was, to some degree, determined by the men. During hunting season fewer showed up; the same thing sometimes occurred during planting season since many employees farmed in their spare time. In cold weather more of them complained of sprains or other ailments so they could be transferred to the "sample room," where the work was light and the room was warm, until they were feeling better. This was preferable to staying at home and using up sick leave or to living off unemployment compensation. Mining operations fell off considerably on Mondays because of hangovers among the heavy-drinking miners. As a mill foreman explained, "You can't ride the men very hard when they are your neighbors. Lots of these men grew up together."[3]

Many employees used the plant materials and services freely. Men took dynamite home with them to explode in ponds (an easy way to fish), and for construction. They appropriated quantities of wallboard, even truckloads, for their personal use. They brought in broken items such as furniture to be fixed by the carpenters. And both employees and farmers in the area brought in broken parts for free welding.

---

[3]Ibid., p. 65.

For the workers, the plant was a pleasant and comfortable operation. One could hardly "get ahead," but few desired to go wherever "ahead" was. Those who showed a desire to advance in the company got transfers to company plants in different areas. Others left for the big city.

But for other interested parties, the plant was not all that satisfying. A jobseeker found it difficult to get work if he was not well known, did not have relatives in the plant, or did not measure up to the vague standards of the personnel man—which had little to do with the ability to do the job. The customer found deliveries erratic. He might also suspect that if all gypsum plants were run this way, he would be paying a surcharge to cover the purloined materials, repair work, and general laziness. Top managers in the company headquarters, faced with intense postwar competition from other companies and competing products, were apparently climbing the walls.

When the plant manager died ("Old Doug," he was affectionately called), headquarters sent in an aggressive new manager with orders to tighten things up—increase productivity and cut costs. According to Gouldner's account, this man was not blessed with bountiful tact and insight, even though he was an otherwise efficient manager. He cracked down rather hard and accumulated much ill will. He activated dormant rules, instituted new ones, demoted the personnel man, and brought in one who applied a "universalistic" standard—the only thing that counted was a man's ability to do the job. The new manager also successfully "bureaucratized" the surface plant (though not the more dangerous mine, for there was too much uncertainty and unpredictability in the work, and teamwork was extremely important). However, some time later he was faced with a wildcat strike.

What had been a "traditional" form of organization, or in the terms of Max Weber,[4] a "traditional bureaucracy," became a "rational-legal bureaucracy." A rational-legal bureaucracy is based

---

[4]The famous German sociologist, writing in the early decades of this century, laid out the model of bureaucracy and described and explained its origins. Weber's writings on bureaucracy appear in two different parts of an uncompleted draft of his opus, *Economy and Society*. The first part is presented in Max Weber, *The Theory of Social and Economic Organization*, trans. A. M. Henderson and Talcott Parsons (New York: Oxford University Press, Inc., 1947), pp. 324–340. The second part, which was actually written first and is a more discursive section, appears in Max Weber, *From Max Weber, Essays in Sociology*, trans. and ed. by Hans Gerth and C. Wright Mills (New York: Oxford University Press, Inc., 1946), pp. 196–244. A newer edition of *Economy and Society*, ed. Guenther Roth and Claus Wittich (New York: Irvington Publications, 1968) has been prepared. The relevant pages there are vol. 1, pp. 212–225 and vol. 3, pp. 956–1001.

upon rational principles (rational from management's point of view) backed up by legal sanctions and existing in a legal framework. A miner fired for taking a case of dynamite, for example, was unsuccessful in his appeal that "everyone did it" and that the foreman "told him he could." Tradition or precedent was not binding; the material belonged to the company, not to the miner or the foreman.

Not all elements of the rational-legal bureaucracy are represented in this brief case history, but several are. The bureaucratization of the plant involved the following:

1. Equal treatment for all employees;

2. A reliance upon expertise, skills, and experience relevant to the position;

3. No extraorganizational prerogatives of the position (such as taking dynamite, wallboard, etc.); that is, the position was seen to belong to the organization, not to the person. The employee could not use it for his personal ends;

4. The introduction of specific standards of work and output;

5. The keeping of complete records and files dealing with the work and output;

6. The setting up and enforcing of rules and regulations that served the interests of the organization;

7. A recognition that rules and regulations were binding upon managers as well as upon employees; thus employees could hold management to the terms of the employment contract.

The rational-legal form of bureaucracy developed over many centuries in Western civilization. It grew slowly and erratically since the Middle Ages and reached its full form on a widespread basis only in the twentieth century.[5] Most all large, complex organizations in the United States, for example, are best classified as bureaucracies, though the degree and forms of bureaucratization vary.

Its "ideal" form, however, is never realized for a variety of reasons. For one thing, it tries to do what must be (hopefully) forever impossible—to eliminate all unwanted extraorganizational influences upon the behavior of members. Ideally, members should act only in the organization's interests. The problem is that even if the interest of the organization is unambiguous, men do not exist just for organizations. They track all kinds of mud from the rest of their lives with them into the organization, and they have all kinds of interests that are independent of the organization.

The ideal form also falls short of realization when rapid changes in some of the organizational tasks are required. *Bureaucracies are set up to deal with stable, routine tasks; that is the basis of organiza-*

---

[5]See Reinhard Bendix, "Bureaucracy," in *International Encyclopedia of the Social Sciences* (New York: The Free Press, 1977).

tional efficiency. Without stable tasks there cannot be a stable division of labor, a prescribed acquisition of skills and experience, formal planning and coordination, and so on. But when changes come along, organizations must alter their programs; when such changes are frequent and rapid, the form of organization becomes so temporary that the efficiencies of bureaucracy cannot be realized. (The price of the output then goes up.) The gypsum mine could not be bureaucratized to the degree that the surface plant was because the unpredictability of the seams and the dangers and variability of the raw material made continual change and improvisation necessary.

Finally, bureaucracy in its ideal form falls short of its expectations because men are only indifferently intelligent, prescient, all-knowing, and energetic. All organizations must be designed for the "average" person one is likely to find in each position, not the superman.

Whatever the limitations imposed by extraorganizational influences, changing tastes, and the variability of human capacities, most large organizations are bureaucratic; the rational-legal form of bureaucracy is the most efficient form of administration known. It may not be, as Weber claimed, that all else is dilettantism; but some of the alternative forms are clearly very expensive, unstable, short-lived, or rare.

Bureaucracy is a remarkable product of gradual, halting, and often unwitting social engineering. Most elements were in place before the spurt of industrialization in the nineteenth century; it was this spurt and the associated control over employees that destroyed most other forms of large-scale organized activity. Without this form of social technology, the industrialized countries of the West could not have reached the heights of extravagance, wealth, and pollution that they currently enjoy. In the rest of this chapter, we shall explore the essentials of bureaucracy by examining what takes place when the principles are violated by organizations, and by illustrating the difficulty of achieving complete bureaucratization of organizations.

First, however, I would like to state my own biases. After twenty years of studying complex organizations, I have come to two conclusions that run counter to much of the organizational literature. The first is that the sins generally attributed to bureaucracy are either not sins at all or are consequences of the failure to bureaucratize sufficiently. In this respect, I will defend bureaucracy as the dominant principle of organization in our large, complex organizations. My second conclusion is that the extensive preoccupation with reforming, "humanizing," and decentralizing bureaucracies, while salutary, has served to obscure from organizational theorists the true nature of bureaucracy and has diverted us from assessing its impact upon society. The impact upon society in general is incalculably more important than the impact upon the members of a particular organization, that most critics concern themselves with.

The conventional criticisms of bureaucracy fall into two categories. First, they are said to be inflexible, inefficient, and, in a time of rapid change, uncreative and unresponsive. This is the social engineering or planning attack. I would only note at this point that these criticisms are possibly more applicable to the gypsum plant Gouldner studied before it was bureaucratized than afterwards. The second criticism is that bureaucracies are said to stifle the spontaneity, freedom, and self-realization of their employees. This is the "human relations" attack, and at this point I would only observe that such stifling is inescapable but may occur more in traditional than bureaucratic organizations. The two criticisms, the social engineering and the human relations, are often combined by a single author. The criticisms of bureaucracy found in social science literature are echoed by such diverse groups as the radical right, the radical left, the man in the street, and the counterculture.

Less often seen in the organizational literature, at least until very recently, are the charges that by its very nature, and particularly because of its superiority as a social tool over other forms of organization, bureaucracy generates an enormous degree of unregulated and often unperceived social power; and this power is placed in the hands of a very few leaders. As bureaucracies satisfy, delight, and satiate us with their output of goods and services, they also shape our mentality, control our life chances, and define our humanity. They do so not so much in our role as members of one or more of these organizations, but as members of a society that is truly an organizational society. Those who control these organizations control the quality of our life, and they are largely self-appointed leaders.[6]

Let me be quite clear about my position, since it guides this book: in my view, bureaucracy is a form of organization superior to all others we know or can hope to afford in the near and middle future; the chances of doing away with it or changing it are probably nonexistent in the West in this century. Thus, it is crucial to understand it and appreciate it. But it is also crucial to understand

---

[6]Carl Kaysen makes this point about self-appointed leaders with respect to the large corporations in our society in "The Corporation, How Much Power and How Much Scope" in E. S. Mason, *The Corporation in Modern Society* (Cambridge, Mass.: Harvard University Press, 1960), pp. 85–105. It is generally true of powerful organizations in other areas, including political ones. For an assessment of the political realm, see G. William Domhoff, *The Higher Circles* (New York: Random House, Inc., 1971) and his earlier book, *Who Rules America* (Englewood Cliffs, N.J.: Prentice-Hall, Inc., 1967). See also Seymour Melman, *Pentagon Capitalism* (New York: McGraw-Hill Book Company, 1970). Most such assessments have come from nonsociologists.

not only how it mobilizes social resources for desirable ends, but also how it inevitably concentrates those forces in the hands of a few who are prone to use them for ends we do not approve of, for ends we are generally not aware of, and more frightening still, for ends we are led to accept because we are not in a position to conceive alternative ones. The investigation of these fearful possibilities has too long been left to men of letters, journalists, and radical political leaders. It is time that organizational theorists began to turn their expertise toward the true nature of bureaucracy. This will require a better understanding both of the virtues of bureaucracy, despite its critics, and of its largely unexplored dangers.

In this volume, then, I will examine the customary view of the sins of bureaucracy in Chapters 1, 2, and 3; construct a more realistic (and appreciative) model in Chapters 1 and 4, turn to some forebodings in the course of Chapter 5, and some hopeful new developments in Chapter 6. Specifically, in this first chapter I will explore, defend, and extend the Weberian skeleton of the structure of bureaucracy. In Chapter 2 I will examine the historical occasion for the attack upon this structural, "mechanistic" view and examine the views of the principal prophet of an alternative view of bureaucracy as a cooperative system—Chester Barnard. In the third chapter I will critically examine the full flowering of that view as found in the works of the various members of the human relations school. In Chapter 4, I will add some flesh and muscle to the Weberian structure by observing the unobtrusive means of control in bureaucracies (largely drawing upon the second half of James March and Herbert Simon's volume, *Organizations*) and by discussing the bases for conflict and of multiple goals. Then I will qualify it all by reference to variations in structure stemming from technology. This will provide a rough synthesis of much of the theory of the internal workings of organizations. In the fifth chapter I will turn to the matter of the organization and its environment. We will examine the institutional school, which emphasizes the interaction of goals and environment, and the failure of this school to come to terms with the possibility of viewing organizations as tools in the hands of their masters. The final chapter will review recent work on the environment, emphasizing "network" analysis, and the recent interest in the popular culture industry.

PURGING PARTICULARISM

One of the many dilemmas of organizations is that they attempt to be efficient in producing their output of steel, court convictions, reformed delinquents, legislation, or whatever, and yet they seek to be quite particular about who shall enjoy the pay and the honor of doing the work. *Particularism* means that irrelevant criteria (e.g., only relatives of the boss have a chance at top positions), in contrast to universalistic criteria (competence is all that counts), are employed in choosing employees. The criteria of efficiency and particularism are likely to clash, since the most efficient workers may lack the particular social characteristics desired. Organizations are profoundly "social" in character, in the sense that all kinds of social characteristics go into their operations by *intent*. They discriminate in memberships. For example, few Jews ever rise very high in such industries as steel;[7] few blacks have thus far been able to break into many skilled trades in the construction industry. In a study of one manufacturing firm, Melville Dalton found that membership in the Masons was a prerequisite to advancement in management, even though it is hard to imagine what there is about Masonic membership that would increase managerial efficiency.[8] Ambitious managers were smart enough to join the fraternal order. Some strata, work groups, and even whole plants are uni-ethnic—that is, all Irish or all Poles. One of the distinctive characteristics of voluntary associations such as patriotic societies or clubs is that they often specify membership criteria openly, while economic or governmental organizations can only do so informally. The Daughters of the American Revolution was founded at a time when many native-born Anglo-Saxons had parents who had lived during the days of the Revolution; the unqualified, then, were conveniently all immigrants. Today, some fraternities and sororities still insist upon the option of social criteria for membership, as do segregated private schools in the South or as did lunch counters in the South before the sit-ins of the late 1950s.

We view these claims with suspicion because of democratic ideals of equality. But we also view them with suspicion because we dimly recognize that organizations draw upon resources provided by society in general and thus are beholden to all of society. There is, for example, a flourishing and baroquelike structure of courts, laws, and law enforcement facilities which are available to organizations for protecting their interests. We all support these through taxes. Fraternities and sororities have special access to university facilities and special protection—and are tax-exempt. The factory is fairly free to pollute the air and water, to enforce its law through its

---

[7]And not just steel, of course. In Detroit, only two thirds of 1 percent of the white-collar jobs at the three major auto companies are filled by Jews. A study in 1960 of 1500 U.S. corporations showed that although Jews made up 8 percent of all college graduates and, even more important, 15 percent of the graduates of professional and business schools, yet they account for only 0.5 percent of management. See "Has Bias Locked Up the Room at the Top?" *Business Week*, January 24, 1970.

[8]Melville Dalton, *Men Who Manage* (New York: John Wiley & Sons, Inc., 1959).

own police force and its access to the courts, to hire and fire (and thus provide or deny livelihood), to utilize the services of the local chamber of commerce (which is tax-exempt and may even receive local tax support), and to draw upon tax-supported services of many state and federal agencies. These things cost us all money. No matter that the factory pays taxes in return, or that the sorority provides housing and surveillance that the university might otherwise have to build and provide. Common resources are drawn from society, whatever the specific products returned. Thus, we feel the services should be common to all who desire them. Particularism or discrimination is frowned upon.

But these are political rather than bureaucratic reasons for particularism. The bureaucratic reason for frowning on particularism is that efficiency is foregone if recruitment or access is decided upon grounds that are not related to the members' performance in the organization. For most organizational goals or roles, social origins (race, ethnicity, and class) are not likely to be a measure of competence. The steel company or bank that bars Jews from middle management is possibly depriving itself of superior talent at the higher levels. The appointment of a large political campaign donor to the position of Ambassador to the Court of St. James's suggests that the criteria are not knowledge of foreign affairs and skill in foreign diplomacy, but party loyalty and personal wealth. The son of the president of a corporation may well start out on the shop floor, or as a sales trainee, but it is not his competence that moves him quickly to a vice-presidency. Moreover, the frequent practice of a professional person hiring staff members from the same university he attended suggests something other than universalistic criteria. One finds this in university departments ("only eastern schools have a chance there," or "that's where Michigan sends its run-of-the-mill Ph.D.'s"), research and development labs ("someone from M.I.T. doesn't stand a chance in that company"), social agencies ("they only give supervisory positions to Chicago graduates" [University of Chicago School of Social Work]), and hospital medical staffs ("that's a Johns Hopkins shop").

The problem with these practices is not only that there is little relationship between the social criteria for hiring or promoting people and the characteristics that affect performance in the organization. More serious, the particularistic criteria are likely to be *negatively* related to performance—the more these particularistic criteria are used, the poorer the performance. By hiring only Chicago graduates, one may have to take some who were among the poorer students, missing out on the good Michigan graduates. More serious still, one may end up with only one way of seeing the world and only one way of approaching a problem. By using broad or universalistic hiring criteria, the chances of getting different perspectives, and thus more ideas, is increased.

That particularistic criteria are often equivalent to favoritism also means that corruption is a likely accompaniment. The agency head who hires or favors primarily people from his own region, state, or university, may get subtle returns in the bargain. He may be favored as a consultant to his former university or to the state government and receive handsome fees; he may place himself at the head of the line for bigger and better appointments. Competence is hard to judge, so we rely upon familiarity. The corruption may be less discreet, as in the political spoils system whereby the elected official hires only people who are willing to contribute to his election campaign or to provide him with kickbacks.

Tenure and the Career Concept

Political patronage reached such a corrupting extreme in the late nineteenth century that the merit system and civil service examinations were instituted in the federal and most state governments. Of course, we now pay a price for that sweeping change, since merit systems may have little to do with merit. Once a civil service appointee receives his "tenure," it is very hard to remove him for lack of competence, one reason President Carter in the late 1970s attempted to reform the civil service. Over the years, as the organization changes and the demand for new skills increases, the person who may have once been a very competent employee may turn out to be quite incompetent. But the organization is stuck with him. One need look no further, for example, than university departments where skills change quickly, promise does not materialize into productivity, or men simply pass their prime. Should research-oriented universities change to the extent that teaching ability became a prime criterion for competence, rather than a secondary one, many tenured people might be found incompetent.

It is a tenet of the bureaucratic model of organizations that a man is expected to pursue a "career" in the organization. Thus, if he burns out too quickly or, more likely, if the skills demanded of the position change without the occupant changing (e.g., more emphasis upon teaching and less on research), the organization is expected to retain him. He has tenure. Despite the frequency with which this annoyance is met in organizations, the career principle is a sound one. Men would not be likely to master sets of skills through long technical training or experience in an organization if they knew they could not perpetually draw upon the capital of their investment. There must be some guarantee that if the demands of the job change radically in the future, a man will still be credited with having met them in the present. Otherwise, personnel might be less willing to make large investments in skills.

In short, the benefits of universalistic standards clearly appear to exceed the costs; tenure may be a necessary inducement for mastering obscure skills and a necessary protection against arbitrary rulers. There are costs, but the alternatives are worse.

Universalism and Organizational Goals

Universalistic criteria, then, would appear to be a proper goal in organizations, and few would fault the bureaucratic model in this respect. But the situation is not that simple. To establish the standards, one has to know the real goals of the organization. Suppose a manufacturing firm favors members of a certain fraternal organization when it hires and promotes its managers. On the face of it, this sounds particularistic. Upon closer examination, though, one might well find that the manufacturing organization receives a variety of tax benefits from the local government, and the local government is heavily loaded with Masons or Lions, or Legionnaires, or whatever. If the firm gives preference to Masons, should that be the dominant group in the city government, it may avoid paying its fair share of the sewage system; it may get special arrangements for power supplies; zoning ordinances may have been drafted so that it does not have to pay a heavy school tax; it may be able to get certain city streets closed to permit convenient expansion; and a good share of its security protection may come from the city's police department, rather than from plant guards. Furthermore, the local authorities may see that other plants are discouraged from coming in, through zoning ordinances or restriction upon transportation uses or available power supplies. Competing industry, particularly, would up the demand for skilled labor in one field and drive up wages. Moreover, the city planning commission may ensure that a new superhighway comes close to the front gate of the plant, even at the expense of cutting a residential district into two sections.

Showing favoritism within the manufacturing company to this fraternal organization is hardly, then, a particularistic criterion from the *company's* point of view. Any loss in managerial competence that may result from using selective criteria is more than offset by the gain of having sympathetic friends in the city administration. For similar reasons, defense industries have a disproportionate number of former military officers in their top echelons, even though it is questionable whether former procurement or inspection officers are particularly good managers of large aerospace firms or conglomerates. For defense industries, political ties to the Pentagon are a universalistic criterion. Similarly, experience in the major corporations and investment houses is often crucial for top civilian positions in the State Department, the Defense Department, the CIA, and the Atomic Energy Commission; Richard Barnet found that seventy of the ninety-one top men in those agencies from 1940 to 1967 had such backgrounds.[9] The Polish foreman who favors the Poles under him is acting no differently.

This reasoning also applies to voluntary associations such as fraternities and sororities. If the "real" goals of the Greek-letter societies were auxiliary support for the university, good fellowship, recreation, character building, and efficient housing, then discrimination against Jews and blacks would be unwarranted. However, if the goal of the fraternity or sorority also includes promoting social class and ethnic solidarity, ties that will lead to business or marital advantages, and reinforcement of religious, ethnic, and class sentiments, then the discrimination is certainly efficient. The Jew or the black is an inappropriate resource for the organization; he does nothing for the group.

We may deplore the particularism of the Greek-letter society or the manufacturing firm and call for the universalism that is explicit in the bureaucratic model. There, at least, bureaucracy is virtuous in its impersonality. But to deplore particularism is only to advance an ideal and to neglect the reality of organizational affairs. The real cause for concern is not just the failure to apply universalism; rather it involves the goals of the organization which determine just what are universalistic or particularistic criteria. We are being naive when we deplore patronage, collusion, and snobbery in our political, economic, and voluntary organizations as if those traits stemmed from a failure to apply sound organizational principles or even general moral principles. A more realistic view would question the goals to which these organizations are directed by their owners and managers, for these goals define what is efficient. The bureaucratic ideal can be a mystifying device, disguising the real interests of the masters.

The Contest for Control

Much inefficiency in organizations and much annoyance shown by members and observers of organizations stem from a less wholesale brand of particularism, namely, nepotism—giving preferred treatment to relatives—and personal favoritism on the part of particular managers. Both forms of particularism are extremely common in economic organizations; they are also found in noneconomic or-

---

[9]Richard Barnet, *Economy of Death* (New York: Atheneum House, Inc., 1969).

ganizations. To some extent, nepotism stems from the belief that one's own incompetence can be better protected if one offers positions to nieces, nephews, daughters, sons, aunts, uncles, and other relatives of the owners. To some extent, favoritism takes place because subordinates learn that expressing obeisance to the boss is one way of protecting their security, lightening their workload, and ensuring advancement. However, if incompetence and laziness were adequate explanations for nepotism and favoritism, the matter would be settled by weeding out people with such traits, or, more sensibly, resigning oneself to the fact that organizations draw upon the general population for their personnel. The general population, by definition, has its share of venality, stupidity, sycophancy, etc.; so not much can be done.

There is a deeper reason for particularism in organizations; this reason, which does not rest on the inadequacies of human resources, illustrates the characteristic tensions that exist in large, complex organizations. It involves one of the dominant themes of the book: *Organizations must be seen as tools.* Particularism is one means of gaining or maintaining control over the tool.

A tool is something you can get something done with. It is a resource *if* you control it. It gives you power that others do not have. Organizations are multipurpose tools; there are a great many things that one can do with them. For example, through an organization you may get your ego flattered by subordinates; or you may be able to provide a respectable place in the occupational system for your relatives or friends. More important, however, *organizations are tools for shaping the world as one wishes it to be shaped.* They provide the means for imposing one's definition of the proper affairs of men upon other men. The person who controls an organization has power that goes far beyond that of those lacking such control. The power of the rich lies not in their ability to buy goods and services, but in their capacity to control the ends toward which the vast resources of large organizations are directed.

Such power is naturally contested. People attempt to achieve control of organizations or even parts of an organization in order to gain that power. "If I were in charge I would do it this way." "What we really should be doing is such and such." "Top management should never let the union [or suppliers, or customers, or medical staff, or the prison guards, or the government, or middle management, or whatever] get away with this." "The trouble with top management is that they are only interested in immediate profits and not in long-term growth; I want to see this organization strong over the long run." "This agency should be serving lower-class people, not the middle class." "Top management is too tied to the industry way of doing things; they are preoccupied with traditions that are no longer relevant, and they do not want to rock the boat." "We should be revolutionizing things in this industry." "We don't want people of *that sort* in our company." "Business has a responsibility for protecting the American way of life. We should make it clear to these groups that they can't get away with this." These are statements about power and the uses to which it can be put.

Retaining or gaining power is difficult because it is almost always contested, and the contest is not decided by measuring the "efficiency" or "productivity" of the contenders. The criterion is not narrow and testable, but general and vague. The principles of bureaucracy have little to do with the contest. One decidedly unbureaucratic principle is crucial—personal loyalty or loyalty to a superior rather than to the organization and its goals. One of the best ways to seize or retain control is to surround oneself with loyal people. If a person has a certain charisma or force of personality, the loyalty may be freely given by strangers and acquaintances. If one lacks this rare quality, there are other means of ensuring loyalty. The most powerful is dependence. The subordinate who is a relative of a superior or a friend of the family is more dependent than one who is not; his or her superior has privileged access to "significant others" in the social world of the subordinate. The marginally competent manager who is promoted over others is vulnerable and thus had better be loyal.

Of course, one purchases some inefficiency along with this loyalty. Inefficiency means that the costs of doing business are increased. But the difference between a small increase in the operating cost and a threat to losing control of all or some of the resources of the organization is enormous. In most cases, the exchange of loyalty for competence is in the executive's interest.

Even less-than-exemplary subordinates can perform very well for their superiors. A man may lack good judgment in setting policies, be inefficient in organizing his work and his staff, and even spend an excessive amount of time on the golf course or traveling about at company expense. However, if he manages to sniff out potential sources of opposition within the organization, nominate loyal subordinates and identify those who cannot be trusted, and generally keep track of the activities of "internal enemies," he is worth a great deal to the executive. Such functions are commonplace in organizations of all types. As we have said, organizations are tools; they mobilize resources that can be used for a variety of ends. These resources and the goals of the organization are up for grabs, and people grab for them continually. Internecine warfare, often involving court suits, is a very prominent news item in the business press; it generally concerns the uses to which organizational power is to be put.

Finally, what critics view as incompetence often is merely a different set of goals. It is said that former Treasury Secretary George Humphrey in the Eisenhower administration, an old friend of the President, played havoc with the American economy. Inflation went up while unemployment was high, economic growth was stagnant, and the national debt was increasing—all without the excuse of a war. Or, it has been held that Secretary of State John Foster Dulles under the same President left behind a discredited patchwork of alliances, commitments, and promises of enormous supplies of weapons for undemocratic regimes in his fanatic effort to stem what he viewed as communism. Even if one shares these judgments, they do not mean that either man was necessarily incompetent. Each had different views of the way the world should be than his critics. Each used the enormous power of his organization to implement these views. Subordinates in those organizations were well advised to be loyal. The extreme case of Richard Nixon as President is not necessary to make the point.

In conclusion, we have explored particularism in organizations, indicating the desirability of the bureaucratic ideal of universalism—hiring and promoting upon the basis of performance ability (skills, competence, diligence, etc.) rather than upon agreement to support the goals of the organization. We deplore particularism for several reasons. It goes against the values of a liberal society—i.e., it yields racial or religious discrimination; it involves using public resources for the advantage of specific groups; it promotes inefficiency in organizations. But we also have been suggesting that much of the particularism we frown upon is particularistic only if we think the goals of an organization should be other than what they are; from the point of view of those who control the organization, the criteria may really be universalistic and promote the efficiency of the organization. Better personnel practices, or standards, or screening criteria are irrelevant when only changes in goals would meet the criticisms. This is because organizations are tools designed to perform work for their masters, and particularism or universalism is relative to the goals of the masters. Because organizations generate power to get a variety of things done, people contend for that power, and favoritism and nepotism help insure loyalty to the contenders.

We also briefly touched upon one other characteristic of bureaucracy—tenure, or the career principle; we argued that the costs of this principle, as seen in the frustration of dealing with incompetent personnel who have civil service protection, incompetent tenured professors, or burnt out vice-presidents, are more than made up for by its advantages. These include freedom from arbitrary authority, protection from changes in skill demands and declining ability, and assurance that one's investment in skills and experience will be secure. The bureaucratic model emphasizes efficiency in the long run, not the short run.

It is a tribute to the bureaucratic model as it developed since the Middle Ages that it gave at least a partial answer to the problem of particularism and pursued it with vigor. Loyalty to the king or lord or chief was once everything; incompetence counted for little. With the rise of the university-educated scribes, jurists, and mathematicians, a class of presumably professional, neutral, and loyal personnel arose, the business administration students of yore.[10] The kings and chiefs could use these and get both competence and loyalty (through dependency) in their administration. The eunuch in the harem is the prototype of the modern professional; he can be trusted with everything except that which really counts: the uses to which the masters put the organization. We have come so far from the particularism of medieval days that nepotism and favoritism today are frowned upon as both subversive and inefficient. A substantial residue of these practices remains in organizations simply because organizations, then as now, are tools in the hands of their masters; thus, control over them is a prize which many men seek. Particularism is one weapon in that struggle, but it must be masked.

FEATHERING THE NEST

Organizations generate a great deal of power and leverage in the social world, power and leverage far beyond their ostensible goals. But one of the problems of organizations is that they are very leaky vessels. It is quite easy for a member of one of them to use some of his power and leverage for his own ends rather than for the ends of the organization. (The ends of the organization, we may say for the present, are those of a small group at the top of the organization or, in many cases, a small group outside the organization who control those at the top.) In the ideal world of the ideal bureaucracy, it should be possible to neatly calculate, and thus control, the relationship between a person's contribution to an organization and the rewards he or she receives. Theoretically, too, the rewards the organization has to pay should not exceed the contribution of the person. In practice, this is very difficult because it is hard to control

---

[10]As Lewis Coser notes in *Greedy Institutions* (New York: The Free Press, 1974), slaves, Jews, and others excluded from society could also be used because they owed to their lord their promotion from nonpersons to quasipersons.

people that closely and because organizations have permeable boundaries. People tend to act as if they owned their positions; they use them to generate income, status, and other things that rightfully belong to the organization. Bureaucracy has made great strides in reducing the discrepancy between a man's contributions, on the one hand, and the inducements necessary to keep him in the organization and make him work, on the other.[11] It was during the time when bureaucracies were just beginning to form that the problem was most acute.

During the late Middle Ages, the king who wanted revenues from the land and the people he controlled would sell a tax franchise to someone, generally a nobleman. This official would agree to pay the king a set fee; he was then free to collect as much money as he could from the people and keep anything beyond the set fee. The king benefited because he did not have to organize and maintain a large bureaucracy for the purposes of tax collection. However, there were problems. The collector might extract such a heavy toll that the subjects would revolt. Or the basis of the economy might be ruined so that fewer and fewer taxes could be collected. Or the collector might become so rich that he could challenge the power of the king. Eventually, the king or the state took control of taxation, centralized it, hired personnel on a salaried basis to run the system, and used the army to back up the collectors. In this way, the imbalance between the effort and reward of the tax collector was markedly reduced. The tax collectors were paid what they were worth on the labor market at that time.

Today, we do not find tax collectors paying a franchise fee to the state to collect as much as they can, but problems still remain because governmental units are empowered to force people to pay taxes. This power is a source of leverage for the officeholder. For example, local assessors (those who determine the value of property for taxation purposes) have been known to make deals with business firms or other interests such that certain property is assessed at a lower value than it would normally be. Then the assessors receive a percentage of the reduction from the organization that is being assessed. Internal revenue agents have been known to make deals with taxpayers whereby the latter's taxes are reduced and the agents get a portion of the savings. The Internal Revenue Service spends a good deal of money on various forms of surveillance to

---

[11]The contributions-inducements theory of organizations was first formulated by Chester Barnard in the late 1930s and subsequently greatly refined by James G. March and Herbert A. Simon in their book, *Organizations* (New York: John Wiley & Sons, Inc., 1958). Both of these contributions are cited as landmarks in organizational theory, despite the simplicity of the idea or perhaps because of it. We shall take them up later.

keep this practice to a minimum and to keep the agent from using the power of that organization for his private purposes.

The medieval system of selling franchises is still legally practiced in some of the less-organized areas of our economy. For example, small businessmen, particularly doctors and dentists, "sell" delinquent accounts to a tax collecting firm; the tax collecting firm gives the businessman, say, 40 percent of the value of the account and then keeps anything beyond that which it collects. Most businesses are wary of using all the powers legally or illegally at hand to collect debts because they do not want to alienate people who might be future customers or clients. For the tax collecting firm, however, this is not a constraint, so their methods of extracting money from debtors are more severe.[12] Of course, the agencies also do not care whether the debtors feel that the debt is unjust or not. It is irrelevant to the agency if the debtor failed to pay his full bill because he was overcharged or because he did not receive the goods or services. Furthermore, agencies stand to gain a great deal by collecting all or 70 percent of the debt rather than 40 percent, so they pursue their task with vigor. Agencies also find it easier to extract money from the poorer and less well educated parts of society since those with few resources are more easily intimidated.

Another example of ancient practices in the less well organized and rationalized sectors of our economy is the selling of professional services. Normally, one thinks that the client of a doctor, dentist, or lawyer goes to the professional on a voluntary basis. However, for a number of reasons clients do not have effective choice in these matters. In varying degrees, professionals have captive clients. There is not much competition between doctors, for example, because clients have few ways of judging doctors and have to consider geographical accessibility; also, doctors have restricted entry to their profession to keep the numbers low. If the patient has been going to a particular doctor for any period of time at all, he has a "sunk cost" in this relationship—the doctor knows him and has X rays and other records. What happens, then, when a doctor or lawyer or dentist retires or moves away? If he has any sizable practice at all, he will "sell" it to another professional. Indeed, if he dies

---

[12]One of the most frequent consumer fraud devices is for a collection agency to send a fake social survey questionnaire out. Along with the usual attitude questions ("How do you feel about law and order?"), the unsuspecting debtor is asked about his place of employment, the value of his car and other property, and whether his wife works or not. The agencies also send letters on official-looking stationery saying that a heavily insured package is being held for them by the post office, and they should fill out the identification papers and mail them in to receive the package. Debtors thus disclose the information that the collection agency can use as leverage. Both practices are forbidden by law but are very hard to police.

his beneficiaries can sell his practice. Patients are not literally sold to the new buyer, but in practice they may have little choice; and in any case the new buyer has quite privileged access to them. Practices are put up for competitive bidding and go to the highest bidder. Of course, there is no guarantee that there is any relationship between ability and reward since an incompetent doctor, for example, may be able to pay more for a practice than a good one. Given the highly entrepreneurial, even medieval, character of our independent professions, there is little that can be done to rationalize or bureaucratize them in order to control the relationship between effort and reward.

Feathering one's nest from the copious amounts of down floating around in an organization is often taken for granted as a part of the income from the position. No professor in his right mind (and they all have right minds in this regard) would think of buying his own paper, pencils, carbon paper, and so on to write a book, from which he hopes to gain substantial income in the form of royalty. It does not occur to him that he should pay for the privilege of using a huge library that caters to his exotic tastes and allows him to keep books out for months or years without paying fines. Nor do many universities question his use of secretarial time that is officially budgeted as an educational expense. When pressed, professors may insist that while they draw royalties on their books (which range from a few dollars a year to over $100,000), they are really contributing to the educational resources of the society and that this is an inexpensive way of producing knowledge and teaching materials. This is true enough, but it is still remarkable that very few universities have attempted to require professors to pay back to the school some percentage of any outside income that comes from exploiting resources that are tax exempt or derived from students and, in public universities, from the taxpayers. A few have tried and fewer actually do it; it meets with considerable resistance. In addition to royalties from books, there are the matters of lecture engagements and consulting jobs. A professor at a prestigious university is able to demand very high fees for consulting and lecturing and will get many opportunities to do these things. Since few prepare for these tasks only on Saturdays and Sundays, spending the other five days of the week busily teaching, these activities undoubtedly divert one from teaching duties.

Virtually all organizations offer opportunities for feathering one's nest. Recall the dynamite that was readily taken from the gypsum mine described at the opening of this chapter. A more dramatic example would be the scandals in the Chicago police department and other police departments in the early 1960s that were referred to as the "cops and/or robbers" syndrome. These scandals involved policemen who, by knowing when people were going to be away and when on-duty policemen were not likely to be around, were able to effectively burglarize stores and homes.

We may not expect a great deal of rectitude in police departments, but we might in voluntary hospitals supported by government funds, private donations, community chest funds, and, of course, patient fees. Nevertheless, I was not surprised to find that in some voluntary hospitals it was the custom for top-level administrators and top-level physicians and surgeons to receive expensive filets and other food from the hospital kitchens for use at home. Also, the maintenance staff occasionally remodeled or maintained the private houses of key executives, key doctors, or prominent board members. The illustrations are trivial but the principle is not. Organizations generate surpluses and leverage in our world, and those who have any power in them can use these for their own ends. The device of bureaucracy was designed to prevent *any but the masters* of the organization from doing this.

We might think that the more bureaucratized and rationalized the organization is, the less nest-feathering will occur. This may be so, at least at the lower levels, but we have no research on the subject. However, to the extent that business and industrial organizations are among the most bureaucratized and rationalized, the generalization probably would not stand. Highly placed executives of business and industrial firms sometimes profit handsomely from giving lucrative contracts to suppliers in which they have invested their personal funds. These arrangements rarely become public because it is very difficult to gain such information. One did become public in 1960 when an aggressive busybody stockholder pursued the matter with the Chrysler Corporation. Eventually, the president of Chrysler resigned, and, after being sued by the corporation, returned $450,000 to the company. He allegedly favored suppliers in whose firm he had a personal financial interest. (It is not often, however, that a stockholder with only a pittance of stock can bring down the administrative head of a large corporation.) Perhaps the reason that such an "unbureaucratic" practice could occur in a highly bureaucratized firm is that, as Max Weber noted long ago, the top of an organization is never bureaucratized. It always belongs to somebody. In this case, though, the board of directors and stockholders insisted that the organization was also theirs; it did not belong just to the president.

The practice of feathering one's nest in large part reflects the problem of separating the interests of the person from the interests of the organization. In our organizational society, this becomes increasingly difficult. For example, to whom does the experience of a woman belong? Does it belong to her or to the organization in which she acquired that experience? The growth of bureaucracy was equivalent to putting a label of "company property" upon the skills, experience, and creativity of the employee. It is a measure of our socialization into a society of bureaucratic organizations that we no longer question this extraction at all in the case of blue-collar workers and most white-collar ones. But consider industry at the turn of the century. Most of the work in the large, mass-producing factories and mills (except textiles, which had been "rationalized" long before) was done by work crews who were recruited, organized, and paid by independent contractors.[13] They used the company's facilities, supplies, and tools, but worked under yearly contracts to produce so many rifle barrels or parts of sewing machines or whatever. The contractors sometimes made very large profits, and paid their men presumably what the market would bear, or more likely, what the local custom dictated. The system was apparently quite efficient—technological changes were rapidly introduced and were in the interests of the contractors. It flourished in factories producing highly engineered products on a mass basis. Owners supplied the capital and organized the final assembly and marketing.

The genius of F. W. Taylor and others in the scientific management movement (see Chapter 2) was to convince the owners that they should employ engineers to go around and find out how the men and women drilled the rifle barrels or made the gears for machine tools, or cast the locomotive parts, centralize this information in a planning room and study it, then break the tasks down into small parts so as to remove as much of the skill and accumulated experience as possible, hire a foreman who would supervise the crew for a wage, and assign the highly specialized "deskilled" tasks to the men and women and pay them at a much lower wage rate. The owners "expropriated" the craft skills and craft system, and put the label of company property upon the ingenuity, experience, and creativity of the workers. Only now are we beginning to painfully rediscover and recommend giving back to the workers a small part of what had been their own property, in the form of such schemes as job enlargement, workers' participation, workers' autonomy, or group incentives.

What was settled for workers and most managers long ago (sometimes through bloody strikes)[14] still appears for top executives and scientists in new fields today. What happens when a team of

---

[13]Daniel Clawson, "Class Struggle and the Rise of Bureaucracy" (Ph.D diss., State University of New York at Stony Brook, 1978) whose excellent work I am drawing upon here. See also the more general discussion of this issue in Harry Braverman, *Labor and Monopoly Capital* (New York: Monthly Review Press, 1975).

[14]Katherine Stone, "The Origins of Job Structures in the Steel Industry," *Radical America*, 7:6 (November-December 1973): 19–64, describes the process and conflicts for the steel industry. See also the seminal piece by Steven Marglin, "What Do Bosses Do?" *Review of Radical Political Economics* 6, no. 2 (Summer 1974): 33–60.

researchers or an executive and three or four subordinates who have been working together for a long time leave the organization? There are at least two issues involved. One is the raiding of personnel that have been trained by the organization; the other is the knowledge of the technology, business operations, market strategies, and so forth developed within the organization. In both cases, the organization loses heavily. Such incidents have become frequent enough to produce a number of court rulings. The principles are still obscure, but in general the court has been ruling in favor of the former firm in requiring, for example, that the departing manager or scientist not work in the same product area for a period of five years. If he goes to work for firm B after having worked in firm A, and firm B comes out with a product that is similar to the one he was working on in firm A, firm A can sue firm B on the grounds that the man took specific knowledge with him and gave it to the second firm.

The man and his subordinates need not go to another established firm, taking with them the fruit of years of experimentation, trial, gestation, and stimulation. They may start their own company. In a recent case, an engineer for IBM took thirty-six people with him and started a competing company for the purpose of making integrated circuits for memory cores for large computers. IBM sued. Even if a large firm had little hope of winning such a suit it could help persuade others that it is not wise to leave with so many company-provided resources in their hands. It is a measure of our organizational society that the courts are able to rule in favor of the organization rather than the creative individual.[15]

The case of the scientist who decides that what he has in his head belongs to him and not to the organization, even though organizational resources were used to develop it, is a borderline case in the basic question of who owns the office. As such it is illuminating. For, intrinsically, there is no difference between such a case and the executive who makes sure that the supplier in which he has a financial interest gets contracts from his company even though that supplier's products may be inferior. In both cases, the organization provides the resource which is then exploited by the individual for his own benefit and to the disadvantage of the organization. It does not matter whether the organization is considered a socially valuable one or whether the individual is moral or immoral. We are stuck with the organizational logic of our time; the official

---

[15]But on the other hand, it is striking that few creative individuals appear to start on their own, forming their own companies. Generally, they work first for a large firm. Only then can they attract the necessary capital from those arbitrators of the business scene, the banks.

does not own his office—as Weber put it, and as the gypsum plant employees discovered, and most workers long before that. The organization takes precedence over the individual.

"THERE OUGHT TO BE A RULE"

Restricting particularism and featherbedding and protecting people in their careers are fairly noncontroversial aspects of bureaucracy. Other matters, however, have drawn much criticism from scholars as well as from the man in the street. One of these is the question of rules in organizations. A multitude of rules and regulations appears to be the very essence of a bureaucracy. The term "red tape" adequately conveys the problem. Rules govern everything; one cannot make a move unless one does it by the book or, to use military slang, by the numbers. Every office in every department has seen to it that its autonomy is protected by rules. If one attempts to change one rule, he immediately runs into the problem that half a dozen other rules are connected to it; to change these, a geometric proportion of additional rules will be affected, and so on.

While it is obvious that some rules are needed in organizations, it is generally felt that most organizations have far too many rules. How might these be eliminated?

Reducing Rules

There are a number of ways to reduce the number of rules. One way is to mechanize as much as possible. A typewriter eliminates the need for rules about the size and clarity of script and the way letters will be formed. Rules on these matters were common before the appearance of typewriters. Any machine is a complex bundle of rules that are built into the machine itself. Machines ensure standardized products, thus eliminating rules regarding dimensional characteristics. They ensure even output time; they also indicate precisely what kind of material can be fed into them. The larger the machine, presumably the more people it replaces, and this eliminates rules about how workers are to interact and cooperate and coordinate their activities. The thoroughly automated factory, of which we have none as yet, would be one with few or no written rules or regulations.

Another way to cut down on the number of rules is to insist upon near uniformity of personnel in an organization. If we could hire people with the same physical characteristics, intelligence, amount of self-discipline, personality traits, and so on, we would need far fewer rules to govern the range of differences that usually obtains among personnel. If none of them had families, ever got sick, or needed vacations, and if all were thoroughly trained before they arrived at the office, plant, or agency, that would also simplify matters greatly.

If we could seal the organization off from its environment so that nothing ever affected it, we would need very few rules regarding relationships with the environment. We would also need few or no rules regarding changes in procedures—because nothing would change. Once things were started in the proper manner, they could run that way forever. Finally, if we could produce only simple products in our organizations, rather than complex ones in various sizes, shapes, and colors and with a lot of custom-made attributes, this would eliminate the need for a lot of rules.

As these comments suggest, we might not care for organizations that eliminate the need for rules—they would be rather dull, mechanized, inflexible things. Rules are needed in organizations when complexity increases due to variability in personnel, customers, environment, techniques of producing the goods and services, and so on. When these matters are complex, it is not possible to allow personnel to "do their own thing," no matter how much we might prefer that. And every time variability in handling personnel is introduced by these complexities, rules are required to limit the discretion of those with power to handle people under them. There will be rules about favoritism and nepotism and discrimination on irrelevant grounds, rules about transferring people, rules about expectations regarding pay, promotion, accrued leave, and so on.

Of course, rules in the sense of formal written procedures can be essentially eliminated, thus giving the impression of a place that operates with few rules, even though the impression is bound to be mistaken. Wilfred Brown, an experienced and successful manager, discussed this matter at some length in connection with the industrial firm of which he was president in England.[16]

Many managers feel that "freedom" lies in the sort of situation where their supervisor says to them: "There are not many regulations in this place. You will understand the job in a month or two, and you make your own decisions. No red tape—you are expected to take command; make the decisions off your own bat as they arise. I am against a lot of rules or regulations, and we do not commit too much to paper." In my experience a manager in such a situation has virtually no "freedom to act" at all. He starts making decisions and his boss sends for him to say:

---

[16]Wilfred Brown, *Exploration in Management* (New York: John Wiley & Sons, Inc., 1960), pp. 97-98.

"Look here, Jones, I am sorry to tell you that you have made two rather serious mistakes in the course of reorganizing your work. You have promoted one man to supervisor who is not the next man due for promotion in the factory, and you have engaged five additional machinists, a decision you should have referred to me because we have some surplus men in this category in an adjacent factory." Now Jones might well say: "You said there were no regulations but, in fact, you have already mentioned the existence of two; one concerned with promotion and the other with increase of establishment. Please detail these regulations to me precisely, so that I can work to them in future, and let me know now of any further regulations which bear upon my work."

In practice, Jones probably says nothing of the kind, because he does not think in this way; to him regulations are stumbling blocks in the path of those wishing to display initiative. He will proceed, over the years, to learn, by making mistakes, of the whole array of regulations which, by the very nature of Executive Systems, do in fact exist. His boss will have to say to him frequently: "Yes, Jones, freedom for subordinates to act on their own is the policy here, but surely it must have been obvious that you should have seen me before doing *that.*" Jones is thus in a situation where he does not know what decisions he can or cannot make, and when in doubt he is likely to follow a course of doing nothing at all. In three years he will have got through this difficult period; he will know when he can or cannot act, because he has learn[ed] by testing what his boss was unable to give him in writing—*the prescribed component of his job.* Thereafter, Jones will be a staunch supporter of the "no-red-tape" policy, and so the situation will continue.

It is much more efficient to delineate as precisely as possible to a new subordinate all of the regulations he must observe and then say: "You must take all the decisions that seem to you to be required, so long as you keep within the bounds of that policy. If, keeping within those bounds, you take decisions which I think you should have referred to me, then I cannot criticize; for such a happening implies that some part of the policy which I wish you to operate has not been disclosed to you. I must, then, formulate that policy and add it to the prescribed content of your job." If, in addition, the manager can give his subordinate a rounded idea of the discretionary component of his job by stating the types of decisions which he must make, then that subordinate is in a real position to act on his own initiative in the prescribed area.

I have found, however, particularly in discussing jobs with external applicants, that the array of policy represented by our Policy Document, Standing Orders and Directives, causes people to assume the precise opposite of the real situation, i.e., that this extant written policy will deprive them of the right to make decisions. In fact, it is only by delineating the area of "freedom" in this way that a subordinate knows when he can make decisions. The absence of written policy leaves him in a position where any decision he takes, however apparently trivial, may infringe [upon] an unstated policy and produce a reprimand.

Professionalization and Rules.   Buying and installing machines, as indicated above, is one way of reducing the number of rules in an organization. The rules are built into the machine itself, and the organization pays for those rules in the price of the machine. A quite similar means of reducing the number of written rules is to "buy" personnel who have complex rules built into them. We generally call these people professionals. Professionals, such as engineers and scientists, psychiatrists, doctors, social workers, teachers, and professors, are trained on the outside, usually at great public expense, and a large number of rules are inculcated into them. They bring these into the organization and are expected to act upon them without further reference to their skills. While accounting practices differ more widely than some might expect, accountants in general are expected to be familiar with the rules and techniques of accounting. Doctors know when they should give certain drugs or what kinds of drugs should not be given to certain kinds of people; medicine is a complex body of rather imperfect rules. Professors, through long, arduous, and heroic training, learn rules about plagiarism in their writing, truth in their teaching, and deference to their more senior colleagues.

Professionals, like machines, cost a lot of money. There is a high initial investment in training that someone must pay, and the care and feeding of machines and professionals is expensive. Therefore, we tend to use them only when the economies are apparent or when there is no real choice. We charge more for services produced by complex machines or professionals than simple ones, other things, such as volume of production, being equal. It costs more to go to Harvard or to an outstanding hospital than it does to attend a city college or go to a poor hospital. Were we able to thoroughly routinize the tasks performed by professionals and get around the restrictions that professionals are able to place on their positions, we would substitute machines for them. We are trying, for better or worse, with teaching machines. *& computers*

Expressive Groups.   One other example of a way of avoiding rules in an organization is rare but interesting. This involves organizations where all members agree upon the goals of the organization (or, to put it more accurately, where the goals of the individual members are identical) and the techniques for achieving these goals are within the ability of all members. In such cases, few or no rules are required. Each will do his own thing, but his own thing will fit with the thing of all other members. Such organizations are generally quite small and usually oriented around expressive needs. Few organizations have members solely upon this basis. Most of the so-called voluntary associations rely on services to the members for which members pay in one form or another through dues, allowing their name to be used, or doing some work.[17] Since most voluntary associations provide services to members, they, like other organizations, also have a proliferation of rules and regulations.

Interdepartmental Regulations

So far, we have been talking about rules with respect to the whole organization. A quite different dimension of rules appears when we examine the relationships among units in an organization. Here it is clear that many rules are the basis of self-protection, predictability, and autonomy for the units in an organization. Take the matter of distribution requirements in a university. The rule that students shall take a certain number of credits in various departments of the university exists because students are not homogeneous when they enter the university; all cannot be expected to "know their own best interests." Only some would be motivated enough, the argument goes, to sample the sciences if they are majoring in the humanities or to sample the humanities if they are in the sciences; so a rule is promulgated. However, the matter does not end there. Departments, knowing there will be a big influx of students into their courses, want to control which courses the students come into. So they set rules regarding which courses are to be utilized for distribution requirements. This protects departmental autonomy and provides scheduling benefits and staffing economies. To change these rules when the characteristics of students or advances of knowledge have changed may prove to be quite difficult because a host of other practices have grown up in the department which depend upon the designation of certain courses appropriate for distribution requirements. For example, perhaps only instructors and assistant professors are assigned to teach these courses. Also, majors may be steered into more high-level courses where enrollment is kept down. A dean who attempts to force the department to make what seems to be eminently sensible changes from his point of view, or the point of view of the students or other departments, may run into serious opposition from the department. The change would threaten the department's whole fragile structure of work assignments and course requirements. The department might turn around in retaliation and change some of its rules on its own. For example, it might limit the enrollment in certain courses. Soon, if not immediately, a first class *political* situation has evolved which has little to do with

---

[17]Charles Perrow, "Members as a Resource in Voluntary Organization," in *Organizations and Clients,* ed. W. Rosengren and M. Lefton (Columbus, Ohio: Charles E. Merrill Publishing Company, 1970), pp. 93–116.

the original problem and can only be solved by political bargaining. But bargaining threatens the status quo, involves other departments, and ramifies the changes. Because rules protect interests and groups are interdependent, changing the rules is difficult.

Rules are like an invisible skein which bundles together all the technological and social aspects of organizations. As such, rules stem from past adjustments and seek to stabilize the present and future. When things are different in the future, an attempt to change these tough, invisible threads means that all kinds of practices, bargains, agreements, and payoffs will tumble out of the web and must be stuffed back in again. As a result of these kinds of interdependencies, changes in organizational rules (which go on continuously, if only informally)[18] are generally incremental—a little bit here and there. The hope is that somehow the whole structure of the organization will gradually, painlessly, and, most of all, *covertly* change over time. It generally does.

In sum, rules protect those who are subject to them. Rules are means of preserving group autonomy and freedom; to reduce the number of rules in an organization generally means to make it more impersonal, more inflexible, more standardized. But granted this, rules are still a bore. We would all prefer to be free of them, or so it would seem. Actually, only *some* rules are bores. The good, effective rules are rarely noticed; the bad ones stand out. Bad rules are inevitable. Some merely reflect the fact that people make rules, and people are not generally geniuses. The problem is not rules in general, but particular ones that need changing.

Rules as Scapegoats

Rules are the scapegoats for a variety of organizational problems. Complaints about excessive rules or bad rules generally are symptomatic of more deep-seated problems that cannot be solved by changing rules. During the unhappy days of the breakdown in telephone service in New York in 1969–1970, a number of "stupid" rules surfaced and were held to have caused the difficulties. Actually, the difficulties appeared to be that the system in New York was designed so that it would operate with a good deal of inefficiency and slack. Such an operation is easy when an organization has a monopoly and, despite the lack of risk, a guaranteed high rate of return. Savings from technical advances need not result in significant rate decreases, but simply in more inefficient ways of doing business—which is, after all, the easiest route. No one in the com-

---

[18]Peter M. Blau, *The Dynamics of Bureaucracy*, 2nd rev. ed. (Chicago: The University of Chicago Press, 1973).

pany gets upset, and since the public is uninformed and the rate-setting agencies are weak and generally captives of the utilities, the lack of rate reduction is not noticed. (The same appears to be true for the gas and electric utilities, which also are very profitable, inefficiently regulated monopolies.) When greater demands were made on the company than it could fulfill, it became apparent that, for example, the business-office side of the company in the New York area was not talking to the plant or operations side; both hid under a complex set of rules and regulations which governed their inter-relationship and the operations within each of the divisions. As long as there was sufficient "fat," or surplus, in the system, it did not matter; when more efficiency was needed to meet demand for services, these inefficiencies surfaced, and rules got the blame. The rules were not bad in themselves. For example, they probably reduced contact and thus antagonisms between the operations and customer-service branches. A more efficient operation would require more contact, however, and under these situations the rules were inappropriate. But—the whole premise upon which the system operated would have to be changed; rules would be only one aspect that would be changed.

In a similar fashion, hide-bound government bureaucracies are not unresponsive to their clients because of their rules but because of the premises they operate on and the system designed around those premises. The New York public school system[19] and the Bureau of Indian Affairs are two outstanding examples. In both cases, professionals have captured the organization and made it too difficult or expensive for policy makers—board members, staff of the Secretary of the Interior, politicians, etc.—to wrest control and change practices. The incredible rules of these agencies are only by-products and symptoms of a commonplace fact of organization life: those who can will seize control of an organization and use it for their own ends, in these cases security, power, and expansion.

Good rules are often those that are rarely noticed. They may be written down or just a matter of custom, but they are rarely challenged. They just make sense. Some other good rules are those that cut the Gordian knots that inevitably bind organized endeavors of any complexity. Frequently, there is no clear ground for doing A instead of B; both will have unpleasant outcomes. Rather than agonize over a decision, a rule cuts the knot. Another function of good rules is to justify unpleasant decisions or actions: "Sorry, old boy, but I will have to discipline you for that." "I know it's not fair, from your point of view, but it's the rule." "It took a lot of extra work, and I made some enemies in the agency, but the rule is that these

---

[19]David Rogers, *110 Livingstone Street* (New York: Random House, Inc., 1968).

kinds of clients are entitled to more service." Without the rules, these necessary but unpleasant actions might not be taken.

The greatest problem with rules is that organizations and their environments change faster than the rules. Most bad rules were once good, designed for a situation that no longer exists. Nepotism was apparently a problem in university departments of the past, when they were dominated by one man who made all the decisions as to what the courses would be, what texts would be used, who was to be hired and who promoted. It was easy to extend this power by putting one's wife on the staff. Today, departmental chairmen have much less power, and there are more finely graded criteria for performance. Yet, as more women once again come into the job market, and have husbands who are also teachers, the nepotism rule becomes more burdensome and discriminatory. It is often stoutly defended, though, by those who resent women professors anyway, since they are a threat to male hegemony.

In sum, "there ought to be a rule" is as valid as saying "there are too damn many rules around here." Rules do a lot of things in organizations: they protect as well as restrict; coordinate as well as block; channel effort as well as limit it; permit universalism as well as provide sanctuary for the inept; maintain stability as well as retard change; permit diversity as well as restrict it. They constitute the organizational memory and the means for change. As such, rules in themselves are neither good nor bad, nor even that important. It is only because they are easy scapegoats for other problems that are more difficult to divine and analyze that we have to spend this much time on them. Social scientists, no less than the man in the street, love to denounce them and to propose ruleless organizations. But ruleless organizations are likely to be either completely automated, if they are efficient and have much output, or completely professionalized, turning out expensive and exotic services. Only a tiny fraction of organizations fit either case.

"WHO'S IN CHARGE AROUND HERE?"

For many social scientists, rules are a nuisance; the emphasis upon rules in organizations is bad enough, but the existence of a hierarchical ordering of offices and authority is a barely tolerable evil. The principle of hierarchical ordering of offices and authority says that for every person there shall be one person above her to whom she primarily reports and from whom she primarily receives direction. The organization is structured in the form of a pyramid, with the top controlling everything. Power is centralized. Though all aspects of

bureaucracy—rules, universalism, impersonality, tenure, and stability—are criticized, hierarchy, the most characteristic aspect of
bureaucracy, is judged its worst. It is the negation of individual
autonomy, freedom, spontaneity, creativity, dignity, and independence.

The Collegial University

When we think of organizations with elaborate hierarchies, we often
have the government and its bureaus in mind, or perhaps the large
corporation. Professional organizations, according to theory, are not
so arranged—colleagues are at more or less the same level.[20] This
author would probably be considered a professional, as a full professor of sociology in a university, so let us see what I might have
had to go through at the University of Wisconsin in 1970 in order to
make a suggestion, take up an issue, make a complaint, or whatever, if I wished to touch all bases. Theoretically, I would first go to
the assistant chairman of my department, who would send the
matter on to the chairman. The chairman might wish to consult with
the departmental executive committee to be on "solid ground" before proceeding. The departmental chairman would then take it up
with one of the appropriate assistant deans (there are eight to
choose from) in the College of Letters and Science, who would refer
it to one of the associate deans (there are four of them), who would
take it up with the dean of the College of Letters and Science (there
are Colleges of Agriculture, Engineering, etc., each of which has its
dean and associate and assistant deans). If the matter involved the
graduate program at all, it should next go to one of the two assistant
deans, and then to one of the five associate deans of the Graduate
School; then it would be taken up with the dean of the Graduate
School (who would, of course, confer with the dean of the pertinent
college). The Graduate School dean might consult with a student-
faculty committee in the process. After that, it would be taken up by
one of the two assistants to the chancellor, who would refer it to one
of the two vice-chancellors, who would take it up with the chancellor
of the Madison campus (there are other campuses—Milwaukee,
Green Bay, and Parkside among them). The chancellor of the Madison campus would send it along to one of the vice-presidents of the
university (he has seven to choose from), who would take it up with
the president of the university. Supposing that the matter is still
unresolved and has not lost its power of ascent, the president would

---

[20]Talcott Parsons, "Introduction," in Max Weber, *The Theory of Social and
Economic Organization*, pp. 58–60. Amitai Etzioni, *A Comparative Analysis of Complex Organizations* (New York: The Free Press, 1961), pp. 218–261.

take it up with the university's regents. They, in turn, might have to refer to the State Coordinating Council for Higher Education (which has several staff layers of its own). It, though, receives its power from the legislature, whose actions can be vetoed by the governor. Were the matter important enough to go as far as the Coordinating Council, it would have gone through five major levels of authority, each with about three internal levels of authority, for a total of at least fifteen steps in the staircase.

Of course, it is not that simple. We have assumed that the matter did not involve any of the numerous interstitial fiefs, which is highly unlikely. There are numerous councils, committees, divisional organizations (e.g., a chairman of social studies), administrative units (such as the admissions office with its director, associate director, and four assistant directors), the libraries (an Egyptian-sized pyramid in itself), a jumble of business offices, the computing center, counseling services, and offices concerned with public relations, parking, physical plant, protection and security, purchasing, registration, student affairs, and so on—each of which could be involved. A professor has occasion to deal with all of these at times. In addition, much power is exercised by the campus university committee, the senate, the all-university faculty assembly, the university faculty council, the course committee, the divisional executive committee, the social studies committee of the graduate school, the research committee, the honors committee, various student-faculty committees (at the time an area of exponential growth in form, though with little substance), and various all-university committees. These committees plug the interstitial areas of the fifteen levels above me very effectively and relieve all the assistant deans or whatever of their backbreaking loads.

Of course, even with fifteen levels of authority and a tropical jungle of committee growth to go through to get to the top, I would not be at the bottom of the heap. Below me are strung out the associate professors, assistant professors, instructors, lecturers, teaching assistants, graduate students, and, somewhere down there, undergraduates. This is not a chain of command; undergraduates have been known to talk directly to full professors without going through a teaching assistant, for example. But these levels come into operation in numerous ways. For example, if two full professors desire the same office, the one who has been "in rank" longer will generally get it. We cannot really add six more levels below a full professor in terms of authority, though we can in terms of status.

In addition, I might have a secretary, research assistant, undergraduate work study people, and graduate student trainees in a training program, i.e., another little empire. (I have left out the enormous informal power of the head secretary of the department, other directors of training programs or of the graduate program, renowned colleagues, and those who somehow just manage to amass power.) Just to grasp this social structure intellectually, let alone maneuver in it, is a demanding task.[21]

So much for the myth that the university is a collegial body having a minimum of hierarchy and status difference. Nor should one assume that other professional bodies such as the medical staff of a hospital, the Senate of the United States, or the lawyers in a large law firm also enjoy the advantages of lack of hierarchy. The medical personnel in hospitals are generally highly organized with a structure that parallels that of the administrative staff of the hospital. The medical staff has its own nursing committee, outpatient department committee, pharmacy committee, etc., and in between the major ranks of junior and senior attending staff are several clear distinctions in grade, with appropriate powers and entrance criteria.[22] The U.S. Senate is also more highly structured than one would expect on the basis of the contrast between bureaucratic and professional organizations, and it takes a new senator a long time to learn all the aspects of this structure. Even law firms are highly structured.[23] Indeed, any group with a division of labor, professional or not, will be hierarchically structured.

The Sins of Hierarchy

What is the consequence of this ubiquitous structuring of even "professional" organizations? For the critics of bureaucracy, the consequence is that the bulk of people in the lower and middle levels are prevented from really giving their all for goal achievement; they turn, instead, into infantile, fearful robots. The argument runs like this:

---

[21]I wish to thank Robert Taylor, former vice-president of the University of Wisconsin, for constructive comments on this material. As he points out, the chain of command works in a variety of ways, depending upon who or what is involved. "Very little (maybe no) 'traffic' moves up or down this chain in this fashion. The fact is that most of it moves as your letter [to me] did—from professor to vice-president and back with all the other levels left in blessed ignorance. And, of course, no modern student would countenance such a chain for a moment—he'd pick up the phone and call the president or the president of the board of regents, if he thought either of these officials capable of acting on his request." (Private correspondence.) This is true, but in a crunch, the chain is there for those higher up to use it. As we shall see, much short-circuiting of the chain occurs in organizations that are not made up of "professionals."

[22]Charles Perrow, "Goals and Power Structures: A Historical Case Study," and Mary E. W. Goss, "Patterns of Bureaucracy Among Hospital Staff Physicians," in *The Hospital in Modern Society*, ed. Eliot Freidson (New York: The Free Press, 1963).

[23]Erwin O. Smigel, *Wall Street Lawyer*, rev. ed. (Bloomington, Ind.: Indiana Univ. Press, 1970).

The hierarchy promotes rigidity and timidity. Subordinates are afraid of passing up bad news,[24] or of making suggestions for change.[25] (Such an action would imply that their superiors should have thought of the changes and did not.) They also are more afraid of new situations than of familiar ones, since with the new situations, those above them might introduce new evils, while the old ones are sufficient. The hierarchy promotes delays and sluggishness; everything must be kicked upstairs for a decision either because the boss insists or because the subordinate does not want to take the risk of making a poor decision. All this indecision exists at the same time that superiors are being authoritarian, dictatorial, rigid, making snap judgments which they refuse to reconsider, implementing on-the-spot decisions without consulting with their subordinates, and generally stifling any independence or creativity at the subordinate levels. Subordinates are under constant surveillance from superiors; thus they often give up trying to exercise initiative or imagination and instead suppress or distort information. Finally, since everything must go through channels, and these are vertical, two people at the same level in two different departments cannot work things out themselves, but must involve long lines of superiors.

At this point one may wonder how organizations can function at all, but it becomes even more alarming when we consider a contrasting series of complaints frequently made by members of a hierarchy. These are complaints about people in one department making decisions which affect other units without checking first with their respective superiors, and about the *lack* of clear lines of authority, the *failure* to exercise authority or to be decisive, and the *lack* of accountability. Some typical complaints:

1. Who's in charge here? Who am I supposed to take this matter to?

2. That bureau gets away with murder; no one will exercise authority over it, and it is not clear what their authority is supposed to be;

3. Some technician in engineering went ahead and made these design changes in conjunction with a department head in production, but they never bothered to check with the sales manager and the account supervisor in finance;

4. We make changes, and before we can see how well they are working out, we are making more changes;

---

[24]Harold L. Wilensky, *Organizational Intelligence: Knowledge and Policy in Government and Industry* (New York: Basic Books, Inc., 1969), pp. 42–48.

[25]Victor A. Thompson, *Modern Organization*, 2nd ed. (University, Ala.: Univ. of Ala. Press, 1977), Chapter 8.

5. What this place lacks is decisive leadership;

6. No one told me.

In such cases we hear of too much flexibility, too little attention to the hierarchy, too little forceful decision making. According to one survey,[26] managers in industrial firms are decidedly in favor of more, rather than less, clarity in lines of authority, rules, duties, specification of procedures, and so on. Only when the structure is clear can authority be delegated, they indicate, as did Wilfred Brown in the earlier quote regarding rules (see pp. 24–25).

If both the presence and the absence of hierarchy can be faulted, and if authority can be both excessive and absent, change too rapid and too infrequent, employees both fearful and aggressive, gutless and crafty, and flexible and rigid, it suggests that the problem does not lie in hierarchy per se. Some degree of hierarchy is needed in any organized endeavor, but how much and in what kinds of endeavors? We are only beginning to phrase the problem in this fashion, and to get a glimpse of how hierarchies actually work.

Research on Span of Control

Take the matter of "span of control"—the number of subordinates that a superior directly controls. This is the building block of hierarchy. If each superior controls few people—has a narrow span of control—there will be many levels in the organization; if he controls many, there will be few. For twenty to thirty years, social scientists and management theorists debated regarding the optimum span of control—was it four, six, eight, or what? If we only knew, we could design our organizations properly. Embedded in this discussion was the assumption that if a manager had many people under him, he could not supervise them closely, and thus they would have more autonomy.[27] This assumption was furthered in an influential piece of reporting by a personnel man with Sears Roebuck who described how morale and efficiency improved when the number of levels in the organization was reduced.[28]

Of course, as is true of most "principles" of organization, there was an alternative view—rarely stated as a principle, but acted upon by management consulting firms. This principle said that if a man had a lot of people reporting to him, he was centralizing power

---

[26]Charles Perrow, "Working Paper on Technology and Structure," mimeographed, February 1970.

[27]William F. Whyte, "Human Relations—A Progress Report," in *Complex Organizations, A Sociological Reader*, ed. Amitai Etzioni (New York: Holt, Rinehart & Winston, Inc., 1962), pp. 100–112.

[28]James C. Worthy, "Organizational Structure and Employee Morale," *American Sociological Review* 15 (1950): 169–179.

and would not want to give it up. Such a man should establish an intermediate level in order to give his subordinates some leeway. A wide span of control meant reluctance to delegate, rather than delegation.

Few theorists took the rule-of-thumb wisdom of the management consultants seriously, however. One of the best theorists, for example, is Peter Blau. He and his associates conducted a study of 156 public personnel agencies, starting with "a few plausible considerations" which led to inferences "which appeared straightforward and perhaps even self-evident." They reasoned that if a person was well trained, he would need little supervision. The span of control would be wide. If personnel were not well trained, they would need more supervision, and the span of control would be narrow and the hierarchy higher. (In the language of journal articles, it reads like this: The inferences suggested, "as an initial hypothesis, that expert requirements decrease the ratio of managerial to nonsupervisory personnel in organizations, which widens the average span of control."[29])

To the admitted surprise of Blau and associates, the hypothesis was found to be incorrect. The more qualified the people, the *less* the span of control. They then suggested that the explanation might be that a narrow span of control—only two or three subordinates for each superior—allows easy consultation on difficult problems and permits common problem solving. Though they did not state it directly, this would suggest that wide spans of control could mean close supervision but little consultation.

Actually, as is so true in much of organizational research, the resolution of the dilemma lies in distinguishing different types of organizations or situations. In some cases, a span of control of ten can mean close supervision through highly routinized controls over people performing routine tasks; in others, it can mean very little supervision, with the ten subordinates working out things with each other and only occasionally seeking the advice or direction of the boss.[30] The span of control, then, can be independent of the close-

---

[29]Peter Blau, "The Hierarchy of Authority in Organizations," *American Journal of Sociology* 73 (January 1968): 453–457.

[30]See, for example, the various discussions by Joan Woodward, *Industrial Organization: Theory and Practice* (London: Oxford University Press, 1965). In discussing span of control, Lorsch generally finds a broad span is associated with nonroutine tasks, contrary to Blau. But on the other hand, in the routine production department of one of his companies, Lorsch also finds a broad span of control. See Jay W. Lorsch, *Product Innovation and Organization* (New York: The Macmillan Company, 1965), p. 53. For a good discussion and additional evidence supporting Blau's view see Gerald Bell, "Determinants of Span of Control," *American Journal of Sociology* 73, no. 1 (July 1967): 90–101.

ness of supervision. Supervision can be direct or indirect with either a wide or a narrow span of control.

The span of control, in turn, affects the degree of hierarchy, or the number of levels of supervision in an organization. Where spans of control are wide, the organization tends to be "squat"—there are not many levels of authority. Where spans of control are narrow, the organization tends to have a narrow, "tall" hierarchy, with many levels of authority. But we have argued that a squat organization does not necessarily mean either close or distant supervision. There are a number of factors which might affect the closeness of supervision (beyond, of course, the personality and leadership style of a manager), and they are worth listing to indicate the complexity of the matter:

1. The degree to which tasks are routine or nonroutine;

2. The difference between the expertise of the manager and that of his subordinates; the amount of interdependence among tasks under one manager; and the interdependence of these tasks with those performed under different managers;

3. The interdependence of the department as a whole with other departments in the organization, and the varying kinds of routine and nonroutine mixes of the departments;

4. The degree to which written rules and regulations or machines can reduce the need for personal supervision;

5. The extent to which flexibility and rapid response is necessary to the organization.

Given these relevant sources of variation, it remains to be seen whether, as Blau maintains, the relationship they suggested between span of control and supervision is likely to hold in all organizations.

Using the same data, Marshall Meyer concludes that there are two strategies available to organizations—control through direct supervision, utilizing a wide span of control, which promotes flexibility of response since the manager can change things quickly; and control through rules, regulations, and professional expertise, utilizing a greater number of hierarchical levels with a narrow span of control, which promotes more "rational" administration and more stable operations.[31] Blau also concludes that there are two types of organizations, but he labels the first the "old-fashioned bureaucracy." It has a "squat hierarchy with authority centralized at the top," little automation, and personnel rules that emphasize managerial discretion, seniority, and personal judgment. The second he calls the "modern organization" with a "tall, slim hierarchy with

[31]Marshall Meyer, "Two Authority Structures of Bureaucratic Organizations," *Administrative Science Quarterly* 13 (September 1968): 211–228.

decentralized authority," relying upon experts, automation, and universalistic personnel procedures (objective merit standards).[32]

Meyer's data show only weak support for Blau's conclusions; the differences between the two types of strategies are in the predicted direction but are quite small. The important thing, however, is that they are *not* in the *opposite* direction; that is, the usual view of hierarchy would indicate that the higher the degree of hierarchy the greater the centralized control.[33] But that does not hold here. If anything, the greater hierarchy is associated with decentralization. Blau handles his data somewhat differently and finds somewhat stronger relationships, but more important, he finds the relationships consistent over three types of organizations: personnel departments, finance departments, and state employment agencies. Thus, even though the differences may not be large in any one sample, the consistency over the three is impressive.

Furthermore, a quite independent and large study in England, generally referred to as the Aston Study because the team, headed by Derek Pugh, was then at the University of Aston in Birmingham, came to very similar conclusions.[34] In the Blau and the Aston studies, the gap between the indicators used and the concepts these indicators were supposed to represent is often very large. For example, the items that are used to measure the degree of delegation of authority, or decentralization, refer only to decisions which are visible, binary (either-or) and capable of clear statement in official rules, such as the level at which a certain amount of money can be spent without prior authorization. More subtle, basic, and certainly more powerful decisions are not measured; these may be quite centralized. We refer to this as the problem of "operationaliza-

---

[32]Blau, "Hierarchy." There are complex problems here of different degrees of "tallness" in different units of an organization which are not relevant for these agencies, but would be for most organizations.

[33]See, for example, Worthy, "Employee Morale." It is noteworthy that in a study of school teachers that used, by and large, unloaded questions to tap bureaucracy, it was found that, quite contrary to the authors' expectations, "Teachers in highly bureaucratic systems had a significantly higher, not lower, sense of power than those in less bureaucratic systems." See Gerald H. Moeller and W. W. Charters, "Relation of Bureaucratization to Sense of Power Among Teachers," *Administrative Science Quarterly* 10, no. 4 (March 1966): 457. These authors were as surprised as Blau and his associates but fell back upon the influence of other factors which might have clouded or reversed a relationship predicted by most schools of thought.

[34]The best summary and introduction to these studies is that of John Child, "Predicting and Understanding Organization Structure," *Administrative Science Quarterly* 18:2 (June 1973): 168–185. For a sample of the criticisms of this important survey see Howard Aldrich, "Technology and Organizational Structure: A Reexamination of the Findings of the Aston Group," *Administrative Science Quarterly* 17:1 (March 1972): 26–43, and Sergio E. Mindlin and Howard Aldrich, "Interorganizational Dependence: A Review of the Concepts and Reexamination of the Findings of the Aston Group," *Administrative Science Quarterly* 20:3 (September 1975): 382–392.

tion," or making the measurement of concepts operational. The operationalization of the concept of hierarchy in the Aston Study was particularly controversial. Nevertheless, one can have some confidence in the findings of the Blau and Aston studies for three important reasons: (1) they are independently arrived at, using different measures; (2) they were unexpected by both research teams; and (3) they are counterintuitive.

In short, we cannot assume that the more hierarchical the organization, the more centralized it is. If the limited data show anything, they indicate an inverse relationship. More important, the very characteristics that both Blau and Meyer ascribe to their tall, hierarchical, and decentralized organizations are those which Weber stressed in his bureaucratic model: expertise, written rules and regulations, clear ordering of positions, and hierarchy. The characteristics of the squat centralized organization are personal rule, personal evaluations, and low expertise. These are closer to the traditional model which the development of bureaucracy attempted to supplant.

Hierarchy and Timidity

Another attribute often associated with tall hierarchies is timidity and caution on the part of subordinates who fear criticism from superiors and thus fear to pass unpleasant information up the line. That such an attitude exists in bureaucracies is clear, but that it is an inevitable concomitant of hierarchy, and thus its product, is far from clear. Timidity and caution appear to vary greatly among bureaucracies, on the basis of casual impressions. Peter Blau, in his study of two government agencies, commented that he found little evidence of this behavior.[35] It certainly does not show up among the more successful managers in Dalton's study,[36] nor among all managers in Gouldner's study.[37] Why, then, the variation?

It would seem that tendencies toward conservatism and self-protective behavior are natural outcomes of all organized activity that is not spontaneously coordinated and based upon wholehearted cooperation, but that organizations have mechanisms to minimize the danger and even reverse the tendency. For example, people can be rewarded for passing up critical items of information; the reward may have to be high if it reflects upon one's superior, but if it is that important to the organization it can be done. Actually, the opposite is sometimes a problem—a man gets ahead by showing up his superior. Between these two stances—timidity and cun-

---

[35]Blau, *Dynamics.*
[36]Dalton, *Men Who Manage.*
[37]Gouldner, *Industrial Bureaucracy.*

ning—there is the far more usual situation where constructive criticisms are encouraged and rewarded because the boss can get the credit. Accounting departments are generally rewarded for critical information, which is why, in the organization Dalton studied, it was so essential for aggressive managers to neutralize or bribe the accountants. Innovative and risk-taking behavior may be harder to reward than conservative behavior, but it is possible to do it.

Timidity and caution appear to be functions of the technology and market of organizations, rather than of their degree of hierarchy. In some market situations—e.g., social security administration, aid to dependent children, railroads, public utilities, mining (especially where there are oligopolistic situations such as with sulphur mining)—there is little perceived need for risk-taking. In other large and equally bureaucratic organizations—the Agency for International Development in its golden days of the late 1950s and early 1960s, the federal rehabilitation agencies during the 1950s and early 1960s, which used the money dumped upon them by an uncomprehending Congress to upgrade physically healthy but untrained blacks, and the electronics and chemical industries—risk-taking is much more in evidence. There is no evidence that these organizations had fewer levels of authority than more conservative organizations.

Still, problems remain. Some officials do insist that a great many minor matters be brought to their attention before action is taken. The explanation may be that they are poor administrators, insecure administrators, or have incompetent subordinates. This happens all the time, but it can hardly be attributed to hierarchy alone. Sometimes it is impossible to get an answer out of a higher officer; the explanation may simply be that he does not know and unfortunately will not admit it, or that he is still searching, or that he is perhaps hoping that the lower officer will go ahead and make the decision (and take the blame if it is wrong). But someone has to decide, and the principle of hierarchy at least specifies *who* should decide if ambiguity exists. Wilfred Brown observes that the principal function of a hierarchy is to resolve disputes or uncertainties; things go on well enough without slavishly going through channels if there is no dispute and no uncertainty.[38]

The Official and the Unofficial Hierarchical Order

One of the true delights of the organizational expert is to indicate to the uninitiated the wide discrepancy between the official hierarchy (or rules, for that matter) and the unofficial one. It is a remarkable phenomenon in many cases, and well known to most people who

---

[38]Wilfred Brown, *Exploration in Management.*

have to spend their working lives as managers in organizations. Departmental secretaries in many universities have power far beyond their status. David Mechanic's well-known essay, "Sources of Power of Lower Participants in Complex Organization," touches on this and other examples.[39] Melville Dalton, in his excruciatingly unsettling study of a manufacturing plant, reveals top people with no power and those three or four levels below with extensive power.[40] Sociologists have been particularly fond of the contrast between the official and the unofficial because it indicates that organizations are natural systems rather than artificial or mechanistic ones—living things that the men within them create out of their own needs, rather than rational tools in the hands of a master. They are right, of course: between the conception and the reality, as the poet tells us, falls the shadow. The first thing the new employee should learn is who is really in charge, who has the goods on whom, what are the major debts and dependencies—all things that are not reflected by the neat boxes in the table of organization. Once he has this knowledge he can navigate with more skill and ease.

For the organizational theorists, however, a different kind of question is required: What are the systematic bases for the deviations? We should not expect the official map to be completely accurate because:

1. It is never up-to-date—it does not reflect the growing power of a subordinate who will be promoted over his boss in a year or two, or the waning power of a boss who has been passed by because of changes in technology or markets;

2. It does not pretend to make the finely graded distinctions that operating personnel have to live by—e.g., three departments may be on the same official level, but one of them is three times the size of the other two and may carry a commensurate increment in power;

3. It does not reflect all transactions in the organization, but primarily those disputes that can be settled formally;

4. Most important, the hierarchy functions primarily for routine situations; when new ones come along, someone two levels down may have more say for this or that situation, but unless the new situation itself becomes the persistent or frequent one, his authority will only be temporary. If it persists, he may well move up fast;

5. Finally, hierarchical principles are sometimes violated intentionally; when, for example, the head office cannot get enough information about a division's operation, it sends in a spy. Dalton describes such a case. The man involved had a relatively unimportant job of manager of industrial relations, but his power over

---

[39]David Mechanic, "Sources of Power of Lower Participants in Complex Organization," *Administrative Science Quarterly* 7, no. 4 (December 1962): 349–364.

[40]Dalton, *Men Who Manage*, Chapter 2.

many other aspects of the organization was substantial because everyone knew that he was there to find out what was going on.

Few organizations keep an official chart of offices ranked by authority for very long or, if they do, such charts are rarely referred to. (Some organizations even refuse to draw them up.) Positions and units move up and down in authority over time, and the lag with the official chart is always there. Thus, we should not be surprised at the discrepancy, nor should we assume that the unofficial is necessarily a more accurate rendition than the official. The two are just different and only briefly join hands in their mutual evolution. While the "natural" or "living" system is important, it may only be a wistful and touching part of a rather mechanical and imperative whole. The fact that the dean and I (or the chancellor and I, or the president and I) are both professors in a collegial body of equals is as much a romance of the actual situation as the view that only the yeasty, vital, living, informal system counts in an organization. The official hierarchy is there, and no one who is not kidding himself forgets it. He must know it to survive it.

THREE USES OF HIERARCHY

Perhaps the most common criticism of hierarchy (and related aspects of bureaucratization, such as the emphasis upon rules) results from the failure to attribute to hierarchy the successes that it enjoys. If things are going well, we talk of cooperation; if they are going badly, we speak of the "emphasis upon hierarchy" or this "goddamned bureaucracy" with all its red tape and gutless or overbearing people. Three semifictional examples of problem solving in organizations will illustrate this. (These are composites of situations I observed while studying industrial firms.)

Example A: Task Specialization

A foreman in the rolling mill of a steel company (where hot strips of steel are passed between heavy rollers to reduce their width, lengthen them, and change their molecular structure) is having difficulty with cracks in the ends of steel bars. The ends must be cut off, his scrap rate rises, and longer bars than are necessary must be rolled. He is not personally held accountable for the waste, but it is an annoyance, requires explanations, and offends his sense of craftsmanship. He decides on the basis of past experience that the problem may be due to the length of time the bar spends in the annealing furnace (which gives it a slow bake) before it reaches

FIGURE 1   SIMPLIFIED CHART FOR EXAMPLES OF HIERARCHY

Level					
II	V.P. Production		V.P. Research & Development	V.P. Sales	
III	General Superintendent of Production		Research Director Metallurgy	General Manager	
IV	Superintendent of Melting	Superintendent of Processing	Superintendent of Process Research	Account Supervisor	Tool Steel Sales Manager
V	Melting Supervisor	Rolling Mill Supervisor	Research Group A Supervisor	Regional Sales Manager	
VI	Foreman Furnace A	Foreman 10-Inch Mill	Technician	Salesman	

him. If the time were longer, he feels, the bars would not crack. He asks his supervisor to request the annealing unit to leave them in longer. His supervisor says, "We better check with the metallurgical department in Research to see if this will make it more difficult to grind and shape the bars for the customer. I will call the director of metallurgy; he will know who to ask." (Note that the supervisor thereby skips a level in the hierarchy *and* crosses departmental lines. See the accompanying chart which presents a simplified version of an official chart, omitting many departments and functions not relevant here. The level is noted at certain points in my narrative as an aid in judging the fit between hierarchy and interaction.) The metallurgy director (Level III) says, "I'll have Charley check it and he will let you know." Charley is a technician (VI) in Research and Development (R&D) and happens to be more or less at the foreman level (it is difficult to compare the levels of authority in departments like R&D or Sales with those in Production). But he knows these problems better than his own immediate supervisor of Research Group A (V), who is new, or the superintendent of Process Research (IV), who coordinates several groups and is out of touch with detailed problems. (Note, then, that the research director (III) has skipped two levels of authority in his own organization.)

At this point, Charley might say to the rolling mill supervisor, "We don't know. It very well might and it is a good thing you checked. But it would take a week of research to find out, and since we have all these other projects it would have to be spread out over a month or two. To get this entered into our schedule would require the authorization of the Group A supervisor, and I know that he will have to check with the superintendent of Process Research because things are tight right now. The latter is away for a week visiting customer plants, but we could estimate the amount of delay to other projects and call him." If this were the response, the cry of "bureaucracy" or "hierarchy" might go up, and the foreman would think twice about making another suggestion. Nevertheless, the response would be perfectly proper and in the interests of the organization.

To simplify matters, though, let us assume that Charley says, "I doubt that it would have any effect upon machineability. But if this steel is being used to make cutting tools for numerically controlled machining tools [highly automated devices], it might affect their cutting life because of the heat generated. Someone better check to see what this grade is used for." So the supervisor of the rolling mill calls the account supervisor in Sales to find out who handles this particular account. The account supervisor gives him the name of a salesman (VI). The salesman is out, but he is finally located on the other side of the country. He does not know what the customer is using this grade for, but he will check. In a couple of days he finds out. "It would be all right, though we should probably let them know about the change so they can do a tool-life check; they are a big customer and are quite particular about these things. But the main problem is that there are some touchy negotiations going on with that company. I am not affected by them; they concern stainless steel. But I picked it up from the secretary of the vice-president of Sales. You had better check with the manager of Tool Steel Sales" (IV).

Parenthetically, to have information about the touchy negotiations is not part of this salesman's responsibility, but it is an important bit of gossip for him to have picked up. If he had not picked it up the minor change in steel characteristics would endanger a large order, as we shall see. But any manager in any organization picks up all the rumors he can about these sorts of things; the official lines of communication, strung up and down the official hierarchy, are designed less to inform than to record action, less to initiate than to justify and protect action. "Do it first, and let the paperwork and official authorizations follow" is a frequent injunction when time is at a premium or novel events are being dealt with. On the other hand, much communication outside the official lines is only occasionally important and utilized, such as this bit of gossip. To design a communications system to handle all the informal bits of information formally would create a monster.

The matter now goes to the tool steel manager who says, "Yes, we are trying to negotiate a contract with Universal to buy our new type of stainless steel. It involves a different part of the organization than tool steel, of course, but the purchasing agent who is in on these negotiations also handles tool steel purchases. I (IV) will check with the vice-president of Sales (II) about the status of the negotiations, or even with the president (I) if the V.P. is not around this week. We cannot, of course, put anything in writing, and we better stay off the phone, too." (That is, they could not call the V.P. at a customer's plant because the customer probably had bugged the line; industrial espionage is a very big and serious business.)

The whole thing might fall apart at this point because the negotiations have been touchy, and if word got to the purchasing agent that the customer would be subjected to the nuisance of a tool-life check, he might be a little more cool than he already is to the deal. He is already cool because the steel firm did the very unusual thing of refusing to hire his college-going, hell-raising son again for a plush summer job. Purchasing agents do not expect such treatment. But the lad was so unreliable and stirred up so much trouble that the steel company gave him a company car and told him to stay away the rest of the summer. Putting this aside, however, let us say that the vice-president of Sales (II) tells the tool steel manager (IV):

"The purchasing agent hasn't got a thing to say about this, it is up to their vice-president of Production and we can promise better deliveries than the competition. Anyway, I hate the purchasing agent's guts. Tell production to go ahead if they want." (He then mumbles to himself, "Why do they have to bring every little thing to me? What is the V.P. of Production doing anyway?")

The foreman of the 10-inch rolling mill, who has been wondering what has been holding up such a simple matter for two or three weeks, finally gets his go-ahead, providing the annealing department will agree. The salesman has to be informed so he can tell the customer when a slightly different type of steel will be coming through. (He decides to tell the customer that this constitutes a minor breakthrough in increasing quality, since he suspects that if the customer views it in this light, the tool-life checks are more likely to be positive—a sound judgment which conforms to social science experimental evidence on perception and "experimenter effect.") The foreman then tries the new method out and finds that it makes no difference at all in terms of the degree to which ends of the bars crack and have to be scrapped.

We have just described a moderately hierarchical organization. But our remarks about hierarchy were asides. We also described a series of specialized functions, tasks, and sequences—which we could have done without reference to the hierarchy. The V.P. of Sales (II) knew about some negotiations; the lowly salesman (VI) knew about product usage. The V.P. of Production (II) probably will never hear of the event, and would not even if the technique had worked. (If it might have resulted in large savings, the superintendent of Production (III) would have heard about it from the superintendent of Processing (IV), who would have been told by the rolling mill supervisor (V), so that all could claim credit. The V.P. of Production, then, of course, would have kept the president (I) informed at all stages. The hierarchy is always involved when rewards are at stake.) Had anything gone wrong at any point, it might have occasioned curses about the hierarchical aspects of the company. ("Everything has to go up to the manager of metallurgy, and he is so scared of his position that he refuses to approve anything"—a doubtful, if useful, generalization, since he probably would not last long if that were true, or else he would be ignored and someone else would make the decision.) But the hierarchy was important, if only implicit, in this example. The supervisor relied upon the metallurgy manager to decide who in his group would know about the consequences of annealing times; the tool steel manager had to buck a decision about relationships with the customer up to his superior, the V.P. of Sales. The hierarchy established routes of communication where information was needed and levels where certain kinds of decisions could be made. The foreman could not undertake all these inquiries himself since he did not have the access to the hierarchy that his supervisor did, and also because he was too busy rolling steel. His supervisor exists to handle such communications. Thus, in this commonplace example of organizational problem solving, we find specialized tasks and hierarchies merged; one could not function without the other. Though the hierarchy was crucial because it identified knowledge sources and decision powers, the participants would never think to praise its existence. Most of the times that it serves its function, it is unnoticed.

Example B: Hierarchy

Let us imagine another situation, however, where this hierarchy and division of labor would not function well. Let us assume that the impetus for change comes from outside. The aforementioned customer, along with other customers, has installed new machinery, and the type of steel the firm had used before for drills and routers no longer works very well. The customers thus need tougher steel and longer bits, but there is no economical grade they can shift to. They put it up to their suppliers (they undoubtedly buy from more than one supplier to hedge against poor deliveries or changes in quality). Whoever supplies it first will have a substantial competitive edge for some time. They tell the salesman (VI) and also the tool steel manager (IV). This creates a crisis in the supplying organization—a crash program is needed to develop a steel with somewhat different characteristics. In a highly structured, hierarchical organization the sequence would be something as follows:

The tool steel manager (IV) would contact the general manager of Sales (III) who would tell the V.P. of Sales (II), since this is an important matter. The latter would contact his opposite number in Research—the V.P. of Research (II). He, in turn, would bring in the manager of metallurgy (III) and others on his staff, and order a research program. Other projects would have to be dropped or slowed up, so the head of Research or his metallurgy manager would contact other parts of Sales and Production, telling them of the impending delays. The research program would then go ahead, and after a few weeks, or even months, Research would come up with a likely steel. The V.P. of Research (II) would take this to the V.P. of Production (II), who would pass it on down the line of his organization until, after a few days, it got to the melting, cogging, and rolling work stations. The melters would try out the new recipe, no doubt running into trouble, send the message of "trouble" up the production hierarchy to the V.P., who would inform the V.P. of Research, who would send it down his side. After the trouble is corrected, the cogging mill might find that the new steel is too hard to shape on the press usually used for this purpose, so they must get permission from Production to put it on the larger press (which means delaying other work). After all that is settled, rolling will probably run into problems, and will inform the plant superintendent or the V.P. of Production, through channels, who will take the matter up again with his counterpart in Research. And so on.

The hierarchy is involved at almost every step, on the grounds of task specialization. But, in fact, the manager of metallurgy or the V.P. of Production may not need to make all the decisions he does, since all he decides is that the usual, official lines of communication and authority shall be utilized. If so, this is a misuse of the hierarchy. Once the decision has been made to go ahead with the program—a decision that must move up the proper channels for authorization—it should be defined as a matter for the experts involved. Their superiors must be informed of what they are doing so they can monitor the task, but they do not need to make any further decisions unless, of course, the budget is to be exceeded or there is a clash with other priorities that cannot be settled at a lower level. Why, then, would the managers behave as they did in example B, treating a novel event as if it could traverse the hierarchy in the same manner as a routine one? There might be many reasons. Unfamiliarity with an event like this (lack of precedent) can cause insecurity. A struggle for power or prestige may turn upon the failure of one or another group to do its job well, so that constant surveillance is required, and since lower level managers do not want to get blamed for something when the stakes are so high, they seek unnecessary authorization. Or it might be simple job insecurity or even ineptitude on the part of someone in the hierarchy, which forces all to play his game.

Example C: The Task Group

In contrast, let us say that after receiving the signal from the customer, the manager of Tool Steel Sales (IV), perhaps familiar with this sort of problem, suggests to the director of metallurgy (III) and the superintendent of Production (III) the setting up of a special task force. They decide who should be on it, what its mission should be, and probably set up at this time two or three other groups to be activated later on. Research starts to work on the problem, but while doing so consults with the superintendent of Melting, the superintendent of Processing, and someone from Sales who knows about the various other schedules that might be disrupted. Research, rather than pushing to a final elegant solution, gets Melting to try out a variety of plausible mixes in one of the small melting furnaces when they are not in heavy use. A few of these are tried out in the intermediate press and other cogging and rolling operations. These decisions are made without reference to anyone higher in the hierarchy than the members of the task force, and in most cases they are made by people considerably lower—e.g., the foreman of the 10-inch rolling mill, whom we met before, is brought into the matter, and he tells the melters that if they add a little sulphur it might help, and the research technician, whom we also met before, is sitting there and says that that would louse everything up, but if you cooled it faster it might work, and so on. Meanwhile, when normal production runs are about to be slowed up by these special efforts, the representative of Sales finds out what would be the least costly way of handling it and talks to people—perhaps two levels above him in the sales hierarchy—so they know why things will be delayed and why they will have to do a little extra selling to keep their customers happy. Back and forth the experimentation goes on, with the metallurgical lab and research people in continual contact with those on the shop floor, until a steel that meets the customer's requirements and can be made on the firm's equipment at a reasonable price emerges. Only then do people from Levels II and III need to be contacted.

Discussion

In our first example, a fairly routine change was made in procedure, and hierarchy and task specialization merged easily; they were coterminous. The organization was set up to handle just such events. In the second example, the hierarchy took precedence over task specialization and expertise. A routine, noncrisis solution was applied to a nonroutine crisis situation. At the same time, the hierarchy was made to bear the load of insecurity or mistrust or ineptitude. This meant that the volume of official communication was high (e.g., things had to go back and forth from Production to Research) and efforts were wasted (e.g., a solution from Research would be scrapped because it would not work in Melting, and a new one started). But everyone did what he was trained to do and, presumably, quite efficiently. In the third case, hierarchy is de-emphasized and task specialization is emphasized. This was defined as a special event; a new temporary unit was set up to deal with it, and it was designed to interfere as little as possible with the routine flow of events that went on around it. The organizational structure for handling routine events was not changed or affected. Indeed, the official hierarchy could not be abandoned since it serviced routine work.

PROFESSIONALISM AND DISCIPLINE

The final criticism of bureaucracy that we shall consider is one of the most attractive and widespread. Virtually every discussion of bureaucracy mentions this point. It concerns the discrepancy between the expertise of the subordinate and that of his superior. That is to say, it involves the manager or official who knows less about things than the people that work for him, yet who exercises authority over them. This is an attractive criticism because we all resent, more or less, those who have authority over us when we suspect that we know more about things on the firing line than they do. The outstanding example of this concerns professionals in organizations. The manager of professionals often simply cannot be as well informed as those highly trained people under him. Social scientists have always been preoccupied with the plight of professionals and have defended their interests extensively.

This whole line of thought started with a footnote in Talcott Parsons' introduction to his translation of parts of Weber's *Economy and Society*. Weber, Parsons said, confused two types of authority in his discussion—the authority that is based upon "technical competence," and the authority based upon "incumbency of a legally defined office."[41] Could there not be a discrepancy between the two? Could there not be officials who were not experts but who directed the work of those who were? Indeed, there were examples, asserted Parsons. Unfortunately, his main example had little to do with organizations, and his second example was something less than relevant. Since this is possibly the most important footnote in the history of organizational theory, it is worth digging into at some length.

Parsons' main example was the physician whose "authority rests fundamentally on the belief on the part of the patient that the physician has and will employ for his benefit a technical competence adequate to help him in his illness." The trouble with the example is that in this role the physician does not function in an organization. Parsons recognizes this, but adds that where he does function in an organization, "instead of a rigid hierarchy of status and authority [hierarchies are always rigid, one gathers] there tends to be what is roughly, in formal status, a 'company of equals,' an equalization of status which ignores the inevitable gradation of distinction and achievement to be found in any considerable group of technically competent persons."[42] However, the evidence from studies of hospitals indicates that medical staffs are quite bureau-

---

[41]Parsons, "Introduction," in Weber, *Theory of Social and Economic Organizations*, p. 59.
[42]Ibid., p. 60.

cratic in their organizational functioning, with hierarchies that are apparent; moreover, they are quite sensitive to "inevitable gradations of distinction and achievement."[43]

His other example concerns "powers of coercion in case of recalcitrance." It is not logically essential, he says, that the person with this power "should have either superior knowledge or superior skill as compared to those subject to his orders. Thus, the treasurer of a corporation is empowered to sign checks disbursing large funds. There is no implication in this 'power' that he is a more competent signer of checks than the bank clerks or tellers who cash or deposit them for the recipient."[44] The example is irrelevant because the power of the treasurer rests in his knowledge that certain checks should be made out and sent, not in his ability to sign his name.

Nevertheless, despite these two quite weak illustrations, the idea took immediate root. (Many earlier writers had noted the possible discrepancy between authority and expertise, of course, but Parsons made it famous.) Everyone, it appears, could think of superiors who were less competent than their subordinates, and the bureaucratic dilemma of expertise and discipline was firmly established. Alvin Gouldner used it as the organizing basis for his previously mentioned study of a gypsum plant, *Patterns of Industrial Bureaucracy*.[45] In his hands, it became the explanation for two contrasting bureaucratic patterns—representative bureaucracy, which relied upon expertise "based on rules established by agreement, rules which are technically justified and administered by specially qualified personnel, and to which consent is given voluntarily," and punishment-centered bureaucracy, "based on the imposition of rules, and on obedience for its own sake."[46] He, too, thought that Weber saw things two ways; in one, administration was based upon expertise, and in the other "Weber held that bureaucracy was a mode of administration in which obedience was an end in itself."[47] (That Weber held nothing of the sort regarding obedience is not important here; it is the distinction that is. Gouldner's representative pattern, incidentally, is based upon the slim reed of a safety rule.)

Stanley Udy, studying records of organizations in primitive societies, and Arthur Stinchcombe, in his discussion of the organization of the construction industry, come to much the same conclusion—that there are two fundamentally different forms of organiza-

[43]Perrow and Goss in Freidson, ed., *The Hospital in Modern Society*.

[44]Parsons, "Introduction," in Weber, *Theory of Social and Economic Organizations*, p. 60.

[45]Gouldner, *Industrial Bureaucracy*.

[46]Ibid., p. 24.

[47]Ibid., p. 22.

tions, rational or professional organizations and bureaucratic ones.[48] But data on primitive organizations, and the statistics from the construction industry, have dubious relevance for modern large-scale organizations, though both of these studies are excellent for other purposes. The latest use of the distinction is by Peter Blau in the article cited above, where it sets the stage for his analysis.[49] But it is apparent that the professionalized (and more hierarchical) organizations are the closest to the Weberian ideal, as we have seen. Blau's data thus support the opposite conclusion—professionalism is consistent with bureaucracy. While Weber asserted the importance of strict discipline, he was much more emphatic about the critical importance of expertise.[50]

But the real use of this distinction has been in the voluminous literature on professionals in organizations, certainly the hottest single topic in the field of organizational analysis during the early 1960s. With the increasing importance of university-trained scientists and engineers in organizations, the expense of these people, and the need to keep their morale high in a highly competitive employment market, a number of social scientists began to study their adjustment to industrial organizations. Some of these studies were concerned mostly with research laboratories, where the work was complex, innovative, unstructured, and unpredictable. These were truly new organizations that were difficult to cut to the bureaucratic mold. Some sense of the enormous importance of charismatic leadership, individual autonomy, and serendipity can be gleaned from the fascinating account of the way J. Robert Oppenheimer directed the large Los Alamos laboratory, where the first atomic bombs were built, during the Second World War.[51] The ef-

---

[48]Stanley H. Udy, Jr., "'Bureaucracy' and 'Rationality' in Weber's Organization Theory," *American Sociological Review* 24 (1959): 591–595; Arthur L. Stinchcombe, "Bureaucratic and Craft Administration of Production," *Administrative Science Quarterly* 4 (1959): 168–187.

[49]Blau, "Hierarchy."

[50]See Weber, *Theory of Social and Economic Organizations*, pp. 337–339, for the following: "The primary source of bureaucratic administration lies in the role of technical knowledge. . . . Bureaucratic administration means fundamentally the exercise of control on the basis of knowledge. This is the feature of it which makes it specifically rational. . . . Bureaucracy is superior in knowledge, including both technical knowledge and knowledge of the concrete fact. . . ."

[51]Nuel Pharr David, *Lawrence and Oppenheimer* (New York: Simon and Schuster, Inc., 1968), Chapters 6 and 7. General Groves is reported to have said, "Here at great expense the government has assembled the world's largest collection of crackpots," (pp. 173–174). He proceeded to run it like an asylum as well as a factory. Group leaders were required to turn in reports on the daily hours worked by Nobel laureates and other top scientists. The purpose, which they did not know, was to keep down absenteeism. "The payroll office did not know what to do with work reports ranging up to a preposterous and unreimbursable eighteen hours a day." The mili-

forts of General Groves (under whom Oppenheimer worked) to bureaucratize the enterprise—to treat it as if it were turning out Sherman tanks—had disastrous effects on morale and productivity. This example is more pertinent for understanding professionals than, say, studies of such research labs as Bell Laboratories or the DuPont experimental station, since in the Los Alamos case a single product was turned out—a bomb. In the labs, the administrative organization is an umbrella over scores of individual or small-group projects that produce diverse outputs unrelated to one another. To generalize from this highly decentralized type of operation to the usual case of large groups of professionals working on various aspects of one problem or product is misleading.

Many of the studies of scientists in industry, however, did deal with actual industrial organizations with a common problem focus rather than with universitylike basic research labs. They revealed, in keeping with antibureaucratic views, that scientists did indeed resent the constraints placed upon them by the organization in general, and by their superiors in particular, and preferred the luxuries of academic life such as flexible schedules, few deadlines, uninhibited bull sessions, conference-going, freedom to publish, and so on. This is not surprising. If you present yourself as a sociologist or a psychologist from a university and ask if these things are not valued more than profits, production deadlines, and restrictions on publications and inability to study whatever problem one is interested in, the answer is very likely to be yes. The hypothesis is confirmed: there is a conflict between professional values and bureaucratic ones.

However, if one asked a question such as the following, the answer might be quite different: "Would you sooner spend most of your time working on a basic problem that might result in an academic journal publication, but be of little value to the company, or on a problem the company is interested in which might bring you a handsome bonus and a promotion?" Such a question has not been asked, but it poses the dilemma in realistic terms. I suspect that the

---

tary police closed up the labs at five o'clock every afternoon. Said a physicist, "Apparently they didn't have orders to throw us out, but they did have orders to lock up the supplies. We sawed around the locks on the stockroom doors and just stayed and worked. We kept a refrigerator full of sandwich stuff because everybody was pretty hungry by four in the morning, our usual quitting time. After a while, whoever was directing the M.P.'s caught the spirit of the thing and stopped replacing the locks" (p. 181). Another scientist contrasted the University of California lab at Berkeley, run by Ernest Lawrence, with the Los Alamos complex. They were similar only in the long hours put in. "The difference was the atmosphere. There you did whatever task they assigned you and learned not to ask why. Here (Los Alamos) you asked what you liked and at least thought you did what you liked. There the pressure came from outside. Here there didn't seem to be any pressure" (pp. 181–182).

majority of scientists and engineers in industry would choose the profitable project. The reasons are close at hand. The education these men receive in a university is from departments that are vocationally oriented.[52] Engineering departments and such science departments as chemistry and geology are designed to meet industrial needs, at least at the undergraduate level, and in many places at the graduate levels. Professors in these departments judge the quality of their teaching by the status of the companies in which their students obtain jobs. The professors also consult with industrial firms. The curriculum is designed to be relevant to industrial employment. The large majority of the students go into industry. Once there, they find that the route to power, prestige, and money is through serving the company and, in particular, through getting out of technical work and into management. Dalton has observed that the action and the rewards are in line positions rather than in staff (professional) positions.[53] A study by Fred Goldner and R. R. Ritti of recent engineering graduates, conceived without a bias in favor of a conflict between scientists and managers, found that "from the start of their business careers many engineers have personal goals that coincide with the business goals of the corporations."[54] Business-oriented goals, dealing with power and participation in the affairs of the company, were ranked far above professional goals.

Furthermore, although it is rarely noted, managers also are usually college-trained, for example in law, business administration, and economics. Are they not professionals, too? Presumably they would prefer to work in a university-like atmosphere if they could have the power and the pelf provided by industry at the same time. They, too, resent supervision and discipline and if asked the proper questions would probably question the profit goal of business even as do scientists. In fact, the student with a masters' degree in business administration will hear more about the "social responsibilities" of business than the scientist.

Finally, the distinction made by Parsons and invoked by so many since then fails to recognize the *technical* character of ad-

[52]See Harold L. Wilensky, "The Professionalization of Everyone?" *American Journal of Sociology* 70 (September 1964): 137–158, for a discussion of the role of the training institution in the process of professionalization.

[53]Dalton, *Men Who Manage;* see also "Conflicts Between Staff and Line Managerial Officers," *American Sociological Review* 15 (1950): 342–351.

[54]Fred Goldner and R. R. Ritti, "Professionalization as Career Immobility," *American Journal of Sociology* 73 (March 1967): 491. This article contains a good discussion of the issues raised here, as well as citations and review of the literature that views the goals of professionals and managers (or the company) as in conflict. See also the critical review of the literature in Norman Kaplan, "Professional Scientists in Industry," *Social Problems* 13 (Summer 1965): 88–97.

ministration. That is, though the scientist promoted to a supervisory position will soon lose some of his *scientific* technical competence (he cannot keep up with the field; the new graduates know the latest things in some cases; he loses touch with the practical, daily problems), he is probably promoted upon, and expected to exercise and increase, his *administrative* technical competence. The job of the scientific manager is to manage, not to do research. It is a very common observation in industry that the best scientists do not make the best managers; the skills required are quite different, even though the manager of scientists must know a good bit about the technical work of these specialists. The same is true of the manager in marketing, finance, personnel, and even production. By assuming that official incumbency of a supervisory role has no relationship to expertise (expertise in management, in this case), it is possible for critics of the bureaucratic model to suggest a hiatus between expertise and occupancy of an official position. It was Weber's simple but enduring insight to see how crucial expertise was as a requirement for holding office throughout the hierarchy. The critics of bureaucracy have failed to utilize that simple insight when they propose that the official is not an expert in anything but survival. Far more damning would be the criticism that bureaucracy, by enfeebling so many workers, has made management a specialized skill demanding expertise.

SUMMARY

When we attribute the ills of organizations and the ills of our society to the bureaucratization of large-scale organizations, as we are so wont to do, we may be only fooling ourselves. We may be talking about specific instances of maladministration, of which there will naturally be a multitude since people are more or less imperfect, or we are talking about the uses to which the power generated by organizations is put. The presence of hierarchy, rules, division of labor, tenure provisions, and so on can hardly be blamed for maladministration or abuses of social power. Indeed, the bureaucratic model provides a greater check upon these problems than do nonbureaucratic or traditional alternatives once you have managerial capitalism. Critics, then, of our organizational society, whether they are the radicals of the Left emphasizing spontaneity and freedom, the new radical right demanding their own form of radical decentralization, or the liberals in between speaking of the inability of organizations to be responsive to community values, had best turn to the key issue of who controls the varied forms of power generated by organizations rather than flail away at the windmills of bureaucracy. If we want our material civilization to continue as it is, and are not ready to change the economic system along the drastic ways of, say, China, we will have to have large-scale bureaucratic enterprises in the economic, social, and governmental areas. The development of industrialization has made this the most efficient way to get the routine work of a society done. (I will elaborate on the controversial point that bureaucracy is more closely tied to capitalism than industrialization, despite the appearance of bureaucracy in socialist countries, in a future volume entitled *A Society of Organizations*.)

In this long discussion, we have, in effect, ranged over the model of bureaucracy drawn up by Weber, extending it in many places but rarely if ever modifying it greatly. Since the next two chapters deal with the attack on bureaucracy as a mechanistic, unfeeling, authoritarian system, I will summarize the basic Weberian model here. In Chapters 4 and 5 we will extend it.

Weber's model of bureaucracy contains three groups of characteristics: those which relate to the structure and function of organization; those which deal with means of rewarding effort; and those which deal with protections for the individuals.

Regarding the structure and functioning of the organization, Weber specified that the business of the organization be conducted on a continuous basis; that there be a hierarchy of offices, with each office under the control of a higher one; that this hierarchy entail a systematic division of labor based upon specialized training and expertise; and that the division of labor specify the area of action for which the official is competent, the responsibilities he has in this regard, and the amount of power or authority he has. The performance of duties is to be governed by written rules, imposed or enacted, and by written records (the files) of acts and decisions already taken. This cluster of characteristics did two things for Weber's model: (a) it provided mechanisms for control over performance of individuals, and (b) it provided means for specialization and expertise and means for coordinating roles and preventing them from interfering with each other.

The second group of characteristics, dealing with rewards, specified that officials receive fixed salaries, graded by rank; and that officials did not own the means of production or administration, could not appropriate their offices, had to separate their private affairs and property from the organization's affairs and property, had to render an accounting of the use of organizational property, and that the official's office should be his sole or primary occupation. The provision of salary rather than other forms of reward and the clear role separation contrasted sharply with charismatic and traditional forms of administration, but charismatic and traditional forms of rewards still linger in bureaucracies.

Finally, in contrast to other forms of administration, the rights of individuals are protected in the Weberian bureaucratic model. This is necessary not only to insure a source of personnel, but also to prevent the arbitrary use of power in the service of nonorganizational or antiorganizational goals. Officials serve voluntarily and are appointed; service constitutes a career with promotions according to seniority or achievement; obedience is owed to the officeholder, not to the man; officials are subject to authority only with respect to their official obligations; compulsion can be exercised only under definite conditions; and there is the right of appeal of decisions and statements of grievances.

2

Managerial Ideologies and the Origins of the Human Relations Movement

CLASSICAL MANAGEMENT THEORY

The actual writings on bureaucracy by Max Weber did not reach either social scientists or those concerned with business administration until the 1940s. The material was not translated, and there was not much social science interest in the matter. Meanwhile, a theory of industrial and business management was being developed by practicing managers and professors in the growing business schools of the United States, drawing at times upon some influential European authors such as Henry Fayol. We will not discuss this body of literature, which is referred to as classical management theory or, sometimes as the literature of the scientific management school; it is well summarized by Massie.[1] Two points need mentioning, however, since this school of thought is scorned by social scientists today. First, though the classical theory was derided for presenting "principles" that were really only proverbs,[2] all the resources of organizational research and theory today have not managed to substitute better principles (or proverbs) for those ridiculed. Second, these principles, which amount to pious directives to "plan ahead," pay attention to coordination, refrain from wasting execu-

---

[1]Joseph Massie, "Management Theory," in *The Handbook of Organizations*, ed. James March (Chicago: Rand McNally & Company, 1965), pp. 387–422.

[2]See the slashing criticism by Herbert Simon in his *Administrative Behavior*, 3rd ed. (New York: The Free Press, 1976).

tive time on established routine functions and instead to deal with the exceptional cases that come up, served management very well. As obvious as "plan ahead" sounds, it took a lot of saying back in the 1920s, for business rarely did any planning.[3] (Today the injunctions parade under the name of "Management by Objectives," and in more mathematical terms, PERT.) It was also quite a struggle to separate the chief executive (often the founder, or his relative) from routine affairs—to get him to delegate authority and deal only with the exceptions. It still is. Finally, a successful and durable business of management consulting and an endless series of successful books rest upon the basic principles of the classical management school. These principles have worked and are still working, for they addressed themselves to very real problems of management, problems more pressing than those advanced by social science.

The problems advanced by social scientists have been primarily the problems of human relations in an authoritarian setting. The how, when, and why of these concerns is one of the most fascinating stories in the field of organizational analysis and industrial sociology. Why did management to some extent, and social science to an overwhelming extent, become so preoccupied with human relations in the workplace, with treating the worker well and trying to construct a nonauthoritarian environment in an authoritarian setting? Reinhard Bendix, in a fascinating book on the topic of management's justification for ruling in a variety of countries and times, provides the answer for the United States in one of his chapters.[4] His account is the indispensable background for the dominant strand of organizational theory today. I have summarized it here. (All page numbers listed below are references to pages in the Bendix book.)

FROM SURVIVAL OF THE FITTEST TO COOPERATION IN SIXTY YEARS

Classical management theorists, and Weber himself, had little to say about workers in industry or nonsalaried personnel in government. It was not until workers forced themselves upon the consciousness of management by developing unions, or until a scarcity of labor occurred (due in part to the end of massive immigration),

---

[3]For an account of how little they did and how much shock was required to force planning, see Harold Wilensky, "Intelligence in Industry," *Annals, American Academy of Social Science* 388 (March 1970): 46–58.

[4]Reinhard Bendix, *Work and Authority in Industry* (New York: John Wiley & Sons, Inc., 1956).

that those concerned with either organizational theory or principles of management practice began to include the workingman within their purview. Workers had been simply another resource, like the machines that began to replace them in increasing numbers. They were docile, without effective organization, needing jobs, and remarkably content to suffer extensive hardships in the workplace and in the marketplace, where there was an abundant labor supply. Extensive, lasting unionization did not appear in the United States until the World War I decade, in contrast to other industrializing countries.

In this country, there was a special problem facing management, i.e., ideology. On the one hand, democracy stressed liberty and equality for all. On the other hand, large masses of workers and nonsalaried personnel had to submit to apparently arbitrary authority, backed up by local and national police forces and legal power, for ten to twelve hours a day, six days a week. Their right to combine into organizations of their own was severely limited or simply prohibited. How, asks Bendix, could entrepreneurs justify the "privilege of voluntary action and association for themselves, while imposing upon all subordinates the duty of obedience and the obligation to serve their employers to the best of their ability?" This is the most crucial question a social science of organizations could ask, yet it has rarely been raised by students of organizations.

Social Darwinism

Bendix picks up the story in the 1880s when the United States was lagging behind England, Germany, and France in industrialization. From about 1880 to 1910 "the United States underwent the most rapid economic expansion of any industrialized country for a comparable period of time." (254) The rapid expansion was accompanied by ruthless practices toward workers; the United States lagged far behind England in social reforms and unionization. Perhaps for this reason, the doctrine of Social Darwinism—the theory of survival of the fittest applied to social life rather than to animals—found more ready reception here than in England. Success and riches were regarded both as signs of progress for the nation, to be honored and cherished, and as the reward for those who had proved themselves in the struggle for survival. The struggle was a human battle; the "captains of industry" were better fighters than most of us, wrote sociologist C. R. Henderson in the American Journal of Sociology in 1896. (256) They fought on "the battlefield where the 'struggle for existence' is defining the industrially 'fittest to survive.'" Some saw success as the sign of virtue in the Christian mission of business enterprise ("What is the true conception of life but divine ownership and human administration?" asked a man of God); *(257)* some were more ruthless, stressing the role that the "lowest passions of mankind" played in human progress, since civilization would not advance if such evils were always avoided. But all agreed that success entitled a man to command; failure indicated the lack of the requisite personal qualities. And success was only for the few in the struggle for existence. "Many a man is entirely incapable of assuming responsibility," wrote N. C. Fowler in his *The Boy, How to Help Him Succeed* in 1902. "He is a success as the led, but not as the leader. He lacks the courage of willingness to assume responsibility and the ability of handling others." *(259)*

For those who failed the test, so much the worse; they would be weeded out. Elbert Hubbard, whose book *A Message to Garcia* was extremely popular at the turn of the century, made the message clear (the title refers to a lieutenant who carried an important message to General Garcia in Cuba in spite of overwhelming odds):

> We have recently been hearing much maudlin sympathy expressed for the "downtrodden denizen of the sweatshop" and the "homeless wanderer searching for honest employment," and with it all often go many hard words for the men in power.
>
> Nothing is said about the employer who grows old before his time in a vain attempt to get frowsy ne'er-do-wells to do intelligent work; and his long patient striving with "help" that does nothing but loaf when his back is turned. In every store and factory there is a constant weeding-out process going on. No matter how good times are, this sorting continues, only if times are hard and work is scarce, the sorting is done finer—but out, and forever out, the incompetent and unworthy go. It is the survival of the fittest. Self-interest prompts every employer to keep the best—those who can carry a message to Garcia. *(264-265)*

But what if success eluded you? What was needed to ensure it? One answer was provided by the New Thought Movement of the late nineteenth and early twentieth centuries, designed to appeal to the ever hopeful and providing a more civilized explanation than the law of the jungle. The answer was mental power; the power of positive thinking. (It is still very much with us, providing hope for those who cannot accept luck, opportunity, or inferiority as the explanation for their failure.) According to the author of *Thought Force in Business*, "Business success is due to certain qualities of mind. Anything is yours, if you only want it hard enough. Just think of that. *Anything!* Try it. Try it in earnest and you will succeed. It is the operation of a mighty law." *(260)* The book titles tell the story: every backyard, even the lowliest, is strewn with *Acres of Diamonds* if you will only gather them. Just learn about *Your Forces and How to Use Them*; it is the key to *Mastery of Fate*, and *The Culture of Courage*.

By 1925, Orison Sweet Marden had sold some three million copies of his various books, and unfortunate babies were named after him. One 1894 title: *Pushing to the Front, or Success Under Difficulties.*

The ethic was an individual one and the message for the workingman was clear. It was not circumstances, the chance of birth, opportunities provided by wealth and education, nor even luck that guided his fate; it was failure to try. But at least it was not that he was biologically unfit, as in Social Darwinism. The New Thought Movement did not directly challenge Social Darwinism, however, and one even finds the two in an uneasy blend.

The Collective Response of Unions

Meanwhile, workers were constructing their own explanations for the inequities of power and treasure in industry. In 1897 American trade unions had 487,000 members; seven years later there were 2,072,700 trade union members. This enormous increase was accompanied by considerable violence on both sides, in the true form of the struggle for survival. But, in management's hands, the doctrine had not meant that workers *too* could struggle for existence; *that* would not serve society. As the president of the National Association of Manufacturers said in 1903:

> Organized labor knows but one law and that is the law of physical force—the law of the Huns and Vandals, the law of the savage. All its purposes are accomplished either by actual force or by the threat of force. . . . It is, in all essential features, a mob power knowing no master except its own will. Its history is stained with blood and ruin. . . . It extends its tactics of coercion and intimidation over all classes, dictating to the press and to the politicians and strangling independence of thought and American manhood. (266)

One of the objections was that this was collective action, not reflecting individual strength or individual willpower. But that objection soon was overtaken by events, for employers found they could not fight trade unions individually; regardless of the ethic of individual responsibility, they had to band together. They had cooperated before with regard to problems of markets and government, but never to solve a problem within their own firms. Management's response was the "right-to-work" philosophy of the early part of the century—the "open shop" (no union) movement. Bendix analyzes the situation as follows:

> The rising tide of trade unionism forced American employers to acknowledge, however implicitly, that their own individual authority in the enterprise no longer sufficed. It is necessary to appreciate the

novelty of this theme. American businessmen and industrialists were the recognized elite of society. Their great wealth was accepted as a well-earned reward for their outstanding fitness in the struggle for survival. And when these ideas were applied to the relations between capital and labor, the workers were merely admonished to struggle for survival on the terms acceptable to their employers. Yet at this pinnacle of their social recognition, American businessmen were challenged by the trade unions. And they were challenged in the employer's central activity, the management of his "own" plant, where his authority was supposedly absolute. It is not surprising that the ideology of the open shop, the employers' response to this challenge, came to embody all the sacred symbols by which their own fortunes could be identified with the foundation of the social order. (267)

One of the important consequences of the challenge was that the nature of the employers' authority was in doubt. If it had been absolute there would have been no labor problem; the offending worker would have been dismissed. If a labor problem was admitted, authority was not adequate to deal with it, otherwise, the problem would not have existed. The sad fact was that authority was being questioned by the unions. One article compared the machine tool with the "human machine" and found the latter regretfully lacking. The machine tool was "never obstinate, perverse, discouraged," and if something went wrong it could be corrected. "If the human machine could be controlled by the set rules that govern machine tool operation, the world would be a much different place. . . ."

But since it could not, because labor had become a problem, this tended "to eat the heart out of the glorification of success," as Bendix puts it. A change in ideology was in the making, and an article in 1910 admitted that it was not only hard work and the goal of success that mattered, but the employee should also gain the "confidence, respect, and cooperation of his employer." (271–274) The significance of this was that the employer could prescribe the conditions of success or failure; it was not just a question of hard work, jungle laws, or positive thinking. In fact, the insistence upon owners maintaining absolute authority in the plant itself denied the virtues of independence and initiative on the part of the employee.

Enter Science

Even more destructive of the Spencerian struggle for survival as an ideology of management was the rise of "Scientific Management," founded by Frederick W. Taylor in the early part of the twentieth century. Briefly, the goal of scientific management was to analyze jobs very carefully into their smallest aspects, analyze the capabilities of the human machine just as carefully, and then fit the two together to achieve the greatest economy. Job techniques would be redesigned to make maximum use of human abilities; humans would be trained to best perform the jobs.

It is difficult to think of this as a breakthrough, since it seems so obvious; but it was a breakthrough for several reasons. The most important was that it took skills from the hands of the workers and gave them to engineers, decreasing the dependency upon workers. As mentioned in Chapter 1, under the prevalent inside contracting system, workers were responsible for many technological innovations, and through the contractor they presumably reaped some of the rewards. Now, under the deskilling program of Taylor, they found their wages reduced and their ranks split into finely graded distinctions which helped stem collective action. Labor cost saved from deskilling was the crucial benefit to the owners (which Bendix hardly deals with). In terms of justification of authority, there were three advantages of Taylorism for management. First, it applied research (stopwatch clocking of the smallest movements) to work, rather than letting tradition guide it, or letting each work group set its pace. Time-study men and industrial engineers continue this work today in most sophisticated factories. Second, it made some bow, at least, to the interests of the worker, arguing that such research permitted management to explore the possibilities for the worker's development, allowing him to advance to the highest level that his natural abilities would allow. In this view, then, initiative is in management's hand, not the worker's; the struggle for survival is irrelevant if each works up to his own abilities; positive thinking will not affect the outcome of scientific research.

Third, this theory suggested that it was *cooperation* between labor and capital that brought success. In Taylor's view, this was the most important message, for it should take the eyes of labor and management off the *division* of the surplus (higher wages or higher profits) and instead turn them toward the problem of increasing the *size* of the surplus; in this fashion there could be both higher wages and higher profits. Indeed, under this enlightened system there would be no need for unions. Bendix argues that it meant the end of arbitrary power on the part of management; science would decide. The personal exercise of authority would cease. The image of the employer was transformed in the process, notes Bendix. "From a man whose success in the world made him the natural leader of the industrial order, he had become a leader of men whose success depended in part upon a science which would place each man in 'the highest class of work for which his natural abilities fit him.'" (280)

Employers, however, did not embrace the ideology of

Taylorism, though they increased the degree of bureaucratization and control it required. For one thing, it "questioned their good judgment and superior ability which had been the subject of public celebration for many years." *(280)* It reduced their discretion, placing it in the hands of technicians; it implied that management's failure to utilize the skills of workers was the reason for workers' inefficiencies and restiveness. Indeed, Congress conducted hearings on Taylorism, so lively was the debate and so suspicious were managers. But the effect was to break the hold of the old ideologies. Indeed, the ideal of cooperation appeared to many to be a more useful ideological underpinning than Social Darwinism. For one thing, organizations had grown in size and were more complex; it was apparent that sheer initiative or a fighting spirit was not appropriate in increasingly bureaucratized firms. For another, the union movement, while subsiding after the First World War, was a permanent fixture, and employers would have to fight its expansion and its encroachments upon managerial prerogatives with more subtle ideological weapons—even as they continued to use violence. Company unions were established (plantwide organizations of workers set up and controlled by management) and welfare schemes were introduced to counter social unrest and the threat of socialism. Cooperation between capital and labor became a commonplace phrase. Around 1920 an even more sophisticated concept appeared, reflecting the increasing complexity of management and the separation of management from ownership. Suddenly, there were three partners, not just two—capital, managers, and *labor*. The modest rewards and inherent satisfactions of good work, rather than exhortations to emulate their superiors and achieve success, were emphasized for workers. *(285)* By 1928, indeed, a management journal urged: "Treat workers as human beings. Show your interest in their personal success and welfare." *(294)*

The Responsibility to Lead

By 1935 a completely new note had crept in, one that was to figure heavily in the more theoretical works of two grandparents of present-day organizational theorists, Elton Mayo and Chester Barnard: "People are tractable, docile, gullible, uncritical—and wanting to be led. But far more than this is deeply true of them. They want to feel united, tied, bound to something, some cause, bigger than they, commanding them yet worthy of them, summoning them to significance in living." *(296)* That observation is, of course, an ancient justification for leadership (and especially totalitarianism), but it signified a clean break from the previous ideologies. It also plainly said that large-scale, hierarchical industrial organizations were good for people. Left to themselves, people are not much good; in organizations, they can be "summoned to significance in living." So far have we moved!

One implication of the changing emphasis was that employers were now enjoined to do something about or for the workers. Bendix notes:

> As long as they had regarded success itself as the sign of virtue and of superior qualities, no further justification of industrial leadership had been necessary. The counterpart of this belief had been that failure was the sign of vice and incapacity. And since success and failure resulted from the struggle for survival, it was beyond the reach of human interference. Now employers and managers proposed to do something about workers who failed to produce efficiently and to cooperate fully. Apparently they were no longer satisfied to regard such failure as the unavoidable outcome of the competitive struggle. Instead they would investigate the causes of failure and prevent their recurrence by the development of appropriate managerial policies. The qualities of leadership needed for this purpose were necessarily different from, and less self-evident than, those required for success in the struggle for survival. Among American employers the superiority of industrial leaders was as unquestioned as ever, but it had become the subject of discussion as well as of celebration. *(298)*

This meant that, as stated in *American Management Review* in 1924, "The study of the employee's mind alone will not solve, and often confuses, the problem. The mind of management is also an integral part of human relationships in industry." *(299)*

Along with the increasing responsibility of management went a change in the qualities managers were expected to have in order to succeed. In the mid-nineteenth century, those qualities were "industry, arrangement, calculation, prudence, punctuality, and perseverance"—hardly a conceptually oriented list and unrelated to human relations. But industry was not very complex at the time, and such things as prudence and punctuality perhaps needed emphasis and were, perhaps, even decisive. A list from the year 1918 provides a dramatic contrast: intelligence, ability, enthusiasm, honesty, and fairness. Ten years later the lists had gone even further: the leader should be worthy of his authority, eager to acquire new information, willing to learn from subordinates, anxious to see them develop, able to take criticism and acknowledge mistakes. Furthermore, these qualities were not inherited but could be developed through training. *(301)* That managers might submit to training in itself shows how great the change was. This last list would do very nicely today, fifty years later, and could be duplicated in a casual reading of management journals.

Persuasion and Cooperation

It was in such an environment that Dale Carnegie's *Public Speaking and Influencing Men in Business* could flourish. (It was later titled *How to Win Friends and Influence People*, suggesting a more universalistic application.) Dale Carnegie Institutes have become a permanent fixture among the services available to business, and are still widely used. The 1926 volume became the "official text" of many progressive organizations, such as American Telephone and Telegraph (AT&T), and management associations. As with the leadership list, the concerns were interpersonal relations and the handling of people.

Under this new philosophy, workers were urged to cooperate as partners in the enterprise; they should be loyal, have stable expectations, and receive stable rewards. They should even be treated as human beings. "We are leading men, not handling robots," said one author in a 1923 publication. *(311)* But it was up to management to lead. Without this, there could be no cooperative endeavor. The emphasis was upon the human relations skills of management, not on the nature of the workers.

The next major change in the ideologies of management was to assert the basic identity of the nature of management and workers, even though the one, naturally, had developed some aspects of his nature more fully than the other. This came about with the social philosophy of Elton Mayo as applied to industrial cooperation. In contrast to Taylor, Mayo broke with the tradition of regarding each worker as a wage-maximizing individual in isolation. He attacked what he called the "rabble hypothesis" of economic theory that was being used in industry. There were three tenets to that hypothesis, said Mayo: society consisted of unorganized individuals—discrete atoms rather than natural social groups; each individual acts according to his calculations of his own self-interest, rather than being swayed by group norms; and each individual thinks logically, rather than being swayed by emotions and sentiments. The rabble hypothesis is the familiar economic view of man, utilized to explain the market behavior of consumers and entrepreneurs alike.

In contrast, Mayo emphasized the desire to stand well with one's fellows, the role of sentiments, and the instincts of human association. Economic self-interest was the exception rather than the rule. This held for all men, be they owners, managers, or workers. They must all cooperate if civilization was not to fall. But, almost inevitably, the distinction between workers and others came back in. The administrative elite of owners and managers had more capacity to engage in logical thinking and calculation than the workers. It was a capacity born of the necessity of guiding complex organizations. Therefore, the elite had a greater responsibility for providing an organizational environment in which employees could fulfill their "eager human desire for cooperative activity." *(315)* Man found himself in organizations.

After analyzing the functioning of the most extensive human relations programs in the 1950s, Bendix concludes that Mayo's contribution found only limited acceptance in managerial practices but that its influence upon management ideology was pervasive. *(319)* A new vocabulary of motives was constructed out of his view of man as preeminently social and cooperative; it would offer new justifications for management authority and worker obedience.

Mayo's philosophy was severely criticized by a large number of social scientists. His statements about "spontaneous" cooperation and his longing for a medieval past where each man knew his place in a cooperative endeavor made him an easy target, especially in the late 1930s and the 1940s, when labor's chances of gaining power in industry rested not on spontaneous cooperation but upon the legitimization of industrial conflict through collective bargaining and strikes. Mayo's critics felt that his view of cooperation was espoused at the expense of labor and on the terms of management and other legitimate and exploitative segments of society.

SUMMARY

The ideologies of management had gone from Social Darwinism to social cooperation in about half a century. Figure 1 suggests the radical nature of the change. For example, the explanations for employee failure or problems with employees run from biological unfitness to not being handled correctly. The changes in ideology, of course, went hand in hand with the changes in the structure and technology of industry. As it became more bureaucratized, large, and mechanized, interpersonal problems loomed larger and those of the sheer force of will, inventiveness, or effort declined. As responsibility for costly machinery and breakdowns in the assembly lines became greater, even deskilled workers needed to be retained because of their experience, and specialized craft jobs grew. As immigration dried up and capital investments increased (making work stoppages more costly for management), unionization became a more potent weapon. Attitudes of the public and of public officials also changed, of course, making Social Darwinism less acceptable as an explanation.[5]

---

[5]For a good general survey of the social problems of the industrial revolution and the conflicting schools of thought, see Part One of Harold L. Wilensky and Charles N. Lebeaux, *Industrial Society and Social Welfare*, rev. ed. (New York: The Free Press, 1965). Wilensky's introduction to this edition is especially recommended.

FIGURE 1 MANAGERIAL IDEOLOGIES[6]

What is the justification for management rule and worker obedience?

Explanatory Doctrine	Characterization of Owners or Managers	Period and Doctrine	Positive Characterization of Employees	Explanations of Employee Failure
Survival of the fittest	Superior individuals	1870: Spencer's Social Darwinism	Independence, initiative, aggressiveness	Biologically unfit
Survival of the best	Moral superiority and willpower	1895–1915: New Thought Movement	Proper thoughts, willpower	Will not try
The fit dictate conditions of success	Power by virtue of position and success	(Unionization)	Compliancy, worthiness of management's respect	Insubordinate unworthy
Scientific determination	Skillful utilization of labor, efficiency	1915—, Scientific Management	Trainability, utilization of capabilities to the fullest	Will not work or learn
Manipulation	Personality skills	Post-World War I: Dale Carnegie	Cooperation by inducement, stable expectations and rewards	Will not cooperate as a partner
Natural cooperation, rational assessment of whole person	Personality skills, statesmanship, rationality, and logic	Mid-1930s: Elton Mayo	Nonlogicality, desire for security and recognition	Not handled correctly

[6]Largely based upon Bendix, *Work and Authority in Industry.*

The new ideologies of management, however, rested not on fixed qualities of managers or the system; instead, they stressed things that management had to *do*, such as discovering a common purpose, or making a purposeful effort to structure a cooperative system. The eager desire for cooperation was there; it was up to management to give it rein. At the same time as this ideology was born, the instruments for its expression were being created in the business schools and social science departments of the nation. Workers could be studied not only by time and motion engineers, but by psychologists, social psychologists, and sociologists. The vast amount of empirical work undertaken by these academicians in industrial (and military) studies was eventually to culminate in our present-day theories of organizations. The first to construct the theoretical outlines of the major theory of organizations existing today was Chester Barnard.

BARNARD'S COMPANY TOWN

When Barnard was writing *The Functions of the Executive*[7] in the late 1930s, there was hardly anything around to qualify as an academic theory of organizations in the United States. As Bendix indicated,[8] there was a growing emphasis upon the cooperative nature of business enterprises—a vague and uncomfortable ideology that capital, management, and labor somehow had to unite for the good of all. From Social Darwinism—the survival of the fittest—in the late 19th century, management ideology had moved through a number of doctrines which progressively weakened management's justification for authoritarian rule and led management to the uneasy position that it had a responsibility for joining hands with labor in a common enterprise. Classical management theory was hardly adequate as a theory of organizations, since it relied upon "plan ahead" proverbs and assumed that management was there to control the enterprise, divide the work rationally, pay minimum wages to ensure profit, and take advantage of a large and dependent labor market. It did not speak to the issues of unionism and industrial unrest. The Weberian model of bureaucracy would have been adequate because it was more complete, systematic, and theoretical than anything turned out by the management theorists. But this had not even been translated from the German by

---

[7]Chester Barnard, *The Functions of the Executive* (Cambridge, Mass.: Harvard University Press, 1938).

[8]Bendix, *Work and Authority in Industry*, Chapter 5.

the 1930s and thus only had an impact upon organizational theory in the latter part of the next decade. Besides, it was inconsistent with the growing concern with cooperation. The sweeping generalizations of Elton Mayo, offering a medieval order in the midst of a rapidly changing and expanding industrial civilization, were not appropriate. Parts of Mayo as well as classical management theory could be used, of course, but there was no coherent unified theory to encompass the new view of organizations.

The void was filled by Barnard's 1938 volume. This enormously influential and remarkable book contains within it the seeds of three distinct trends of organizational theory that were to dominate the field for the next three decades. One was the institutional school as represented by Philip Selznick (see Chapter 5); another was the decision-making school as represented by Herbert Simon (see Chapter 4); the third was the human relations school (see Chapter 3). The leading theorists of these schools freely acknowledged their debt to Barnard. It would not be much of an exaggeration to say that the field of organizational theory is dominated by Max Weber and Chester Barnard, each presenting different models, and that the followers of Barnard hold numerical superiority. All those simplified, dramatic dichotomies—such as mechanical systems versus organic systems; production-centered versus employee-centered organizations; rigid, inflexible versus adaptive, responsive organizations; and authoritarian versus democratic organizations—stem from the contrast of the Weberian and the Barnardian models.[9]

The Barnardian model went beyond the pious statements that labor and management should cooperate or that conflict would be reduced or productivity raised by cooperation. Barnard was the first to insist, at length, that organizations *by their very nature* are cooperative systems and could not fail to be so.

In a sense that is true. People do cooperate with one another in organizations, or in any enduring social group for that matter. In organizations, the cooperation goes beyond formal rules, is not precisely calculated to conform to the amount of wages or salary, frequently is spontaneous and generous, and, by and large, is in the interests of achieving the goals of the organization. But, in the Weberian view, this is hardly the essence of organizations since basically people are constrained to cooperate because of hierarchy of authority, separation of office and person, and so on. For Bar-

---

[9]Terence K. Hopkins, "Bureaucratic Authority: The Convergence of Weber and Barnard" in Amitai Etzioni, *Complex Organizations* (New York: Holt, Rinehart & Winston, Inc., 1962), pp. 159-167, attempts to reconcile the two but himself comes to the conclusion that only on the most general level—organizations are both coordinated and imperative systems—is this really possible?

nard, however, cooperation is the essence of organizations. As a pioneer theorist, Barnard emphasized cooperation almost to the exclusion of such things as conflict, imperative coordination, and financial inducements. His position is somewhat extreme, but because it underlies so much of organizational theory today, the remainder of this chapter will be devoted to rather close criticism of it.

To read Barnard today is a chore, and I do not recommend it except for historical analysis. Barnard knew he was breaking new ground, and as a careful executive (he was president of New Jersey Bell Telephone Company, a part of the Bell Telephone System which breeds and honors careful executives), he may have felt compelled to examine and classify every lump of soil in tedious detail. The first sixty-one pages of his book consist of an attempt to ground his work in some kind of theory of human interaction, complete with epistemological discussions; this section is most notable for the endless presentation of categories upon categories and the relentless analysis of men moving a stone. Yet to unravel this semi-philosophical treatise is to gain an insight into a basic posture of a good part of organizational theory.

The Setting

Barnard was confronted with a difficult problem. The United States was only beginning to cope with the Great Depression; it did not know that a war was around the corner that would increase productivity as twentieth-century capitalism itself had not. The prospects were grim indeed around 1936 and 1937 when Barnard was writing. Throughout the 1930s social unrest had been high, and the legitimacy of established organizations was being questioned. Radical ideologies were strong among the intelligentsia, and direct and often violent action was apparent among the working classes. Yet to respond to this perilous situation with an authoritarian model harking back to the days of Social Darwinism was not appropriate for a subtle and highly intelligent social philosopher in those years.

That giant web of organizations, the Bell System, was one of the first to adopt the principles of treating workers decently and considering them as partners in a triumvirate of capital, management, and labor. The president of AT&T wrote in a business journal in 1926 of the cooperative nature of the company and its obligations to investors, employees, and patrons. In testimony before the Federal Communications Commission in 1936, he reemphasized this and said that his loyalties were divided as equally as possible among the three parties. The question was raised as to whether labor was not bearing the brunt of the Depression rather than the investors, thus making the partnership hardly equal, since throughout the Depression AT&T had managed to adhere to the principle of the

$9.00 dividend on each share of stock while the number of employees had been reduced by nearly 40 percent.[10] As president of a subsidiary of AT&T, Barnard was of course aware of such issues. In fact, in an earlier position he had performed an essentially political role in dealing with the federal government.[11] Given these kinds of challenges, the state of the nation in the mid-1930s, and the state of organizational theory, what was Barnard's response?

The Moral Organization

First, organizations per se had to be defended and even sanctified. It is significant that the opening sentence of Barnard's book reads as follows: "With all the thought that has been turned upon the unrest of the present day in the literature of social reform, one finds practically no reference to formal organization as the concrete social process by which social action is largely accomplished."[12] That formal organizations were largely responsible for the Depression and the social unrest is, of course, not mentioned. Rather, belief in the power of individual action is alluded to as a basic cause of the trouble. Organizations, Barnard tells us, cannot fail to have a moral purpose. Society itself finds its form, its "structure and process," through formal organizations. The only goal of business, he says, can be service. It is not profit nor power nor political ideology and certainly not personal gain. The common purpose of an organization must always be a moral purpose, and to inculcate this moral purpose into the very fiber of the organization and into the members of it is the only meaningful task of the executive.

This view is important; it is not a mere publicity handout by a corporation executive. Years later a similar position was set forth by one of the three or four leading organizational theorists, Philip Selznick, in his book *Leadership in Administration*, though Selznick wrote in far more sophisticated terms. The idea that power can exist or survive only if it is legitimate, which is found in the writings of Talcott Parsons,[13] represents a similar view. If organizations exist

---

[10]The reduction in workers had begun before the Depression hit AT&T and could not be accounted for by the level of business that the firm had. At the end of 1937 it was doing more business than in 1929, but it still had about 30 percent less employees. Part of this was due to technological change, but a good part of it was due to the "speed-up" on the production line. See the discussion in N. R. Danielian, *AT&T, The Story of Industrial Conquest* (New York: The Vanguard Press, 1939), pp. 200–221. I am indebted to Richard Hamilton for bringing this book by a former staff member of the Federal Communications Commission to my attention.

[11]Ibid., pp. 259, 260, 270.

[12]Barnard, *The Functions of the Executive*, p. 1.

[13]Talcott Parsons, *Structure and Process in Modern Societies* (New York: The Free Press, 1960), p. 121.

and have power, that power must be legitimized by society and therefore given the mantle of morality. To question this would be to question the very "structure and process" of modern society.

Why were organizations moral for Barnard? Not simply because of the key role of the executive inculcating moral purpose, though that is important, but because organizations are cooperative systems. People cooperate in organizations. They join organizations voluntarily. They cooperate toward a goal, the goal of the organization. Therefore, the goal must be a common goal, a goal of all participants. Such a goal could not fail to be moral because morality emerges from cooperative endeavors. Society could not exist without cooperation, and the clearest form of cooperation may be seen in organizations. Thus, in this view, if people cooperate in the pursuit of common goals, there can be no problem with the output of organizations; they must be moral institutions.

The Organization and the Individual

There are a number of thorny problems with Barnard's view. First, if the emphasis is upon the collectivity—the organization or the cooperative *system*—how does one handle the individual? Barnard was worried about philosophies which emphasized the individual and his decisions or acts, since morality was a collective phenomenon. It is the Bell System that counted, not President Gifford of AT&T or President Barnard of New Jersey Bell. But how do you separate the individual from the organization? How can you talk about organizations without talking about individuals? It is a basic and enduring problem for all organizational theory. The "field" theory of Kurt Lewin, developed after Barnard's book came on the scene, drew its strength from Lewin's attempt to discuss fields of forces rather than individuals. The interminable debate in the 1940s and 1950s over the old question of whether the group was more than the sum of its parts, and the almost inevitable but shaky answer of yes, is a similar illustration of this ontological problem. The current faddish term "synergism," indicating that something unique emerges from the interaction of discrete inputs of energy, is a reaffirmation of the reality (and superiority) of the collective character of a system. The persistent and unsatisfactory debate over whether there are such things as organizational goals, when only individuals would appear to be goal-directed sources of energy,[14] is another manifestation.

Barnard was the first, I believe, to confront this problem sys-

---

[14]For a statement on this, see Herbert A. Simon, "On the Concept of Organizational Goal," *Administrative Science Quarterly* 9 (June 1964): 1–22.

tematically and head-on in terms of formal organizations (though Durkheim had done so for groups or society in general). It was essential for Barnard's ideology that the group win out. Therefore, he defined organizations as "nonpersonal." They do not consist of persons, or things such as machinery, or ideas such as technology, or even what he vaguely referred to as "social situations." Instead, the organization consists of "forces." These are given off by persons, but persons themselves are not, strictly speaking, members of the organization. They are part of the environment of the organization, part of a larger cooperative system which includes the organization. He insists throughout the book that organizational actions are nonpersonal in character; even executive decisions do not reflect personal choice. It is because the activities of humans are *coordinated* to make a *system* "that their significant aspects are nonpersonal."[15]

This is an awkward position to hold, and even though Barnard does maintain it throughout the book, he is forced to distinguish between the organizational aspects of people and the personal aspects. He suggests "that every participant in an organization may be regarded as having a dual personality—an organization personality and an individual personality."[16] This is somewhat similar to the concept of an organizational "office," but the difference is important. The concept of office or social position pertains to prescribed duties and responsibilities. The person holds or "fills" the office. But he does not, except in exaggerated cases which are subjects of ridicule and humor, *become* the office, nor is the office an equivalent (except in exaggerated cases) of a personality. For Barnard, the identification is much stronger; the organizational personality is all-pervasive for the person acting as a member of an organization. For the five men moving a stone, he notes, it is not important what this means to each man personally once they have agreed to cooperate; what is important is what each thinks it means to the organization as a whole.[17] The extreme situation is, for him, the best illustration of the concept: "In military action, individual conduct may be so dominated by organization personality that it is utterly contradictory of what personal motivation would require."[18]

This position allows Barnard not only to reify the organization (something which all organization theorists are forced to do to some extent) but to put down the importance of personal choice. The executive makes decisions and thus chooses among alternatives, but these do not reflect personal choice. These actions are nonper-

---

[15]Barnard, *Functions of the Executive*, p. 77.
[16]Ibid., p. 88.
[17]Ibid.
[18]Ibid.

sonal in character because the executive is part of a system of "consciously coordinated activities or forces of two or more persons,"[19] which is Barnard's definition of a formal organization. This allows him to speak contemptuously of "the exaggeration in some connections of the power and of the meaning of personal choice." The "connections" undoubtedly referred to some of the radical ideologies that were floating around during the Depression days. These exaggerations of the power and meaning of personal choice, Barnard says, are "vicious roots, not merely of misunderstanding but of false and abortive effort."[20] True and productive effort will be performed through organizations.

The consequences of extolling the organization over the person are clear when we examine Barnard's insistence that organizations are superior to individuals. Organizations are rational, individuals are not. Or, in Barnard's terms, logicality emerges from the interaction of organizational personalities or the field of forces given off by people. Persons themselves, or individual actions, are likely to be nonlogical in character. Thus, one cannot define organizations as consisting of people, for then they would be nonlogical and by implication nonrational. He speaks of the "superlative degree to which logical processes *must* and *can* characterize organization action as contrasted with individual action. . . ."[21] Logic is not a characteristic of the individual but only of the coordinated relationship of individuals acting in terms of their organizational personality. Only in organization can we have the "deliberate adoption of means and ends" since this is the "essence of formal organization."[22]

This view is held by many organizational theorists. But the solution of Weber and classical management theorists is to see in the organization a means for controlling individuals in the interests of the goals of the leaders of the organization. The organization is more rational than the individuals because order is imposed upon members by those who control the organization, and the order is in the interests of goals or purposes established and guarded by those in charge. It is rationality only in the *leaders'* terms. For Barnard, the organization is more rational than the individuals because the organization is nonpersonal, or supraindividual; it is something that extracts from individual behavior the logic based upon common goals and willing cooperation. The duality that pervades Weber is that of the ruler and the ruled; the duality that pervades Barnard is

---

[19]Ibid., p. 73.
[20]Ibid., p. 15.
[21]Ibid., p. 186. (Emphasis supplied.)
[22]Ibid.

that of the organizational personality and the individual personality.[23]

THE PROCESSES OF ORGANIZATION

Executive Decision Making

How, then, do organizations actually function? First, there is the key role of executive decision making. Not only are leaders supposed to inculcate moral purpose into the very fiber of the organization, but their main activity is to make the key, or, as Selznick put it years later, the "critical" decisions. As obvious as this may seem today, it was not so clear over thirty years ago. The role of the executive in the literature of that time was analyzed in much more general, vague, and moralistic terms. Barnard was groping his way toward an essentially behavioral analysis of leadership by singling out the importance of rational analysis of alternatives and selection of the best one. He felt that the direction an organization takes hangs upon one or two major decisions made by an executive in a year. Possibly what Barnard had in mind were such things as Eddie Rickenbacker's decision, while he was president of Eastern Airlines, to emphasize cost reduction while competitive airlines were emphasizing customer comforts and expansion of service. Rickenbacker's decision made a lot of money for Eastern Airlines for a number of years, but it proved to be the wrong one as the competitors overtook the company.[24] Sewell Avery's decision to sit on millions of Montgomery Ward cash and securities in anticipation of a post-World War II depression and to stick with small stores gave Sears a permanent lead, since the latter expanded by building

---

[23]Only in some forms of conflict theory of organizations is the matter of rationality handled in such a way as to avoid these two positions. If different sets of actors are rationally pursuing different interests and goals, the question of organizational rationality is moot. It is the value, for example, of Goffman's iconoclastic work on mental hospitals that he insists that presumably irrational patients, ruled over by rational staff members, are indeed quite rational in their perceptions and interests. The staff members, in the patients' view, appear quite irrational. In emphasizing this, Goffman tends to describe the hospital as irrational as an organization, but it is in reality only ineffectual. See Erving Goffman, *Asylums* (New York: Doubleday & Company, 1961); and Charles Perrow, "Hospitals: Technology, Structure, and Goals," in *The Handbook of Organizations*, ed. James March, pp. 910–971.

[24]For this and other examples of critical decisions as to goals, see Charles Perrow, *Organizational Analysis: A Sociological View* (Belmont, California: Wadsworth Publishing Co., 1970), Chapter 5.

large suburban stores as quickly as possible. The decision of General William Westmoreland to engage in search and destroy activities in Vietnam, seeking out the enemy wherever he might be, was a critical executive decision which was reversed by his replacement, General Creighton Abrams. Barnard not only saw the significance of such key decisions but he saw the need to analyze executive behavior in these terms, rather than merely in moralistic terms.

Indoctrination

Despite his analysis of executive decision making, Barnard could not see the organization as the shadow of one man. He believed that all people must share the goals which the key decisions both reflect and shape. But if organizations are cooperative systems with all people working toward a common goal, how does one explain the fact that there is conflict in organizations, recalcitrance on the part of some members, lack of cooperation, and so forth? Barnard does admit that sometimes the ends of the person and the ends of the organization are not the same; indeed, they may be in opposition. He indicates that such opposition is most likely to occur in connection with the lower participants in an organization. When faced with such opposition, the answer is not to buy off the opponents with inducements of higher wages, nor to threaten them with loss of employment, nor to let them participate in changing the goals of the organization. The answer is indoctrination.

When common purposes do not exist, the answer is to manufacture them. "The most important inherent difficulty in the operation of cooperative systems" is "the necessity for indoctrinating those at the lower levels with general purposes. . . ."[25] This may actually involve deception. "We may say, then, that a purpose can serve as an element of a cooperative system only so long as the participants do not recognize that there are serious divergences of their understanding of that purpose as the object of cooperation. . . . Hence, an objective purpose that can serve as the basis for a cooperative system is one that is *believed* by the contributors (or potential contributors) to it to be the determined purpose of the organization. The inculcation of belief in the real existence of a common purpose is an essential executive function."[26]

Thus, we have an inconsistency. Organizations consist of forces generated by people acting in concert to achieve common goals,

[25]Barnard, *Functions of the Executive*, p. 233.
[26]Ibid., p. 87.

but it turns out that the goals are not indeed always shared or common. And it is even difficult to identify goals which all would hold in common with the leaders once the leaders' aims are understood. So propaganda and indoctrination are necessary. The leaders apparently set the goals and then try to make sure that they are commonly held.

Inducements and Contributions

Another idea that does not fit with Barnard's cooperative view is that of the balance between "inducements and contributions." Only in recent years has it become fashionable to conceive of organizations as systems with inputs and outputs. Barnard was way ahead of his time when he did so in 1938. Each individual makes an input to the organization (a contribution) and receives some part of the output (his inducement). Work and loyalty are contributions. Wages, prestige, etc., are inducements. If there is an excess of inducements over contributions—if people do not give enough for what they get—the organization will fail. If the two are in balance, the organization will survive and will be in equilibrium.

The distinction between contributions and inducements was utilized extensively by Herbert Simon in his work ten years later.[27] Neither Simon nor Barnard, however, deals with the situation in which contributions exceed inducements. This accounts for profits. Presumably, it is in the interest of the organization, and certainly was in the interest of the Bell Telephone System during Barnard's reign, to make sure that people give more than they receive. Otherwise, the organization could not prosper, grow, and gather power. It is upon precisely this analysis that unions make their case for a bigger share of the profits in the form of wage increases. There are other problems with the contributions-inducements theory. It is hard to escape the impression that it is obvious and tautological. If a man leaves an organization, we say that the balance was upset for him; if he does not, it was not upset. But was it wages that caused him to leave, or other job opportunities, or dissatisfaction with the common purpose, or excess travel time, or the weather in that part of the country, or what? The theory does not tell us; presumably, something must have happened, but that is hardly enlightening.

There is a more serious problem. Why would the employees have to make elaborate calculations of inducements and contribu-

---

[27]Simon, *Administrative Behavior*, 3rd ed. (New York: The Free Press, 1976), and James G. March and Herbert A. Simon, *Organizations* (New York: John Wiley & Sons, Inc., 1958).

tions if the crux of the matter were cooperation in a *common purpose?* The inducements-contributions theory sets more easily with Weber or with the classical management school than with the cooperative school. (The human relations theorists have emphasized cooperation and neglected the inducements-contributions idea; Simon does just the reverse.) However, Barnard appears to minimize this contradiction by listing eight inducements,[28] only one of which is material in character. The other seven include such terms as "the condition of communion" and "associational attractiveness." Furthermore, he repeatedly denies that material inducements are very important to organizations. Thus, the calculations of inducements and contributions can be made in terms of whether employees rank the making of cars, butter, and guns as important common goals or not. One might well wonder whether Barnard seriously believed that the employees' acceptance of the purpose of General Motors, whether that might be profit, producing cars, or whatever, was "essential" for all members. Is such a purpose an important inducement? However, much of organizational theory, especially that encompassed in the human relations approach, appears to share his view.

It is essential to Barnard's view of organizations that the importance of economic incentives be consistently played down. It is striking to find him repeatedly asserting, during the Depression days, "the almost negligible" role of material incentives "beyond the level of the bare physiological necessities."[29] He seems to be saying that workers will work for the wage that will just keep them alive, and they will derive their real satisfaction from such things as the condition of communion. Even the bare physiological necessities, this corporation president and major organizational theorist continues, "are so limited that they are satisfied with small quantities." Though the Depression is not mentioned in this book (social unrest is), in another volume Barnard notes that the food allowance for a person on relief was six cents a meal. Nevertheless, it is "wholesale general persuasion in the form of salesmanship and advertising" which has persuaded employees that money is important.[30] (He does not note that it is organizations which advertise; that would suggest an immoral output.) The logical organization is separated from the nonlogical environment as well as from the nonlogical individual.

---

[28]Barnard, *Functions of the Executive*, p. 142.

[29]Ibid., p. 143.

[30]Ibid., p. 144.

Authority

A plain fact about organizations is that the people at the top have a lot more authority than those at the bottom. Authority to give orders, fire, fine, and otherwise control individuals is an essential part of organizations. This presents something of a problem for those who believe in a cooperative system. Barnard's solution, widely cited and firmly embraced by many theorists, is that authority comes from the bottom. The subordinate makes a decision to grant authority to the person above him. If a subordinate does not accept the legitimacy of an order, the person giving it has no authority.[31] The idea is an old one, probably extending back to the Greeks. Barnard himself quotes Roberto Michels, a friend of Max Weber, to the effect that even when authority rests upon physical force, and is accepted because of fear or force, it is still *accepted*. Weber made much the same point, but he stated it as a limiting case, noting that there is always an irreducible element of voluntary compliance in an authoritarian relationship. But what was a limiting case for Weber is the basic nature of the phenomenon for Barnard. Barnard quotes a "notable business executive" who had been an army officer in World War I to the effect that the army is the "greatest of all democracies" because when the order to move forward is given, it is the enlisted man who has to decide on his own to accept that order.[32]

Barnard also speaks of the "fiction of the superior authority," but it is hardly a fiction if one can be fired for disobeying orders or shot for not moving ahead on orders. And organizations do fire people, Barnard admits, but he prefers to refer to voluntary resignation or to "terminating the connection" when the "attitude of the individual indicates in advance likelihood of disobedience."[33] Indeed, he says at one point that "to fail in an obligation intentionally is an act of hostility. This no organization can permit; and it must respond with punitive action if it can, even to the point of incarcerating or executing the culprit."[34] There is no "fiction" involved in these exercises of superior authority. But to define authority differently would be to

---

[31]Ibid., pp. 163–164.

[32]Ibid., p. 164. This view of authority is not consistent with Barnard's concept of the "organizational personality." As noted earlier, he uses heroic military behavior to illustrate the predominance of the organizational personality. The person who decides on his own to move forward is using his organizational personality, not his individual personality. Since the organizational personality can be based upon indoctrination or propaganda, authority can be a top-down phenomenon. In the present example, authority is considered a bottom-up phenomenon.

[33]Ibid., pp. 166–167.

[34]Ibid., p. 171.

weaken the emphasis upon cooperation. If organizations are primarily or even exclusively cooperative in nature, there is no room for a definition of authority that includes imposed rules and coercion as important aspects.[35]

Informal Groups

One of the most celebrated discussions in Barnard's work is that of the role of informal groups within organizations. Weber and the classical management theorists were, of course, aware of informal relations in organizations, but they saw them as problems to be overcome in the interest of complete control. It was the merit of Barnard's discussion that he saw the functional aspects of informal groups. Such groups are necessary, so to speak, to "oil the wheels" of the formal organization, to provide understanding and motivation in those areas where the formal organization is deficient. Barnard notes that they are responsible for establishing attitudes, understandings, customs, habits, and institutions. They are necessary to the operation of the formal organization as a means of communication, of cohesion, and of protecting the integrity of the individual.

It is to Barnard's discredit, however, that he completely neglected the possibility of negative aspects of informal relations. This had been extensively documented in the Hawthorne study, with which he was familiar.[36] For Roethlisberger and Dickson, the informal organization could and did have disruptive and dysfunctional aspects, such as setting standards for what was considered a fair day's output that were below those of management, or supporting systematic rule violation. But Barnard denied that the informal organization could have common purposes; for him, the purposes, such as they were, were only personal.[37] This would make agreements on a fair day's production, arrived at among workers and policed by them, fall into the category of unorganized activity. Why would this be important for Barnard? Because for him, only the formal organization can be rational. Informal organizations are not; they "correspond to the unconscious or nonintellectual actions and habits of individuals," whereas formal organizations correspond "to their reasoned and calculated actions and policies."[38] Barnard

[35]For Weber, authority in bureaucracies was rational-legal authority, a type of domination based upon legally enacted, rational rules that were held to be legitimate by all members. The rules were either agreed upon or imposed. The fact that members accepted the legitimacy of the authority in no way altered the fact that rules could be imposed, and coercion lay behind them.

[36]F. J. Roethlisberger and William J. Dickson, *Management and the Worker* (Cambridge, Mass.: Harvard University Press, 1947).

[37]Barnard, *Functions of the Executive*, p. 115.

[38]Ibid., p. 116.

comes close, here, to joining Roethlisberger and Dickson in their assumption that management behavior is mainly rational and workers' behavior nonrational.

The Fulminating Executive

Finally, as we have noted, the executive is the key to the organization of society. It is he who bears the moral freight of organizations in society. True, all personnel are important in an organization. "The work of cooperation is not the work of leadership, but of organization as a whole." Cooperation is an attribute of organizations, for the force is given off by all. "But," he continues, "these structures do not remain in existence, they usually do not come into being, the vitality is lacking, there is no enduring cooperation, without the creation of faith, the catalyst by which the living system of human effort is enabled to continue its incessant interchanges of energies and satisfactions. Cooperation, not leadership, is the creative process; but leadership is the indispensable fulminator of its forces."[39]

Of course, for such a superman-leader, material incentives are irrelevant. The most important single contribution required of the executive is loyalty, or "domination by the organization personality."[40] But since this is also the least susceptible to tangible inducements, material incentives play an "incidental and superficial role" in the case of the executive. One wonders why, then, their salaries are high. The functionalist Barnard tells us. In a statement altogether remarkable, especially in 1938, he says that income becomes significant enough to be "an important secondary factor to individuals [top executives] in many cases, because prestige and official responsibilities impose heavy material burdens on them." But, he adds, even though they need material incentives to meet the burdens of prestige, these incentives are still not only insufficient but are "often abortive."[41]

THE THEORY IN PRACTICE

Barnard was an operating executive. He knew organizations thoroughly. He spent his working life in the telephone company, and he rose to one of its highest positions. He was a man who, in contrast to most social scientists, could "tell it like it is"; could give the illuminating example or detail; could use his own experience to

---

[39]Ibid., p. 259.
[40]Ibid., p. 220.
[41]Ibid., p. 221.

convince us of the merit of his model. Illustrations from experience or from events recorded by others do not prove anything about a theory but, in the absence of empirical research, the quality of examples and illustrations is important. If, as in Barnard's book, one finds simple illustrations (men rolling a stone or, in his longest one, five men engaged in woodcutting) coexisting with complex and subtle theory, one is likely to ask which should be believed. Theory illuminates the real world; examples lend cogency to untested theory.

There are practically no illustrations in his book of actual organizations functioning in a situation. In fact, there are only three references to the telephone company. Two of them are trivial and incidental (all the decisions that go into moving a telephone pole, and the height of switchboards). The third is an account of a telephone operator so devoted to her ill mother that she took an inferior post in an isolated area so that, while working, she might watch the house which she shared with the mother. The house burned down one day, but despite her commitment to her mother, she stayed at the switchboard, watching it burn. Her "organizational personality" won out. Says Barnard, "She showed extraordinary 'moral courage,' we would say, in conforming to a code of her organization— the *moral* necessity of uninterrupted service."[42]

Aside from this curious instance, real-life organizations with their conflicts, multiple goals, cliques, and ambiguities are absent from this book. The answer, I believe, lies in Barnard's determination to purge the organization of unseemly, nonmoral, or nonlogical human behavior and to uphold the cooperative model.

Fortunately, in another volume of essays, Barnard has given us a concrete example of organizational behavior and particularly of his own behavior. He first wrote it up for a seminar at the Harvard Business School. (The Bell System has had a long and cozy relationship with the Harvard Business School. Danielian describes the company's overtures to professors who teach—and influence— public utility law and regulation, and the thinly disguised propaganda addresses by executives of the company that are given at the school at the suggestion of the company.[43] Barnard himself spent a good deal of time at Harvard talking with L. J. Henderson and others.)

Barnard in Action

For 18 months during the initial days of the Great Depression, Barnard was the Director of Emergency Relief in New Jersey, and then

---

[42]Ibid., p. 269.
[43]Danielian, *AT&T*, pp. 297–302.

he served in 1935 as chairman of the Relief Council in Trenton, where there had been especially severe problems of unemployment and relief administration. Here, indeed, was a nonroutine situation and an obvious clash of interests. In fact, one key meeting between Barnard and a delegation of workers was abruptly terminated when a large crowd of over 2000 demonstrators, backing up the workers, was broken up by the police. A second meeting was scheduled and took place; the purpose was to hear the grievances of the unemployed. Barnard rejected their demand to meet with the whole Relief Council and instead insisted that only he and eight of the workers' representatives meet. Barnard analyzed the situation for a seminar in sociology conducted by L. J. Henderson and later published the analysis in a collection of papers.[44]

He stressed that the complaints of the men, to which he listened for two hours, were, with few exceptions, "either trivial or related to past history no longer relevant to the existing conditions. As a whole, they were utterly inadequate to explain or justify the organization of the relief recipients, their mass meeting, or the time and effort of the representatives, some of whom could certainly have employed themselves to better advantage materially in the endeavor to obtain jobs or create places for themselves."[45] Rather than attempting to make real complaints about relief provisions during a period of severe unemployment in an industrial city, "what these men wanted was opportunity for self-expression and recognition. . . . To have dismissed the grievances as trivial, however, would have been to destroy the opportunity that was literally more important to these personalities than more or less food for themselves or families."[46] So much for one view of the realities of the situation, more or less food. Really at stake were nonlogical sentiments; why else would they not be out looking for work? Indeed, the problem with relief was obvious; it was not the well-to-do and those who ran the state and city who were opposed to higher payments (Barnard agreed the payments of six cents per meal per person were "insufficient").[47] "The well-to-do," he told the workers' committee, "have lost plenty and are grumbling much about taxes and this or that, and lots of them have lost their nerve. But they're not the people who are opposed to you. . . . The people who are most opposed to you and whom you and I must pay most attention to are those nearest you—those just one jump ahead of the bread line."[48]

[44]Chester Barnard, *Organization and Management* (Cambridge, Mass.: Harvard University Press, 1948), pp. 51–79.

[45]Ibid., p. 71.

[46]Ibid.

[47]Ibid., p. 72.

[48]Ibid., pp. 74–75.

This made the problem one of education of the marginally employed, not deficit spending or higher taxes for the well-off and moderately well-off (such as those with large holdings of telephone stock which continued to pay its $9.00 dividend). Education, of course, would take time.

Unimpeded by nonlogical sentiments, Barnard drove his point home. "What ought to be done either in the way of correction of faults or increases of allowances, I will do if I can, because they ought to be done." Then, pounding the table for emphasis, he continued: "But one thing I want to make clear. I'll be god-damned if I will do anything for you on the basis that you ought to have it just because you want it, or because you organize mass meetings, or what you will. I'll do my best to do what ought to be done, but I won't give you a nickel on any other basis." He would decide what "ought to be done." He added that his position was "based more on your own interest than on anything else. For the kind of behavior which you have been exhibiting is alienating from you the very people upon whom you or I depend to get the money for relief, and I assure you there are many who object to giving it now."[49] So much for cooperation. They were wrong in their method—they would get satisfaction only on Barnard's terms and not theirs—and they were wrong about the source of the difficulty. After another hour's discussion, they left, leaving it all in Barnard's hands. "As I look back on it, I do not think I had ever before made a purely personal accomplishment the equal of this," said Barnard.[50] Presumably Mayo would have applauded too. Characteristically, Barnard never indicated what decision he took about what should be done; it was simply not relevant. This little cameo, concrete and descriptive, of actual organizational behavior and organizational problems bears little resemblance to the cooperative systems analyzed in his classic volume. Once again, we find Barnard violating his cooperative model when the realities of organizational life must be considered.

SUMMARY

What can we learn, then, from this analysis of the cooperative view of organizations as laid out by its most distinguished proponent? First, there is the separation of organization and person which cuts through all his major concepts. He glorifies the organization and minimizes the person, as in his contrasts of decision making (deci-

---

[49]Ibid., pp. 73–74.
[50]Ibid., p. 75.

sions are nonpersonal if they are constructive); of the formal and the informal organization; of the logical processes of the organization and the nonlogical processes of the individual; of authority which is accepted willingly and authority which does not exist if it is not accepted; of ideal motives and incentives versus material ones. In all these contrasts, the second half of the coin, the potentially disruptive, the impediments to organizational functioning, are either seen in solely positive terms (as in the case of informal groups) or minimized to the point of extinction. In this fashion the problem areas of organizations—power, conflict, individual goals, and so on—are outside of his model, to be dealt with summarily by the authoritarian executive.

In their place is the moral organization. Organizations are logical; their common purpose is the purpose of all and they exist in ever-widening circles of cooperative systems. If the army is the greatest of all democracies, we have little to fear from organizations; if they exist in a cooperative system, we need not fear conflict between organizations; if they are oriented toward a common purpose, we need not fear conflict within organizations. Organizations are legitimized by their very definition. They are cooperative and pursue a moral purpose. That which is evil comes from without— even as advertising stimulates artificial desires for economic incentives.

Because of the nonrationality of individuals and their desires, indoctrination, propaganda, inducements, and so forth are needed. Executive leadership will shape these in the proper manner. The organization is not merely made up of persons; it is something greater than that, and personal decisions and personal power are not, or at least should not be, relevant. Where the person comes into Barnard's scheme, it is as the slave voluntarily giving legitimacy to the authority of the master. A manufactured consensus and harmony and the dominance of the organizational personality, even as the house burns down while the operator watches helplessly, are what Barnard has to offer. (He mercifully tells us in a footnote that the mother was rescued.)

The basic weakness of Barnard's model lies in its extreme functionalism, that is, the uncritical acceptance of organizations as functional for all concerned and the moralism that follows from this view. Barnard's central concepts, which are so widely used today, combine to legitimize and justify what should remain forever problematical—the value of imperatively coordinated systems of human effort. Bureaucracy, with all its technical superiority, scared Weber, for here was a powerful tool in the hands of the state and the private corporation that was based on domination, legalized and rationalized. For Barnard, organizations were the measure of man's cooperative instincts and were essentially democratic in nature and benign in their influence.[51]

The road from Barnard's company town, which we will follow in the remaining chapters, went primarily in three directions:

1. There is the institutional view of the executive and his organization. This is elaborated and refined primarily by Philip Selznick in his *Leadership in Administration*,[52] where the interpenetration of the organization and the community is stressed, with the organization having responsibility to protect and reflect the values of the larger society and with the leader-statesman as the catalyst of that process. That the community might have conflicting views from which the organization can select, or that the organization is capable of creating and defining values which are then imposed upon the community, is barely considered.

2. Decision making as the primordial organizational act, and the idea of equilibrium. This is refined and developed primarily by Herbert Simon in parts of *Administrative Behavior*[53] and the first half of James March and Herbert Simon's *Organizations*.[54] It results in an essentially psychological view of organizations, an emphasis upon rational cognition at the expense of structure, and a neglect of the degree to which the nature of the equilibrium is manufactured by the organization as a consequence of the latter's enormous power.[55]

3. The human relations tradition. While this tradition, following the impressive documentation of Roethlisberger and Dickson (see next chapter), has to deal with the negative effects of informal

---

[51]It is quite possible to cite passages from Barnard that indicate a highly structural, even Weberian, point of view (e.g., the sections on communication); that show considerable concern with bases of conflict; and that show that he was sometimes less concerned with cooperation than with coordination by the leader. Perhaps for this reason, some find Barnard insightful and valuable even today. However, this is to argue that when he contradicts himself, he is useful. His legacy was not a structural view of conflict and centrifugal forces in organizations, for then we might have a model of authoritarian organizations. Instead, he is cited for his position that organizations are cooperative systems. The value of his story about the relief agency is not that it reveals Barnard the man, but that this description of a real organization so contradicts his theory. So do his discussions of handling conflict, engineering consent, etc.

[52]Philip Selznick, *Leadership in Administration* (New York: Harper & Row, Inc., 1957).

[53]Simon, *Administrative Behavior*.

[54]March and Simon, *Organizations*.

[55]As we will see in Chapter 4, a quite different orientation can be found in both of these books, especially in the last half of *Organizations*, where a limited-rationality view of behavior is utilized and an essentially bureaucratic structure is fleshed out by analyzing the way the premises of decisions are controlled by unobtrusive means. This alternative view of organizations greatly enhances the skeletal model of Weber and constitutes a major advance in theory. It owes little to Barnard, however.

groups, negative effects are seen as aberrant and pathological; they can be reversed and the true nature of informal groups allowed to assert itself and thus serve the organization. This brings this view into line with that of Barnard. Conflict is also not ignored but is treated in a similar fashion. Bottom-up authority flourishes in the participative management viewpoint. Wages and material incentives have little place in this (or any other) current organizational theory, though no one takes the extreme position of Barnard. The uncritical emphasis upon communication as a manipulative device is maintained. The superiority of group over individual cognition and rationality is acclaimed, even while much human relations theory is dedicated to individual-level phenomena.

Yet, it is ironic that Barnard's extreme position with regard to the cooperative nature of the system "solves" many of the problems the human relations theorists labor over by denying they exist. There is no word in Barnard's book suggesting that organizations should be changed to allow more participation from subordinates nor that people should be treated more decently than they are. (Indeed, he decries such attempts as insincere.) How could this be a problem in organizations when authority is derived only from the subordinate? The only real problem lies in establishing a common purpose, and even the status of that problem is ambiguous since if organizations consist of people cooperating in terms of their economy of incentives, the common purpose must emerge without help; indeed, it would be immoral to be anything but a midwife to it, or it would not then be genuine. Of course, the executive must also make the right decisions and lay out the proper channels of communication, but Barnard tells us nothing concrete about these matters. In short, Barnard is a more extreme apologist for management than the human relations theorists. He continues in the tradition of Elton Mayo, as described by Bendix,[56] though he is far more subtle and insightful than most and far more respected.

---

[56]Bendix, *Work and Authority in Industry.*

3

The Human Relations Model

HAWTHORNE AND ALL THAT

In another part of the AT&T forest, another dramatic event was taking shape in the late 1920s and 1930s that would enrich organizational theory and fill the texts with references to such terms as the "bank wiring group," the "Hawthorne effect," and the "Mica-splitting Test Room."[1]

Picture a grimy factory in Cicero, outside of Chicago, in the late 1920s turning out electrical apparatus for the Bell System. This was the Hawthorne plant of Western Electric, a wholly owned and very profitable subsidiary of AT&T that produced all of the latter's equip-

---

[1]F. J. Roethlisberger and W. J. Dickson, *Management and the Worker* (Cambridge, Mass.: Harvard University Press, 1947). The story of the book has been told many times. I have relied primarily upon Henry Landsberger's sympathetic account, *Hawthorne Revisited* (Ithaca, New York: Cornell University Press, 1958), and with regard to the early history of the research, I have called upon the critical account of Loren Baritz, *The Servants of Power* (Westport, Conn.: Greenwood Press, Inc., 1974). Baritz devotes several chapters to the emergence of psychological testing and morale studies, which preceded the Hawthorne research, in an attempt to show how the social sciences were co-opted from the beginning of time by the industrial elite. It is a one-sided account which neglects the degree to which social scientists were interested in ameliorating conditions in factories and learning about human behavior in general, and it fails to indicate the mechanisms by which so many of them supposedly sold out to business interests. Nevertheless, it is a useful documentary. The most famous (and literate) summary of the major experiments is found in George Homans' *The Human Group* (New York: Harcourt Brace Jovanovich, Inc., 1950), but it is a highly colored account which I find inaccurate.

ment. As we have seen, AT&T management was progressive for its time, and it was looking for ways to increase productivity among the workers. Strong reliance upon simply speeding up the production lines and changing piecework rates was to start around 1928 and 1929. But between 1924 and 1927, managers experimented with environmental conditions such as lighting. Those experiments were remarkably frustrating.

The researchers at Western Electric took two groups of workers doing the same kinds of jobs, put them into separate rooms, and kept careful records of their productivity. One group (the test group) had the intensity of its lighting increased. Its productivity went up. For the other group (the control group), there was no change in lighting. But, to the amazement of the researchers, its productivity went up also. Even more puzzling, when the degree of illumination in the test group was gradually lowered back to the original level, it was found that output still continued to go up. Output also continued to increase in the control group. The researchers continued to drop the illumination of the test group, but it was not until the workers were working under conditions of bright moonlight that productivity stopped rising and fell off sharply.

Patiently, the researchers set out to vary the types of groups they studied and the types of work the groups did. They ran the experiments again. The productivity of both test and control groups increased. Doggedly, the researchers stuck to their initial hypotheses and decided that the increase was caused by the combination of artificial lighting and natural illumination. Next, they used only artificial lighting, but again the results were similar.

It was not until several years later that this phenomenon was explained and labeled the "Hawthorne effect." Lighting had been changed in one group and not the other group, but the researchers had neglected a more important change that had occurred for both groups, namely, that management had put them into special rooms to control the lighting and thus had segregated them from the rest of the workers and treated them as something special. In short, the real change had been that management had taken an interest in the two groups of workers. They were given special treatment and special status as compared to the rest of the workers. The attention apparently raised morale and morale raised productivity. It was a happy thought.

But that was much later. Meanwhile, puzzled by the results, the researchers (an industrial psychologist from Harvard, F. J. Roethlisberger and a member of Western Electric management, R. Dickson) turned to other variables. Elton Mayo had been called in by this time, since he was also on the faculty of the Harvard Business School. Aside from his writings about the crisis of industrial civilization, he had done work on the effects of rest pauses and on "negative reverie" among workers as an impediment to higher productivity. (Jobs were so dull that workers daydreamed about things and did not pay attention to their work; hence Mayo called the reverie "negative.") The new round of experiments introduced rest pauses and altered the length of the working day.

A number of women assembling electrical relays were selected on the basis of friendship choices and put to work in a special room where an observer recorded their conversations and interactions. They were removed from direct supervision and also placed under a modified group-incentive pay rate (each woman's pay depended in part on the productivity of the group). They knew they were the subjects of an experiment and apparently tried hard to do well. Again, as rests were introduced, productivity went up, and the effect persisted whether rests were increased or decreased, the length of the day increased or decreased. The women developed close friendships, and an uncooperative member was replaced by one they chose. The authors exhaustively examined all the traditional variables of industrial psychology—methods, fatigue, monotony, and the wage incentive system—and then started two new experiments, the "Second Relay Assembly Group" and the "Mica-splitting Test Room" to further examine the effect of incentives and rest changes. These results were quite ambiguous. Output no longer soared. There were too many variables to control—the Mica group was on individual piecework, and the women were preoccupied with the increasing layoffs at the plant occasioned by the Great Depression, so perhaps this was why their output did not increase. Moreover, the Second Relay Assembly Group did not do as well as the first and various explanations were offered.

Norms and Sentiments

But in general, the researchers were confused and admitted it. (Their book is a model of frank reporting on the step-by-step stages of the research.) The variations in results seemed to have something to do with the vague factor of employee "attitudes and preoccupations." So they did an analysis on "what's on the worker's mind," a favorite topic of the 1920s and 1930s. They employed a number of persons to interview workers throughout the plant, asking very general questions designed to get the employees to talk.

As Landsberger points out in his book *Hawthorne Revisited*, this was possibly the first attempt at what is now called nondirective counseling. Later, just before *Management and the Worker* was published, management implemented the recommendations of Roethlisberger and Dickson and established a formal interviewing program at the Hawthorne works. A large number of personnel—some 300 or so—were employed to wander about the plant encouraging workers to tell them their complaints in confidence. Management did not act upon the complaints (they were not even told of them), but the workers supposedly felt much better after having blown off steam and having concluded that management was interested.

The interviews conducted during the research led to the analysis of the nonlogical or nonrational (but not necessarily irrational) character of the worker's "sentiments." It also led to the discovery that workers restricted output and penalized those who produced more than the group had informally agreed to; that some supervisors were rated as better leaders than others because they treated the employees decently; and that there were cliques and informal groups. (That these findings should be labeled "discoveries" indicated how little members of management and industrial psychologists—and indeed, industrial sociologists in general, if there were any at that time—knew about actual organizations.)

The researchers decided to return to the study of groups since this appeared to be more important than an analysis of individually held attitudes. They set up the Bank Wiring Observation Room in which they established an already existing group of workers and inspectors to wire banks of equipment. They observed this group carefully for seven months until the lack of work in the section ended the experiment. The observations disclosed that there was deliberate and controlled restriction of output by the men. A "fair day's rate" was established informally and policed by the group; "rate busters" were subject to ostracism, sabotage, and physical reprisals. There was also a political system of falsifying records (to a rather trivial extent as far as the company was concerned; the company was quite satisfied with the productivity of the group). These techniques were used to retaliate against supervisors and inspectors who played favorites, to cover up for certain men, and to discipline others. (Other studies have supported these findings in a variety of settings.)

The sordid picture of group pressures, individual competition, falsification, and reprisals hardly supported the view that productivity was related to rest pauses or, for that matter, that this was a cooperative system in Barnard's terms or those of Mayo. (Mayo's own writings on the experiment seem to miss the point.[2]) But the hostilities and survival techniques of workers were not stressed; instead, the finding that workers formed social groups with elaborate

---

[2]Elton Mayo, *The Social Problems of an Industrial Civilization* (Cambridge, Mass.: Harvard University Press, 1945).

norms and customs was stressed. Underlying this view of groups were the omnipresent explanations of "sentiments": nonrational behavior, lack of cooperation with (rational) management, and lack of identification with the (rational) goals of the company. It was not the fear of producing too much, which could mean that some would be laid off, that led to worker restriction of output (though, honest reporters that they were, the authors noted that the company was laying off workers). Such explanations, they explicitly say, were merely rationalizations. It was group norms and the sentiments of the individuals, rather than objective conditions, that formed the bases for explaining this behavior. The sociological tradition of Comte, Pareto, Durkheim, and Sumner that emphasized nonrational norms and sentiments never received a better press.[3]

The Critics

The Roethlisberger and Dickson volume is firmly established as a classic; indeed, it was obvious from the first that this was to be an extremely influential book. But as soon as it appeared, it was also heavily and widely criticized. The *American Journal of Sociology* gave it a critical review,[4] and Robert S. Lynd (of *Middletown* fame, the first of the modern American community studies) was scathing in his review, published in the *Political Science Quarterly*, of an earlier volume by T. N. Whitehead, *Leadership in a Free Society*, that incorporated some of the same material.[5] As Landsberger put it in 1958, "a most spectacular academic battle has raged since then—or perhaps it would be more accurate to say that a limited number of gunners has kept up a steady barrage, reusing the same ammunition."[6] It was a splendid group of marksmen, including Reinhard Bendix, Clark Kerr (much later to be the embattled head of the University of California), Herbert Blumer, C. Wright Mills, Wilbert E. Moore, Harold Wilensky, and Daniel Bell. As Landsberger points out, many of the criticisms are actually directed at Elton Mayo, rather than at Roethlisberger and Dickson's *Management and the Worker*, which was primarily a research monograph. But while one

---

[3]Only Pareto is mentioned in the book; Mayo knew of him through L. J. Henderson, the Harvard natural scientist. Though any sociologist aware of Émile Durkheim's *Division of Labor in Society* (New York: The Free Press, 1947, first published in French in 1893) would have been prepared for the discovery of group norms and sentiments in industry, no sociologists were looking at the time. The biggest sociological find of the decade was thus left to people in the field of business administration.

[4]*American Journal of Sociology* 46 (1940): 98–101.

[5]*Political Science Quarterly* 52 (1937): 590–592; T. N. Whitehead, *Leadership in a Free Society* (Cambridge, Mass.: Harvard University Press, 1936).

[6]Landsberger, *Hawthorne Revisited*, pp. 1–2.

can find, here and there in the volume, recognition of matters that Mayo neglected, or recognition of contrary evidence and viewpoints, it still seems fair to say that the volume in general is cast in the Mayo framework and reflects his values.

As might be expected, some of the most common criticisms hit at the exclusively negative role assigned to conflict by the authors and their concern with cooperation and equilibrium. The cooperation, say the critics, is to be on management's terms and in management's image. There are no legitimate grounds given for conflict of interests between, say, labor and management. A related criticism is that management is seen as rational, while the worker is seen as nonrational. Kerr states, "We cannot accept the view that rationality and initiative are vouchsafed only to the elite, and that the common man is left only the virtues of faith and obedience."[7]

Another strong criticism was that, in their search for causes of negative attitudes on the part of workers, the researchers gave primary emphasis to the social groups in the workplace. As Daniel Bell pointed out, "There is no view of the larger institutional framework of our economic system within which these relationships arise and have their meaning."[8] Those who took into consideration the larger framework stressed the natural, inevitable, and even healthy conflict between the divergent interests of management and workers, the progressive rationalization and depersonalization of industrial technology, the insecurity for workers of violent business cycles, and the unequal power of the two groups. That such conflicts of interests and inequalities of power might be solved by better face-to-face relations between workers and management, or by the famous counseling system, seemed doubtful. Furthermore, the critics felt, the volume, as well as Mayo's ideology, pointed the way toward manipulation of the worker, who was seen as a child or primitive whose self-protective mechanisms and efforts to reduce monotony and boredom were not in the interests of a cooperative social system. Mayo compared the industrial researchers to physicians, administering to the ills of workers, but it is not at all clear that the efficiency of industrial organization is in the same category as individual good health.

It is both revealing and ironic that the major critics of *Management and the Worker* did not challenge it on empirical grounds, asking whether the evidence was properly gathered and correctly interpreted. The "steady barrage" by the limited number of gunners was restricted to the ideology implicit in the study. Doubtless, that ideology was more pernicious to them than the scientific standards

---

[7]Quoted in ibid., p. 31.
[8]Quoted in ibid., p. 33.

of the study. The social sciences, at least in the area of complex organizations, have been desperate for *ideas*, not data. The practitioners seize upon concepts which will make sense of the world; if the concepts make sense, the social scientists do not inquire too carefully into the empirical support for these ideas or concepts. For those who find the ideas repugnant, the most pressing thing to do is to respond on ideological grounds; only later do some have the "luxury" of patiently reexamining the empirical documentation of the new idea.

The first critical examination of the actual data and the interpretations of Roethlisberger and Dickson that I am aware of was published fifteen years after the original study.[9] The author, Michael Argyle, flatly announced in a later paper that "despite a widespread belief to the contrary, 'social' factors have never been shown to be of very great significance as determinants of productivity differences between otherwise similar departments," and he cited the Hawthorne studies as a case in point.[10] Alex Carey in 1967 came to a similar conclusion: "The results of these studies, far from supporting the various components of the 'human relations approach,' are surprisingly consistent with a rather old-world view about the value of monetary incentives, driving leadership, and discipline."[11]

Carey then asks why social scientists have continued to neglect the discrepancy between the evidence and the conclusions contained in this seminal work. The answer is probably rather simple. After the Hawthorne studies were published, a small-scale social movement got underway—financed by government agencies, business organizations, universities, and business-supported foundations—which sought to find ways to increase productivity by manipulating social factors. Conducting more or less careful, scientific studies of the relationship between such attitudes as morale and such behaviors as productivity, the members of what came to be

---

[9]Michael Argyle, "The Relay Assembly Test Room in Retrospect," *Occupational Psychology* 27 (1953): 98–103.

[10]Michael Argyle, Godfrey Gardner, and Frank Cioffi, "Supervisory Methods Related to Productivity, Absenteeism, and Labour Turnover," *Human Relations* 11 (1958): 24.

[11]Alex Carey, "The Hawthorne Studies: A Radical Criticism," *American Sociological Review* 32, no. 3 (June 1967): 416. See also the methodological criticism of A. J. Sykes in "Economic Interest and the Hawthorne Researches: A Comment," *Human Relations* 18 (1965): 253–263. It is interesting that all of these critics are British. The criticisms cover a host of complicated issues and cannot be easily summarized; the reader is directed to the actual articles and to the original study itself. Inadequate controls, failure to assess the impact of such things as replacement of slow workers by fast ones, changes in incentives, and ignoring the contrary evidence the authors themselves present are frequent themes.

called the "human relations movement" increasingly suffered set-backs. The relationship between morale and productivity, and that between good leadership and productivity, proved to be less than clear and less than substantial. Since their own sophisticated studies of the influence of social factors upon production were in serious trouble, the human relations people did not have much incentive to make a searching critique of the first major study.

We will turn in a moment to the thirty-year history of the effort to link morale and leadership to productivity. Much has been learned about individual and group behavior as a result of the effort, but most of the acquired knowledge, unfortunately, tells us little about *organizations* as such. Why spend, then, the better part of a chapter on something that has been generally unproductive in learning about organizations? For one thing, this is the most voluminous and substantial part of the literature on organizations. Just as one must know something about the Hawthorne studies, one must also know something about current human relations models. Second, the premises of the movement are so sensible, and even compelling, that it is necessary to examine them in detail to see where they might go wrong. Why would happy workers not produce more? Why not allow workers to participate in decisions? Third, we learn a great deal about the complexity of *human* behavior by taking this tour; it should give us some pause when we try, in succeeding chapters, to deal with *organizational* behavior. There are no simple keys to unlock the secrets of organizations; an examination of the "obvious" truths of human relations research will make that clear. In a sense, if truly sociological studies of organizations were as numerous, well done, and well criticized as the social-psychological studies, we, too, might be more overwhelmed than we are by the complexities of organizational analysis.

I wish to emphasize the above points because my criticism of the human relations movement will be rather scathing. I think there are more productive paths for understanding organizations and for gaining some control over the way they shape our lives than those provided by this movement. But the structural or sociological analysis, it must be said, has not been tested by thirty years of accumulated studies bearing upon its central theses. Indeed, one is not quite sure what the central theses of the structural school are, while those of the human relations school are clear.

Finally, the work of those who are generally associated with the human relations school has produced some promising lines of inquiry which constitute departures from the central tenets of the school. The work of Seashore and Yuchtman on organizational goals and, especially, the first part of the volume of Katz and Kahn, which uses a sophisticated "open-system" or "social-system" approach, are two examples.[12] We won't go into them here because we are dealing with the main schools of thought and the basic conceptions of organizations that have been well researched or thought through. The work of these people, like that of Arnold Tannenbaum whom we will briefly consider, is a product of the human relations movement, but it goes far beyond that school.

Our discussion of the human relations school will be artificially divided into two branches. The first is concerned with morale, leadership, and productivity. The second, more sophisticated, branch is concerned with the structuring of groups, and it builds on the premises of the first but applies them to the organization as a whole.

LEADERSHIP AND PRODUCTIVITY MODELS

The general thesis of this branch of human relations theory is that good leadership will lead to increased productivity on the part of employees. "Good leadership" is generally described as democratic rather than authoritarian, employee-centered rather than production-centered, concerned with human relations rather than with bureaucratic rules, and so on. It is hypothesized that good leadership will lead to high morale, and high morale will lead to increased effort resulting in higher production. It will also reduce turnover (leaving the organization) and absenteeism, thus raising productivity by minimizing both training time and the disruption caused by absent workers.

The history of research in this area is one of progressive disenchantment with the above theses and progressive awareness of the complexities of human behavior and human situations. As a result of nearly thirty years of intensive research, we have a large body of information on what does *not* clearly and simply affect productivity (or the intervening variable, morale) and a growing list of qualifiers and conditions that have to be taken into account. The size of this list threatens to overwhelm us before we can, with confidence, either advise managers as to what they should do to increase productivity or develop theories that have much explanatory power.

---

[12]Stanley E. Seashore and Ephraim Yuchtman, "Factorial Analysis of Organizational Performance," *Administrative Science Quarterly* 12, no. 3 (December 1967): 377–395. Daniel Katz and Robert Kahn, *Social Psychology of Organizations* (New York: John Wiley & Sons, Inc., 1966).

Attitudes and Performance

One of the early systematic studies in the field of industrial psychology was conducted in 1930. The investigators used questionnaires and interviews to determine the attitudes of between 200 and 300 young girls tending machines in a mill.[13] They concluded that the girls' productivity had no relationship to their attitudes toward their work, their supervisors, personnel policies, etc. The researchers also examined a number of other variables, such as age, intelligence, education, and emotional adjustment, and found that even when these were taken into account, there was no such relationship. It all might have ended there with this negative finding, except that the result was so hard to believe. Happy employees should be productive employees; that was the sermon that was increasingly preached in the management journals and by social scientists. Starting in the 1940s, study after study sought to prove the relationship.

By 1954, there had been about fifty studies of the relationship between attitudes and performance, and two psychologists, Brayfield and Crockett, paused to survey the studies carefully. The conclusion of the 1930 study was upheld; there was little evidence that attitudes bore any "simple or even appreciative relationship to performance."[14] Personnel who were satisfied with their network of interpersonal relationships were not necessarily highly motivated to produce; indeed, the worker had many goals, and productivity was at best a peripheral one. Satisfactions were related, however, to absenteeism and turnover. This should not surprise us. If anyone is going to leave or be absent, it is likely to be that person who is the most dissatisfied. Staying home on Monday or getting another job is of direct benefit to that worker. Increasing his effort on the job is not.

After the Brayfield and Crockett articles in 1955, the work in this area began to slack off, though studies continued to appear. A review of the literature, published in 1964 by Vroom, concluded that there was a small and fairly consistent relationship between satisfaction and performance.[15] He cited twenty-three correlations from the literature, and in twenty of them there was a positive relationship, even though the median correlation was only .14 (which is

---

[13]Arthur Kornhauser and A. Sharp, "Employee Attitudes, Suggestions from a Study in a Factory," *Personnel Journal* 10 (1932): 393–401.

[14]Arthur H. Brayfield and Walter H. Crockett, "Employee Attitudes and Employee Performance," *Psychological Bulletin* 52, no. 5 (1955): 396–424. Many of the references we will be citing in this section are conveniently included in L. L. Cummings and W. E. Scott, *Readings in Organizational Behavior and Human Performance*, rev. ed. (Homewood, Ill.: Richard D. Irwin, Inc., 1973).

[15]Victor Vroom, *Work and Motivation* (New York: John Wiley & Sons, Inc., 1964).

very low, explaining only about 2 percent of the relationship between satisfaction and productivity). If there is such a low relationship, it would hardly behoove managers to try to increase the work satisfaction and morale of workers, except to reduce turnover and absenteeism.

But the matter has not rested there. Lawler and Porter looked over thirty studies considering the relationship between satisfaction and performance, and they decided that the problem might simply be that the causal relationship should be reversed.[16] Satisfaction might result from high performance, rather than being a cause of it, *if* the employee is rewarded for high performance. The cause of high performance might be any number of things, including good equipment and authoritarian leadership. Lawler and Porter tested their hypothesis using data from 148 lower- and middle-level managers in five organizations, and they found support for it. They concluded that instead of trying to maximize satisfaction in organizations, organizations should pay attention to the requirement that high performance be rewarded by satisfying such higher-order needs as "self-actualization" and "autonomy."[17]

This viewpoint shows considerably more imagination than the standard one of high morale leading to high productivity, but it fails to give enough weight to a much neglected aspect of organizational life. For many jobs there is no room for high performance. The assembly-line worker can only do an adequate or a poor job, not a good one, for he does not control the pace of the work or make any decisions that might increase productivity. He may fail to make an adequate weld, but making one that indicates great skill and craftsmanship will bring him no recognition. In fact, it may bring a reprimand for wasting energy and metal when only an adequate weld is required. I suspect that many managerial and white-collar workers are in the same position. An adequate level of productivity is determined by the volume of input received and the volume of output absorbed. These depend upon other units of the organization. A worker or a manager and his staff may not receive an increase in inputs, or other groups may not be able to handle an increase in outputs. If so, an increase in productivity is impossible, and superior quality is likely to be wasted.[18] The so-called "pride of

---

[16]Edward E. Lawler, III and Lyman W. Porter, "The Effect of Performance on Job Satisfaction," *Industrial Relations* 7, no. 1 (October 1967): 20–28.

[17]Recently Dornbush and Scott have examined the role of rewards very thoroughly, and indicate that the role of evaluation by superiors is not only a key factor in all kinds of organizations, but a neglected one. Sanford Dornbush and W. Richard Scott, *Evaluation and the Exercise of Authority* (San Francisco: Jossey-Bass, Inc., 1975).

[18]For a classic example of this, see the account of the toy painters in William F. Whyte, *Money and Motivation* (Westport, Conn.: Greenwood Press, Inc., 1977), pp. 90–99.

craftsmanship" is systematically excluded from as many jobs as possible because it is difficult for management to control this variable. Productivity, it is safe to say, depends much more upon such things as technological changes or economies of scale than upon human effort.[19]

Leadership and Performance

The relationship between attitudes and performance is a simple statement of the productivity problem. More sophisticated is the attempt to determine the effect of leadership behavior upon human performance. The reasoning here is that if one can find out what makes a good leader, and if one could then teach people to be good leaders, or at least find ways to select good leaders, then presumably most of our organizational problems would be solved. Indeed, we could solve our national and even our international problems for, as everyone knows, "what we need is good leadership." The results of this quest, still going on, have been as disillusioning as the more simple attempt to show that good attitudes result in good performance. As we shall see, the result might be summed up as saying "it all depends. . . ."

Furthermore, the human relations tradition has viewed managerial or supervisory behavior as consisting primarily of leading men and not of making good decisions about such nonpersonal, mundane factors as the market, technology, competition, or organizational structure. But the nonpersonal decisions appear to have far more effect than decisions as to how to lead people. There is some confusion here since we are prone to say that an organization has done well because of exceptional leadership. What we generally mean is that the decisions taken with regard to organizational structure, type of product or service, quality control, new technologies, and so on have been good decisions, not just that the leaders have summoned an extra ounce of cooperation and motivation from the followers or been helpful in planning the workers' tasks or in teaching them skills. Of course, one can handle followers so poorly as to negate the advantages of organizational resources and opportunities, or one can have such an extraordinary personality as to compel loyalty, devotion, and hard work even without superior resources and opportunities. But these are exceptional cases. For most organizations, the impact of moderately good or bad relations with subordinates appears to be small and difficult to separate from other considerations.

---

[19]See, for example, Robert Dubin, "Supervision and Productivity," in Robert Dubin et al., *Leadership and Productivity* (San Francisco: Chandler Publishing Co., 1965), p. 50.

For all practical purposes, the leadership studies began in earnest about 1945 with a ten-year research project at Ohio State University. The researchers, mainly psychologists, started out in a practical and empirical manner characteristic of much of the post-World War II social-science research. They sought to find and catalogue all of the traits that might affect leadership ability and to see which were the most important. Literally hundreds of traits were examined. The focus was upon the leader, not upon the members of the group. Most any leader of any group would do. Little attention was paid, at least initially, to the situation the group found itself in or to the type of organization or task.

After several years of research and with increasingly sophisticated data analysis techniques, two dimensions or "factors" emerged which appeared to account for most of the variation between leadership style and group performance.[20] One was called "initiating structure" and referred to structuring and defining the roles of both the leader and the subordinates. A high-scoring leader would be active in planning, communicating information, scheduling activities, trying out new ideas, and so on. The other factor was called "consideration"—consideration for the feelings of subordinates, respect for their ideas, and mutual trust. A high-scoring individual promoted rapport and two-way communication. (Two other factors were dropped.)

A leader could be high on both of these; they were not viewed as opposite poles of a continuum. This conceptualization represented an advance, for it eschewed the simple dichotomy characteristic of early human relations research—the dichotomy between leaders who practiced good human relations and those who did not. In this earlier view, it was sufficient to contrast the democratic leader with the authoritarian one, sometimes conceiving of a third position, laissez-faire.[21] The Ohio State studies indicated that "structural" or "task-oriented" expertise—planning work, eliciting ideas, scheduling, etc.—was as important as good interpersonal relations.

About the same time, another set of studies began to appear from the Survey Research Center at the University of Michigan. Initially, they conceptualized two styles, employee orientation and production orientation,[22] which were thought to be at the opposite

---

[20]See the studies reported in R. M. Stogdill and A. E. Coons, eds., *Leader Behavior: Its Description and Measurement* (Columbus, Ohio: Bureau of Business Research, 1957).

[21]This trio was the product of the single most influential study of leadership, conducted in 1938 by Kurt Lewin, R. Lippett, and R. White. See R. K. White, *Autocracy and Democracy* (Westport, Conn.: Greenwood Press, Inc., 1972).

[22]Daniel Katz, N. Maccoby, and Nancy C. Morse, *Productivity, Supervision, and Morale in an Office Situation* (Detroit, Mich.: Darel Press, Inc., 1950).

poles of a continuum. The first represented good human relations practices, the second, an emphasis upon the technical aspects of the job. Several years later, it was decided that these were not the opposite poles of a continuum, but independent. Thus, a leader could be high on both. Still other conceptualizations appeared, one of which added the dimension of "modifying employee goals," described as "behavior that influences the actual personal goals of subordinates in organizationally useful directions,"[23] just in case subordinates had the wrong ideas. Recently, Floyd Mann emphasized three skills: human relations skills, technical skills, and "administrative skills."[24] In this case, technical skills are confined to the methods and techniques for getting a task done, while administrative skills include such structural aspects as planning, organizing, task assignment, inspection, coordination, and making sure that the group goals mesh with the goals of the total organization.

Bowers and Seashore came up with a four-factor theory of leadership, something of a modification of an earlier five-dimension theory proposed by Rensis Likert in his *New Patterns of Management* (see below).[25] Traditional human relations theory was covered by two aspects—giving support and interaction facilitation; a third factor recognized the importance of "enthusiasm" for achieving goals; and the last was a work facilitation factor (combining Mann's technical and administrative skills). Others proposed other factors. All of them were more or less compatible with the initiating structure and consideration dimensions discovered in the Ohio State studies, but most offered elaborations and recombinations of elaborations. None dealt with the content of actual decisions—e.g., to change production methods.

Unfortunately, despite these many variations on a common theme, enthusiasm has often outrun careful research. In 1966 Korman published a sober review of a large number of studies which related the various measures of consideration and initiating structure to measures of organizational effectiveness. He concluded that although the concepts had become bywords in industrial psychology, "it seems apparent that very little is now known as to how these variables may predict work-group performance and the conditions which affect such predictions. At the current time, we cannot even say whether they have any predictive significance at all."[26]

[23]Robert L. Kahn, "Human Relations on the Shop Floor," in *Human Relations and Modern Management*, ed. E. M. Hugh-Jones (Amsterdam, Holland: North-Holland Publishing Co., 1958), pp. 43–74.

[24]Mann, in Dubin et al., *Leadership and Productivity*, pp. 68–103.

[25]David G. Bowers and Stanley E. Seashore, "Predicting Organizational Effectiveness with a Four-Factor Theory of Leadership," *Administrative Science Quarterly* 11, no. 2 (September 1966): 238–263.

[26]Abraham K. Korman, "'Consideration,' 'Initiating Structure,' and Organiza-

Many of the correlations reported were insignificant; the correlation between consideration and performance was better than that between initiating structure and performance (the latter was sometimes negative); the research did not take into account the situations of the groups or the possibility of important intervening variables; some correlations for consideration were the opposite of those predicted; and so on. "The piecemeal accumulation of 'two-variable' studies . . . does not provide the kinds of direction needed."[27] The influence of the size of a group (in one case, the more authoritarian leaders were more effective in large groups than the less authoritarian ones), urban versus semirural environments, the role of the wishes and expectations of subordinates, the self-esteem of subordinates, and so on were all held to complicate the relationship.

Such pessimistic conclusions have greeted other articles of faith about the way to increase productivity or organizational effectiveness. In addition to the importance of leadership, most human relations theorists have held that "job enlargement" will increase both satisfactions and productivity. According to the theory, the essence of bureaucracy is the minute division of tasks in order to increase predictability and skills, reduce training time, and make surveillance and evaluation more effective. This division of labor results in simplified, low skill level, short-cycle jobs. This in turn produces monotony, boredom, and job dissatisfaction, which results in absenteeism, turnover, and restriction of output. In 1968, Hulin and Blood reviewed a large number of studies concerned with job enlargement and concluded as follows: "Those which have used acceptable methodology, control groups, appropriate analysis, and multivariate designs have generally not yielded evidence which could be considered as supporting the job-enlargement thesis. Those studies which do appear to support such a thesis frequently contain a number of deviations from normally acceptable research practices."[28] The latter group of studies is the larger group, however, and has "generated the greatest favor and [has] been accepted as gospel by a large number of psychologists and human relations theorists." Nevertheless, the case for job enlargement has been "drastically overstated and overgeneralized."[29] Hulin and Blood note studies which argue that not all workers are satisfied when they are allowed to take part in decision making, and they

---

tional Criteria—A Review," *Personnel Psychology* 19, no. 4 (1966): 349–361. (Quote is from p. 361.)

[27]Ibid., p. 360.

[28]Charles L. Hulin and Milton R. Blood, "Job Enlargement, Individual Differences, and Worker Responses," *Psychological Bulletin* 69, no. 1 (1968): 41–55.

[29]Ibid.

suggest that some prefer routine, repetitious, and specified work methods.

Theories of leadership and productivity more complex than the two-factor theory of consideration and initiating structure, or the comparable three-, four-, and five-factor models, have been offered. Herzberg's two-factor theory, for example, holds that man had two sets of needs which were independent—his need to avoid pain and his need to grow psychologically.[30] Avoidance of pain could be accomplished without necessarily producing happiness. Thus, Herzberg made the intriguing suggestion that some aspects of work, such as company policy, administration, technical supervision, and salary, are hygienic factors which, if personnel are not content with them, will lead to dissatisfaction. But, if employees are content with them, these things will not *contribute* to satisfaction. Other aspects, such as the nature of the work itself and intrinsic rewards of the work, are motivators. If they are perceived positively, they will lead to satisfaction; but their absence will not lead to dissatisfaction.

This theory attracted much attention, perhaps partly because of the potentially powerful suggestion that factors contributing to satisfaction and those contributing to dissatisfaction are independent. If this were so, it could open up a complex area of research and perhaps rescue some of the previous theories. The theory also makes intuitive sense. However, it has been subjected to scathing criticism on methodological and other grounds. For example, only if one adopts the questionable empirical methods of Herzberg and his students does one find support for it. House and Wigdor, in their review, find considerable evidence that what causes job satisfaction for one person need not cause it for another. Job satisfaction is relative to a large number of alternatives available to the individual and affected by job level, age, sex, education, culture, time-dimension, and the respondent's standing in his group.[31] Thus, once more, the number of variables mount.

A far more sophisticated study of leadership, Fiedler's "contingency" theory,[32] is the last we shall consider. Pondering several decades of research on leadership, Fiedler increased the complex-

---

[30]Frederick Herzberg, *Work and the Nature of Man* (New York: T. Y. Crowell Co. 1966). The theory was first put forth in F. Herzberg, B. Mausner, and B. Snyderman, *The Motivation to Work*, 2nd ed. (New York: John Wiley & Sons, Inc., 1959).

[31]Robert J. House and Lawrence A. Wigdor, "Herzberg's Dual-Factor Theory of Job Satisfaction and Motivation: A Review of the Evidence and a Criticism," *Personnel Psychology* 20 (1967): 369–389.

[32]Fred E. Fiedler, *A Theory of Leadership Effectiveness* (New York: McGraw-Hill Book Company, 1967).

ity of the problem geometrically when he demonstrated that the "climate" of the group had a substantial impact upon the effectiveness of leadership styles. If the group situation is either highly favorable or highly unfavorable for the leader, a task-oriented leader does best; if it is in between, a leader skilled in interpersonal relations is best. By a favorable situation, Fiedler meant the extent to which relationships between the leader and the member are good, tasks can be easily programmed, and the position of the leader is clearly established. Apparently, if all these exist to a substantial degree, the best leader is the one who provides task direction and gets on with the work of the group. Interpersonal relations are not problematical and will take care of themselves. If the relationships between the leader and members are bad, tasks are unclear, and the position of the leader is not clearly established (what Fiedler calls low position power), then attention to interpersonal relations will be wasted; what is needed is strong direction. But if the situation is in between, then interpersonal leadership or something close to consideration is critical. Fiedler calls this a contingency theory of leadership—it is contingent upon some nonleadership variables. If true—and he has considerable supporting data from a variety of groups in different countries, though some of these data are less convincing than others—this represents an increase in sophistication and complexity over the prevailing views.

Unfortunately, the matter does not end with the complex interaction of leadership style, group structure, tasks, and relationships in the group. There are still other factors that influence leadership effectiveness. First, Fiedler's findings are more relevant to interacting groups than to those which "counteract" (such as committees that represent different viewpoints) or those which require little member interdependence ("co-acting" groups such as machine operators working side by side). Second, the degree of stress is important since the findings do not appear to hold where group stress is minimal.[33] Another reservation concerns the timing of the leadership style. At what point in the group situation does the leader emphasize task performance or interpersonal relations?[34] (Someone could work on that particular complication alone for five years.) Furthermore, Fiedler notes that other variables—such as member abilities and motivation, group heterogeneity, expertness of the leader, his familiarity with the task, and his familiarity with the group—are likely to be important. No doubt there are others which would turn up when research is conducted on still more groups. If so, with what are we left?

---

[33]Ibid., pp. 189–195.
[34]W. K. Graham, "Description of Leader Behavior and Evaluation of Leaders as a Function of LPC," *Personnel Psychology* 21 (Winter 1968): 457–464.

One is tempted to say that the research on leadership has left us with the clear view that things are far more complicated and "contingent" than we initially believed, and that, in fact, they are so complicated and contingent that it may not be worth our while to spin out more and more categories and qualifications—if we wish to learn about organizations. Already, the task of either training leaders to fit the jobs or designing jobs to fit the leaders, a position Fiedler is led to advocate,[35] appears to be monumental. If leadership techniques must change with every change in group personnel, task, timing, experience, and so on, then either leaders or jobs must constantly change, and this will make predictions difficult. At the extremes, we can be fairly confident in identifying good or bad leaders; but for most situations we will probably have little to say. We may learn a great deal about interpersonal relations but not much about organizations.

Training Leaders

Finally, even if we have vague hunches that good leaders are those who practice good human relations, that most leaders do not, and that we have an idea of what good human relations are, can we train leaders to perform better? A whole industry has evolved around the assumption that we can. Academic social scientists make handsome outside incomes from participating in training programs for management; independent corporations have been set up to do this; business schools derive no small part of their income from conducting training programs. The most famous and financially successful of these programs have been dubbed T-group programs, with the T standing for training. These sessions seek to expand interpersonal consciousness, develop authenticity in interpersonal relations and spontaneous behavior, eliminate behavior that stems from hierarchical positions and substitute collaborative behavior, and develop ability to solve conflicts through problem solving rather than through bargaining, coercion, or power manipulation. Since this training technique has become so widespread and important in the organizational world, extending to non-economic organizations and being incorporated into business school curricula, it is worth quoting from one account to give the flavor of these sessions, which can be both illuminating and devastating for the individuals involved.[36]

---

[35]Fred Fiedler, "Engineer the Job to Fit the Manager," *Harvard Business Review* 43, no. 5 (1965): 115–122.

[36]Robert Tannenbaum, I. R. Weschler, and F. Massarik, *Leadership and Organization: A Behavioral Science Approach* (New York: McGraw-Hill Book Co., 1961), p. 123.

At the fifth meeting the group's feelings about its own progress became the initial focus of discussion. The "talkers" participated as usual, conversation shifting rapidly from one point to another. Dissatisfaction was mounting, expressed through loud, snide remarks by some and through apathy by others.

George Franklin appeared particularly disturbed. Finally pounding the table, he exclaimed, "I don't know what is going on here! I should be paid for listening to this drivel? I'm getting just a bit sick of wasting my time here. If the profs don't put out—I quit!" George was pleased; he was angry, and he had said so. As he sat back in his chair, he felt he had the group behind him. He felt he had the guts to say what most of the others were thinking! Some members of the group applauded loudly, but others showed obvious disapproval. They wondered why George was excited over so insignificant an issue, why he hadn't done something constructive rather than just sounding off as usual. Why, they wondered, did he say their comments were "drivel"?

George Franklin became the focus of discussion. "What do you mean, George, by saying this nonsense?" "What do you expect, a neat set of rules to meet all your problems?" George was getting uncomfortable. These were questions difficult for him to answer. Gradually he began to realize that a large part of the group disagreed with him; then he began to wonder why. He was learning something about people he hadn't known before. ". . . How does it feel, George, to have people disagree with you when you thought you had them behind you? . . ."

Bob White was first annoyed with George and now with the discussion. He was getting tense, a bit shaky perhaps. Bob didn't like anybody to get a raw deal, and he felt that George was getting it. At first Bob tried to minimize George's outburst, and then he suggested that the group get on to the real issues; but the group continued to focus on George. Finally Bob said, "Why don't you leave George alone and stop picking on him? We're not getting anywhere this way."

With the help of the leaders, the group focused on Bob. "What do you mean, 'picking' on him?" "Why, Bob, have you tried to change the discussion?" "Why are you so protective of George?" Bob began to realize that the group wanted to focus on George; he also saw that George didn't think he was being picked on but felt he was learning something about himself and how others reacted to him. "Why do I always get upset," Bob began to wonder, "when people start to look at each other? Why do I feel sort of sick when people get angry at each other?" . . . Now Bob was learning something about how people saw him, while gaining some insight into his own behavior. . . .

In 1968 Campbell and Dunnette conducted a thorough review of the evidence for the effectiveness of T-group training, and their conclusion is melancholy.[37] "To sum up, the assumption that T-group

---

[37]John P. Campbell and Marvin D. Dunnette, "Effectiveness of T-Group Experiences in Managerial Training and Development," *Psychological Bulletin* 70, no. 2 (August 1968): 73–104.

training has positive utility for organizations must necessarily rest on shaky ground. It has been neither confirmed nor disconfirmed. The authors wish to emphasize again that utility for the organization is not necessarily the same as utility for the individual."[38]

Their last point deserves elaboration. As they carefully note in an addendum to their review, many people have enthusiastically testified to the benefits of the experience—for themselves, as persons. The cold scientific criteria that Campbell and Dunnette utilize to judge the effectiveness of something so "life-enhancing" to participants must surely be irrelevant to participants. Their enthusiasm is frequently great. If the effects are not found to carry over into actual organizational situations, it may be the problem of the research, not of the T-group training.

There is something to this posture, though Campbell and Dunnette are correct that it is also quite inappropriate to make claims for the effectiveness of these techniques merely upon the enthusiastic response of some or most participants. One suspects that most managers live drab and muted lives in some respects and rarely come upon those life-enhancing, self-actualization experiences and encounters that others realize through cultural and aesthetic activities. If so, or even if everyone needs more of these experiences, the returns to the individual may be high, and the costs to him and the organization may be quite trivial. We should, then, bless T-groups because they do for managers what pot, psychedelic experiences, encounter groups, and hard-rock music do for the far-out younger generation. The search for authenticity and spontaneity should be never-ending, and if it must occur in the guise of better productivity in organizations, let it. The trainees will return refreshed to a world of hierarchies, conflict, authority, stupidity, and brilliance, but the hierarchies, etc., are not likely to fade away. Most organizations remain highly authoritarian systems; some even use T-groups to hide that essential fact.

Summary of the Research

This completes our review of the research dealing primarily with leadership and productivity models. Most of that research is psychological in theory and orientation. In sheer volume, it constitutes the largest group of empirical studies within the human relations tradition, and perhaps in organizational analysis in general. The research has generally been carried out with more sophistica-

---

[38]Ibid., p. 98. For a spirited exchange between these authors and Chris Argyris on the topic, see Marvin Dunnette, John Campbell, and Chris Argyris, "A Symposium: Laboratory Training," *Industrial Relations* 8, no. 1 (October 1968): 1-46.

tion with regard to control groups, multivariate analysis, replication studies, and so on than any other branch of organizational research. A great deal has been learned about individuals and small groups in the process, but what we have learned about organizations is primarily that our simple models do not hold in all or most cases, nor do they account for much of the variance when they do hold. The models have become increasingly complex, with something like the following progression: high morale leads to high productivity; good leadership ("democratic" leadership, good human relations, consideration, etc.) leads to high morale (and thus to high productivity); effective leadership (combining a concern for people with a concern for task effectiveness) leads to high morale and/or high productivity; effective leadership has to be tailored to the group situation (e.g., group task, structure, member relationship, timing, stress, etc.).

The increase in complexity has resulted in a decrease in applicability and in theoretical power. We are now in a situation where the variables are so numerous and complex that we can hardly generalize to organizations or even types of organizations. Only in extreme cases of very poor leadership or very good leadership can we say much with confidence, except that most situations fall between these extremes.

A similar fate may await the more general theories of sociologists when they, too, amass a large number of sophisticated studies. Or it may be, hopefully, that any theory that has the power to explain a good deal of organizational behavior will have to deal with more general variables than leadership and small-group behavior. It will have to deal with such variables as types of structure, group interrelationships, character of resources, technology, and environmental influences, where the more specific variables of leader behavior and small-group characteristics are held to be randomly distributed and thus have little effect when a large number of organizations are the object of study. The conclusion reached by Wilensky over twenty years ago still stands:

> All this suggests that, at minimum, the practitioner who wants to apply the human relations research has no clear directive as to what to do—and this is true not only of the findings on size of immediate work group, the character of informal work group solidarity, degree of identification with company goals, and type of leadership style as related to productivity; it applies also to the findings on the relation of "morale" (i.e., satisfaction with job and with company) to all of these variables. The evidence is typically inconclusive, the interpretations sometimes contradictory.[39]

---

[39]Harold L. Wilensky, "Human Relations in the Workplace," in Conrad

Perhaps in reaction to this mounting complexity, psychologists have tried to cut the gordian knot in another manner—with the blunt edge of stimulus-response theory. The idea goes back to the Russian scientist Pavlov who taught dogs to salivate at the sound of a bell. It became entwined with more sophisticated learning theory (behavior is a learned response, not an expression of complex inner drives, fixed traits, or need satisfactions), and emerged in the 1950s and 1960s as "operant conditioning" theory, associated with the name of psychologist B. F. Skinner.[40] Its simplicity exceeds that of the leadership-morale-productivity model. Behavior is a function of its consequences, runs the dictum. If you are rewarded for "emitting" a type of behavior, you will repeat it; if the behavior is ignored or punished, the behavior will be "extinguished." Rewards are more powerful than punishments; therefore, managers should emphasize "reinforcers" rather than demotivators. Reinforcements should come immediately after the behavior that one wishes to reinforce, but if repetitive acts are to be rewarded, it is best to reward random, intermittent instances of the behavior, otherwise the person can become satiated with the reward and not connect it to the behavior. Despite the fact that the human relations tradition strongly believes in rewards, the operant conditioning formulation is regarded with suspicion and distaste. It sounds mechanical, dehumanizing, overly manipulative, and treats employees as if they were pigeons, rats in a maze, or at best, children. Operant conditioning advocates deny all this, of course.

For a variety of reasons it has been difficult to apply this theory to organizations in any scientific way. (There are the usual highly publicized cures, based on quite ambiguous situations where a variety of uncontrolled factors could be operating to produce the effects, much as in the leadership area.) Luthans and Kreitner devote a book to the subject of organizational applications, but the examples concern such relatively trivial or simple situations as being late to work.[41] But it is too early to rule this approach out of court. At the least it supports the growing emphasis upon evaluating and rewarding performance,[42] conforms to what we know skilled leaders often do (try to praise good behavior immediately, and avoid punishing bad behavior with immobilizing global assertions such as "you are always doing that"), and finally, agrees with the growing emphasis upon the plasticity of behavior and the deemphasis upon

---

Arensberg et al., *Research in Industrial Human Relations: A Critical Appraisal* (New York: Harper & Row, Inc., 1957), p. 34.

[40]B. F. Skinner, *Beyond Freedom and Dignity* (New York: Bantam Books, 1971).

[41]Fred Luthans and Robert Kreitner, *Organizational Behavior Modification* (Glenview, Ill.: Scott, Foresman and Co., 1975).

[42]Dornbush and Scott, op. cit.

basic character traits, values, and norms. I expect it will soon have a large audience.

THE GROUP RELATIONS MODELS

The second branch of the human relations movement incorporates the assumptions of the first—the importance of leadership, etc.—but is more concerned with changing the total organizational climate than the practices of individual leaders. The assumptions of the psychological model are generalized to larger units, and there is more concern with the interaction of groups, the role of top management in setting a proper climate, minimizing hierarchical differences throughout the organization, and increasing the influence of all groups. The distinction between the two branches is more academic than real, but it will serve our expository purposes.

Whereas the psychological model sometimes views good human relations techniques as only a hygienic device (it is better to treat people decently than poorly), designed to minimize opposition and to encourage cooperation with the superior, it is characteristic of the group-oriented branch to stress the creative aspects of good organizational climates. That is, using the terms proposed by Raymond Miles, the former is concerned with "human relations" while the latter is concerned with "human resources."[43] All organizational members constitute valuable resources, and we should learn to develop, tap, and free these resources. Humans are assumed to desire to participate fully, to solve their "higher needs" of autonomy and self-actualization, and to wish to identify with the goals of the organization. They will do so if the leadership and structure of the organization will permit it.

Miles implies that one of the reasons it was not possible to clearly establish that high morale led to high productivity is that the relationship often goes in the opposite direction. High morale may be due to high productivity, rather than the reverse. He argues somewhat as follows: increased productivity comes from the release of creative energies that reside in the individuals; the way to insure this is to create a climate that allows members to participate fully. When they participate fully, they realize their higher needs and thus have increased morale. But increased morale is a by-product of the "human resources model" rather than a means to higher productivity as in the "human relations model." In the human relations

---

[43]Raymond E. Miles, "Human Relations or Human Resources," *Harvard Business Review* 43, no. 4 (July/August 1965): 148–155.

model, participation is seen as the "least-cost method of obtaining cooperation and getting . . . decisions accepted," but in the human resources model it is a means of moving the level of decision making down to where those most informed make the decision, are able to utilize their experience, and are encouraged to search for novel solutions to problems. Finally, in this more expansive view of cooperation, people not only want to belong, to be liked and respected, as in the more limited human relations model, but they want to "contribute effectively and creatively to the accomplishment of worthwhile objectives."[44]

The expansive view of human nature explicit in the second branch of human relations theory finds its theoretical justification in the work of psychologist Abraham Maslow.[45] Several members of this school cite his work in this connection. Maslow held that there is a hierarchy of needs in the individual—physiological, social, ego, and self-fulfillment. Once the lower-order needs, such as physiological and safety needs, are satisfied, the higher-order needs, such as self-actualization and autonomy, come into play. Each higher-order need is not activated until the one below it is reasonably satisfied.

Despite the lack of solid evidence from research (possibly because vague needs cannot be measured), and the existence of circumstantial evidence that there is no clear hierarchical ordering of the needs, the theory has proved very useful for the human relations (or human resources) movement. It justifies extensive involvement in, and identification with, the organization. A person who participates in an organization only to the extent of the contract, or to the extent of giving what he considers to be a fair degree of effort for the return he receives, is considered to be a stunted individual—even though he may be self-actualizing outside the organization. Argyris, for example, posits a fundamental conflict between the individual and the organization, finding that the organization generally demands dependent, childish behavior from its members and makes it difficult for them to grow and achieve or maintain "maturity."[46] The assumption here is that the organizational context is the principal one for the individual, and if he is not capable of self-actualizing behavior in the organization, he is an immature person. Therefore,

---

[44]Ibid., p. 151.

[45]Abraham Maslow, *Motivation and Personality*, 2nd ed. (New York: Harper & Row, Inc., 1970); idem, *Toward A Psychology of Being*, 2nd ed. (New York: Van Nostrand Reinhold, 1968).

[46]Chris Argyris, *Interpersonal Competence and Organizational Effectiveness* (Homewood, Ill.: Dorsey Press, 1962). He argues that a great service the industrial world can offer to our society is to develop "fully functioning human beings who aspire to excellence." See p. 5.

Argyris calls for radical restructuring of organizations and extensive T-group therapy to permit all those capable of maturity to behave maturely; indeed, it is the responsibility of the organization to develop maturity in individuals.

Such maturity, it would seem, would be on organizational terms. Though Argyris and others note the creative aspect of conflict, there is little in their work which suggests that a proper form of self-actualization might be to organize employees for better working conditions, to advocate more ethical advertising practices, or to expose the cover-up of unjustified expenses in government contracts. Nor, presumably, would it be mature to oppose the development of chemical warfare techniques in a chemical firm or a nonprofit research laboratory,[47] to be in favor of mass transit rather than private automobiles at General Motors, to oppose price-fixing techniques at General Electric, or to call for better testing of drugs and more accurate advertising in a pharmaceutical firm.

In contrast, one might argue that a man may disagree with some or all of the goals of an organization (including the goal of profit maximization) but still find that he can best be reimbursed for his efforts, training, and skills in this rather than other organizations, and so he can continue to be a member without being immature. Probably most employees, at both the managerial and blue-collar level, do not seriously inquire into the objectives and tactics of the organizations that employ them. If so, to "contribute effectively and creatively to the accomplishment of worthwhile objectives" is not an important element in organizational analysis. But for the human relations theorists, such self-actualization, *on organizational terms*, is crucial.

The Likert Model

The two most influential models which represent the second branch of human relations theory are those of Douglas McGregor and Rensis Likert. The McGregor model is the least developed.[48] He simply contrasted "Theory X"—which represented a caricature of bureaucratic theory wherein management is supposed to believe that workers hate their work, will do anything to avoid it, are "indif-

---

[47]For example, when the president of the Stanford Research Institute (SRI) said that no one was forced to work on a project he found morally objectionable, one SRI physicist objected that he was pressured into doing chemical-warfare research. He was fired, and the executive vice-president of SRI said: "People like that have a decision to make—do they want to support the organization or not." "The University Arsenal," *Look*, August 26, 1969, p. 34.

[48]Douglas McGregor, *The Human Side of Enterprise* (New York: McGraw-Hill Book Company, 1960).

ferent to organizational needs," and can only be made to cooperate through the application of heavy negative sanctions—with "Theory Y"—wherein managers assume that such things as the capacity for assuming responsibility, the potential for development, and the readiness to direct behavior toward organizational goals are all present in people. The essential task of management, in this view, is to arrange things so people achieve their own goals by accomplishing those of the organization.

The Likert model also rests simply upon a contrast between the exploitative and authoritative and the "participative management" models, with intermediate points.[49] However, it is more complex than McGregor's model since it specifies more of the variables and is more concerned with the interaction of groups. Furthermore, a vast amount of research conducted by those associated with the Institute for Social Research at the University of Michigan is cited in connection with it. (The Institute, a highly productive organization which Likert headed until his retirement a few years ago, does both basic and applied research on organizations and groups. It is financed by contracts from business organizations and grants from various branches of the federal government and foundations.)

We will limit our attention to the Likert model. It is the most well known of the human relations models, and Likert's first major book, *New Patterns of Management*, published in 1961, received three management awards and a great deal of critical acclaim. A second book, *The Human Organization*, published in 1967, carried the work somewhat further by reporting on some further studies and refining the basic indicators.[50]

Likert's "science-based theory," as he calls it, is summarized by a lengthy table that appears at the end of each of his books; he compares this to a periodic table in chemistry.[51] Across the top of the version appearing in the 1961 book are four "systems" of organiza-

---

[49]Rensis Likert, *New Patterns of Management* (New York: McGraw-Hill Book Company, 1961).

[50]Rensis Likert, *The Human Organization* (New York: McGraw-Hill Book Company, 1967).

[51]Likert, *New Patterns*, p. 234. Three other major aspects of his theory will not be dealt with here. One is a useful statement of the causal links among his groups of variables (*Human Organization*, p. 137); a second is a convincing statement of the need for accounting procedures which reflect human resources (ibid., chapters 5, 6, and 9); the third is a discussion of "organizational families" and the "linking pin function" (ibid., chapter 10). The last constitutes an assertion that the relationships between a superior and, say, four subordinates should not consist of four separate superior-subordinate contacts, but all five should interact as a group, with the superior linking this group to other groups. To the extent that tasks performed by the subordinates are at all interdependent, the need for this is obvious in all organizational theory.

tions, called exploitative authoritative (which corresponds to the Weberian model of bureaucracy or to "Theory X" in McGregor), benevolent authoritative, consultative, and finally, participative group. He then lists forty-two aspects of organizations, and for each one he indicates the values it has under each of the four systems. For example, the first aspect listed is the nature of the underlying motives that are tapped in organizations. For the exploitative authoritarian system these are "physical security, economic security, and some use of the desire for status."[52] The organization in this system depends upon these underlying motives. As one moves from this system to the participative group system, more motives are added—for example, the desire for new experience and motivational forces arising from group processes. The next aspect concerns the manner in which motives are used. At one extreme, this is through "fear, threats, punishment, and occasional rewards." At the other extreme, motives are used by means of "economic rewards based on a compensation system developed through participation, group participation and involvement in setting goals, improving methods, appraising progress toward goals, etc."[53]

Likert proceeds through the forty-two aspects, specifying the differences between the four systems. In the 1967 book the list is slightly revised and expanded to fifty-one aspects. Also, the names for the four systems are dropped, and he labels them only System 1 through System 4. Since the list is used as a research tool, with managers checking where their organization falls on each aspect, he felt it was advisable not to influence the answers by labeling the systems as exploitative authoritarian, etc. (In later uses of this research tool, even the headings, System 1, etc., were dropped, and the order of some of the aspects was reversed, going from good to bad, in order to avoid "response set behavior.")

There are several interesting things to note about this list. First, the theory does not depend upon leadership alone. The fifty-one aspects are divided into eight groups, only one of which deals with leadership processes. There are groups concerned with the character of motivational forces, communication processes, interaction-influence processes, decision-making processes, the setting or ordering of goals, control processes, and performance goals and training. Thus, presumably all of the human aspects of the organization are covered (hence the comparison to a periodic table in chemistry). The theory is not limited to leadership alone.

Second, the vast majority of the items are "motherhood" items. No one is likely to be against most of the System 4 values, just as no

---

[52]Likert, *New Patterns*, p. 223.
[53]Ibid., p. 223.

one is against motherhood and for sin. For example, Likert is encouraged that when asked which system they prefer, managers overwhelmingly choose System 4. But to choose System 1 is to recommend, for example, that the company have no confidence and trust in subordinates, while System 4 indicates complete confidence and trust. Nor are the managers likely to prefer subservient and hostile attitudes toward superiors over cooperative attitudes with mutual trust and confidence. In the case of a few of the items, a manager might have some qualms about System 4. He might feel, for example, that employees cannot be fully involved in decisions related to their work, for a number of reasons. It might be too costly or time-consuming to fully inform them; or they might not possess the technical training to fully understand the decisions that are made and how they interact with other work areas. The manager might be inclined to say it varies with the task and with what is actually meant by being "involved" in decision making. But when presented with the following four choices regarding desired involvement of employees, he has little choice but to select the fourth, perhaps with misgivings: "(1) Not at all. (2) Never involved in decisions; occasionally consulted. (3) Usually are consulted but ordinarily not involved in the decision making. (4) Are involved fully in all decisions related to their work."[54]

Likert himself does not see the items as being "motherhood" items, drawn from a boy scout creed for organizations. He speaks of the "predominance of System 2 concepts in the available literature on management," though he does not cite any examples.[55] Presumably System 1 is out, and while organizations do not exploit personnel as much as before, they still practice benevolent authoritarianism and thus fall into System 2. He says that the readily available concepts in management theory apply to System 2, but not to System 4. We might take the last five items in his periodic table to see what this would indicate. It shows that the literature on management, if he is correct, would *not* be in favor of: excellent training resources; providing a great deal of management training of the type desired; seeking to achieve extremely high goals; using data gathered for control purposes for self-guidance and coordinated problem solving rather than for punitive purposes; having the informal and the formal organization mesh; having all social forces supporting efforts to achieve organizational goals.[56]

Not only does he say the literature is not in favor of such things, which is simply not true, but he adds that those managers who try to

---

[54]Likert, *Human Organization*, p. 207.
[55]Ibid., p. 109.
[56]Ibid., pp. 209–210.

use System 4 techniques have to "keep quiet as possible about it," so low is the faith of management in trust, good communication, high goals, etc.[57] Indeed, he reports that managers are not above deliberately destroying System 4 departments in their frustration over trying to move them to System 2 departments.[58] Thus, Likert decidedly does not feel that all he has done is to name some virtues and vices and allow managers to choose the virtues. Theory itself is predisposed to the vices. Likert is not alone here, by any means; most human relations theorists erect a bureaucratic monster and tilt furiously at it.

Another striking thing about the Likert table is that where these questions have been asked of groups of managers, there is a remarkable degree of consistency among items. The intercorrelations are very high. As Likert points out, if some items are scored System 2, all of them tend to be.[59] It is also the case that where their preferences are asked, the managers all invariably check System 4. (Presumably no one in the various companies where preferences have been asked has read the "available literature on management" which is supposed to favor System 2. Moreover, they have not sought to destroy System 4 departments.) Such consistency might tend to discourage some researchers who attempt to show that their various measures are independent of one another. That is, if leadership, communications, goal setting, decision-making processes, supportive behavior, and so on are separate characteristics of management, then there should be some independence among them. One would expect to find some organizations where communication processes are poor but control processes or the setting and ordering of goals are good. If not, one suspects that only one dimension is being tapped, and there is no point in distinguishing among such factors. The one dimension, for example, might be morale. If things are going well, one is likely to report trust, confidence, decentralized decision making, high goals, participation in goal setting, and so on. If things are going poorly, one backs off from giving System 4 ratings to these items.

However, Likert does not hold this view. Instead, he finds that the very high intercorrelations among the items "and the high split-half reliabilities lead to an important conclusion . . . [i.e., that] every component part of a particular management system fits well with each of the other parts and functions in harmony with them. Each system of management has a basic integrity of its own."[60] For this reason he calls it a "systems approach."

---

[57]Ibid., p. 109.
[58]Ibid., p. 112.
[59]Ibid., p. 116.
[60]Ibid., p. 123.

Finally, it is distinctive of his theory (and most human relations theories) that all organizations are considered to be alike.[61] Differences in size, technology, markets, raw materials, goals, and auspices are irrelevant. While much of management theory is moving to a position that there is no single best way of doing things, Likert, along with many others, continues to advocate one best way. This is especially surprising in Likert because some of the work turned out by his associates at the Institute for Social Research, and cited in *The Human Organization* as evidence for the validity of the theory, runs against this view of one best way. Indeed, Likert himself says as much in two chapters of his earlier book, *New Patterns of Management*. In Chapter 6, he distinguishes repetitive work from varied work, and he notes that in the former there is only a slight relationship between attitudes of workers and productivity, and that "different styles of leadership and management have tended to develop" for the two different kinds of work.[62] The "job-organization" system is generally applied where repetitive work dominates and resembles a bureaucratic model, and the "cooperative-motivation" system where varied work predominates. He says that both systems realize high performance and low costs but that both could be better if the "power of each were combined with the other."[63] The problem is that the job-organization system is highly developed in theory and practice and widely accepted, while the cooperative-motivation system "has never been described or stated formally as a management theory."[64] (This is a remarkable statement considering the volume of literature on cooperation and motivation, commencing with Barnard.) Furthermore, the results obtained by the former system are immediately evident, while those of the latter may not be apparent for years because they involve more subtle, though powerful and lasting, changes.

In Chapter 6 of *New Patterns of Management*, Likert indicates his belief that there are advantages to combining the two systems, and he cites the case of a company that had been operating under a cooperative-motivation system but which should move to the job-organization system.[65] In the following chapter, he also admits that there is no one best way to supervise. "Supervisory and leadership practices, effective in some situations, yield unsatisfactory results in others."[66] In this case, however, he does not refer to the difference between repetitive and varied work demands but to differences in

---

[61]Likert, *New Patterns*, p. 241.
[62]Ibid., pp. 77–78.
[63]Ibid., pp. 82–83.
[64]Ibid., p. 83.
[65]Ibid., p. 85.
[66]Ibid., p. 89.

the "expectations, values, and interpersonal skills of subordinates." Thus, we have two admitted sources of diversity in organizations or subunits—tasks and member characteristics. If organizations differ, then to claim that System 4 is the best for all organizations either indicates that the scheme has little to do with supervisory style or types of tasks confronted, in which case the "science-based theory" is of little relevance, or it indicates that the scheme can only be applied where work is varied and subordinates are "emotionally mature"[67] and have common expectations, values, and interpersonal skills. If the latter is the case, the theory is highly restrictive.

The Evidence

With these comments in mind, let us turn to the empirical evidence for the superiority of System 4. There is probably no other organizational research unit in the world that has more empirical data on a wide variety of organizations than the one Likert headed—the Institute for Social Research. And, in both above-mentioned books he makes voluminous citations to this literature and acknowledges the help in writing the books provided by the many outstanding members of the Institute. Here is no fly-by-night theory supported by one study or by the work of a few of one's graduate students.

In *The Human Organization*, the evidence offered is of many kinds. Some of it comes from unpublished material and is only reported in sketchy terms. Some of it is in the form of numerous citations to the published works of Institute members. These citations refer to research which does not always support the major tenets of the human relations school (e.g., some of it reports that high morale and high productivity do not necessarily go together). In addition, these studies were not designed to test the major proposition of System 4 but are generally studies of single work groups or particular leadership techniques. While they may support the human relations viewpoint, they do not support this specific theory which covers all the human aspects of organization. The most important evidence comes from a separate volume which explicitly uses System 4 measurement techniques and concepts in the study of a pajama factory. Likert cites it frequently as substantiating the theory. One other study is reported upon in some detail in *The Human Organization* and also constitutes evidence for the theory. We will start with the latter.

Life Insurance Salesmen.   The most dramatic and convincing evidence for the effectiveness of System 4 is found in the study of a

---

[67]"Participative organizations require emotionally mature personalities." Ibid., p. 57.

number of owner-managed sales offices of a large, national life insurance company.[68] The national headquarters designated the top twenty performing units and the bottom twenty—out of a total of about one hundred agencies—to be subjects of this study. Likert compared the two groups on a number of measures, and the scatterplots presented in his book show that high performing units clearly had more of the following characteristics than the low performing units: supportive relationships by the owner-manager, high sales goals set by the manager, high goals set by the salesmen, high peer-group loyalty, positive attitudes toward the manager, group methods of supervision, and high "peer leadership."

Peer leadership meant that the salesmen engaged in leadership among themselves, rather than having leadership come only from the manager or a supervisor. The group methods of supervision involved monthly or bimonthly meetings where each man reported on his past work, successes and failures, techniques that he used, and so on. The other salesmen discussed his work and helped him set goals for himself. They shared ideas and information about "new appeals, new markets, and new strategies of selling."[69] Supportive relationships were indicated by positive answers to such paternalistic questions as the following: How much trust and confidence does your superior have in you? Does he indicate he is confident you can do your job well? Does he try to understand your problems and do something about them? Is he really interested in training you and helping you learn better ways of doing your work? Does he keep you informed and fully share information? Does he value your ideas and seek them and endeavor to use them? Is he friendly and easily approached? Does he refrain from claiming all the credit for himself?[70]

Some questions can be raised about the study. By using only the twenty best performing agencies and the twenty worst performing, the effect of leadership on performance is grossly exaggerated. Even the responses of these two extreme groups overlap on most items. Including the intermediate sixty would presumably weaken the contrast between high and low performing groups. In addition, an article by Seashore and Yuchtman dealing with the same agencies reports only ten significant correlations (out of a possible fifty) between several different measures of performance and such things as supportive behavior.[71] An earlier article by Bowers and

---

[68]Likert, *Human Organization*, pp. 52–77.

[69]Ibid., p. 57.

[70]Ibid., pp. 48–49.

[71]Stanley E. Seashore and Ephraim Yuchtman, "Factorial Analysis of Organizational Performance," *Administrative Science Quarterly* 12, no. 3 (December 1967): 377–395.

Seashore finds no correlations between other performance measures and supportive behavior.[72] Thus, it is not clear what role the criteria used by Likert to measure performance played in producing his high relationships.[73]

More important, however, is the nature of the sample. Assuming that all the relationships that Likert found were accurate, we still might wonder if the findings could indeed be generalized and used to support the theory. Life insurance salesmen are presumably a somewhat distinctive breed of men, gregarious, verbal, skilled in friendliness and interpersonal competence, and accustomed to ferreting out new kinds of appeals and selling strategies. The units studied are small, apparently averaging about twenty-five salesmen and managerial personnel, and do not have complex structures. In some cases there is a supervisor between the manager and the salesmen; in some cases there is none. The salesmen are theoretically in competition with each other for prospects, but rarely would they actually compete for the same prospect. They are paid on a commission basis only, so there is a direct correlation between their effort and their reward, with few organizational factors intervening in this relationship. There is no need for interdependence among salesmen (though the sharing of ideas, etc., will presumably prove beneficial), and there is little competition over scarce organizational resources.

Thus, these are unusual "organizations." The close fit reported by Likert (though not clearly supported by the other reports on the survey) between performance and aspects of System 4 might be due in large part to the enormous importance of high morale, enthusiasm, and techniques of interpersonal relations in this kind of work and the low importance of things that usually make organiza-

---

[72]Bowers and Seashore, "Predicting Organizational Effectiveness."

[73]To confuse things further, Bowers and Seashore refer to the forty agencies as "representative." Other discrepancies in the work of the Institute are puzzling. A strong relationship between accepting *company* goals and productivity, reported by Likert in the *New Patterns* volume (pp. 31–32), turns out to actually be a relationship between accepting *union* goals and productivity when one examines the original study by Seashore that Likert cites. In the original study, there was no significant relationship between accepting company goals and productivity. Some of the graphs in *Patterns* are greatly distorted in favor of the thesis, as a student (Garry Meyers) once pointed out to me (see those on pages 11 and 20 of *New Patterns of Management*). Recently it was disclosed that the "results" of an Institute study were published in *Personnel* by a member of the consultancy team (Alfred J. Marrow, whom we will meet on page 124) before the data were even gathered. Neither Likert nor Chris Argyris, the two other members of the team, had anything to do with the misleading article, but the fascinating account of this large effort to reform a bureaucracy reveals the dangers and seductions of the advocate role for social scientists. See the Appendix to Donald P. Warwick, *A Theory of Public Bureaucracy: Politics, Personality, and Organization in the State Department* (Cambridge, Mass.: Harvard University Press, 1975), pp. 219–237.

tional life difficult—group conflicts, divergent group goals, specialization in work groups, competition for scarce resources, daily face-to-face interaction and interdependencies, complex hierarchies, and fixed amounts of remuneration. Likert's statement that the principles illustrated "appear to be applicable to all kinds of undertakings"[74] must be treated with considerable reservation. This is but one more example of the difficulty of generalizing about all organizations.

The problem we have noted with Likert's analysis persists, even after the popularity of "contingency theory" (see Chapter 4) has made it quite clear that the type of work done by a unit must be considered when generalizing about principles of management or organization. Pennings recently argued that there were two contending theories, those such as Likert's and a technology-bureaucratic one such as my own.[75] He examined a number of brokerage firms and found that leadership variables of the type that Likert considers played a decisive role, supporting Likert's view of organizations. But the real message of his work is that if you have a number of small independent work groups "selling" to clients as in these brokerage firms—very similar in many respects to the groups of life insurance salesmen—bureaucratic structures and controls are not very appropriate. In the "back offices" of the brokerage firms, where the work is routine and "salesmanship" counts for little—again, similar to the clerical offices of life insurance companies—a bureaucratic model is far more appropriate.

The Weldon Company Test of System 4.   The Harwood Manufacturing Company purchased the Weldon Manufacturing Company in 1962 and undertook to rejuvenate it. Harwood itself was the scene of many of the most famous studies of human relations in the literature[76] and has benefited from the advice, consultation, and wisdom of Kurt Lewin and many members of the Michigan group. The history of the changes in the Weldon Company from the date of purchase is presented in a book by Marrow, Bowers, and Seashore, *Management by Participation: Creating a Climate for Personal and Organizational Development.*[77]

----

[74]Likert, *Human Organization*, p. 52.

[75]Johannes M. Pennings, "Dimension of Organizational Influence and their Effectiveness Correlates," *Administrative Science Quarterly* 21:4 (December 1976): 688–699; and Johannes M. Pennings and Paul S. Goodman, "Toward a Workable Framework," in Paul S. Goodman et al., *New Perspectives in Organizational Effectiveness* (San Francisco: Jossey-Bass, Inc., 1977), pp. 146–184.

[76]L. Coch and J. R. P. French, Jr., "Overcoming Resistance to Change," *Human Relations* 1, no. 4 (1948): 512–532.

[77]Alfred J. Marrow, David G. Bowers, and Stanley E. Seashore, *Management by Participation* (New York: Harper & Row, Inc., 1967).

The major points are quite simple and clear: The Weldon Company was incredibly poorly managed and staffed; lacked proper machinery, layout, and records system; and had a violent labor history with enormous turnover of personnel. All who supplied chapters to this volume agreed in this assessment, including the board chairman of Harwood Manufacturing Company and the plant manager of the Weldon Company. Literally, almost any sensible change in this organization would have improved it. It is worth quoting at length from only one of the several enumerations of company problems, since it indicates some of the things that can go wrong in organizations. This account is by the board chairman of the Harwood Company, Alfred Marrow.

The Weldon Company, at the time of acquisition, was run by two partners; one of them controlled merchandising, and the other manufacturing. We will ignore the manifold problems of the former partner and his sales organization and staff.[78]

> The manufacturing division under the other partner-owner had five functional department heads. The plant organization, as in merchandising, was unbalanced, with too few people in management and supervision and too many in control and record-keeping. The imbalance was a result of the manager's effort to control activity through multiple and duplicating records. A large number of clerks were needed, also, because of inventory imbalances, to change shipping dates, suggest substitutions, and answer customer complaints.
>
> Noteworthy gaps in staff and method were evident in the manufacturing division. A single industrial engineer with one assistant attempted to handle all problems of rate study and machine layout. There was no program of research and development. Electronic data processing, although economically available, had not been introduced. There was no personnel department to provide essential records and services.
>
> Within the total enterprise, the merchandising and manufacturing divisions functioned independently rather than as coordinated divisions of a single organization. Coordination was blocked by the clashes of temperament of the two partners and by the absence of any authorized coordination by others. Moreover, each partner employed relatives in key positions. The son of the merchandising partner was employed as sales manager and a son-in-law as comptroller. A nephew of the manufacturing partner was employed as plant manager. Each "side" viewed the other with suspicion.
>
> As a consequence, little communication was maintained between manufacture and sales. Each division became unable to see the other's problems. Manufacturing took little or no account of customer pressures upon the sales department. Sales and designing divisions made

---

[78]Ibid., pp. 12–14.

little effort to understand the plant complications created by an unrestricted variation of styles and models. Salesmen agreed too readily to sell any type of styling that customers requested without regard to what the plant could produce at a profit. Salesmen, who were generally paid on a commission basis, promised impossibly fast deliveries at mutually conflicting dates. There was little provision for coordination or plant clearance.

Production schedules were set by the sales department. The recurrent conflicts in delivery promises forced them to demand almost daily changes in production priorities and frequently to demand partial deliveries. The effect in the plant was a daily turmoil of priority changes for goods in process and a need to have many kinds of garments in manufacture in small lots at the same time. Costs were raised excessively. Customers were alienated. Late deliveries led the sales people to accuse the manufacturing people of willful negligence and of misinformation; the plant people accused the others of carelessness in imposing impossible schedules. Quarrels and deep antagonisms had extended over a long time, and neither party seemed able to find a way to coordinate sales and production.

The effect of these conditions on the plant supervisory staff was serious. They ignored the increased costs of labor and material due to small runs, rush deliveries, and unbalanced inventories. Production quotas were set arbitrarily, without regard to the frequent disruptions of the work flow. To produce in required quantity, particularly during the seasonal peak, Weldon often had to hire inexperienced employees for short periods and to pay a guaranteed wage for a low output which, for some lines and seasons, doubled and tripled the unit production cost. Supervisors felt justified in meeting the set quota of dozens by every means within reach, and were kept both uninformed and unconcerned in their cost performance.

Work flow fluctuated widely, and workers sometimes went from overtime to layoff in the same work week. Weldon workers came to regard the plant as a place of seasonal or occasional employment. Many would leave as soon as they could find other jobs, while others would be discharged as soon as the seasonal peak was past. Labor turnover thus was high.

In the postwar transition from sellers' to buyers' market, the consequences became drastic. Having retained outdated tools and methods, Weldon forfeited its competitive advantage. Top management tried to counteract mounting losses by cutting expenditures for capital improvement so sharply that by 1962 even spare parts had to be taken from one machine to fix another. Weldon bought little new equipment and made little attempt to keep up with innovations in the tools or methods of manufacture. Their economies thus took a form that exaggerated rather than solved their production cost problems in the long run.

The partners seem to have believed that if they could hold their markets long enough they could find a way to cut costs to a profitable level. They took conventional steps to reduce payroll costs: cutting down on staff, withholding wage increases, calling on their people to make sacrifices, applying strong pressures. Costs did go down, for a time, and sales and production volume was maintained. But morale suffered, and these "economies" also began to add to cost. . . .

It should be noted that the two partners had built up a very good, sizable business; they made the leading quality line in men's pajamas. Nor had it been a tiny organization; in the mid-1950s it had grown rapidly to include five plants employing about 3500 people. (But there was only one plant with 1000 workers at the time of the acquisition in 1962.) What the two partners had done so well for a number of years, making the organization "one of the recognized and highly respected leaders in the industry,"[79] was no longer appropriate for a large organization under changed market conditions. The highly centralized, authoritarian methods they had used for so long and with such success were not altered under the new conditions, a situation found with melancholy frequency in industry.

The "change-agents" included a team of consultants, some of them from the Institute for Social Research. They introduced a number of eminently sensible changes. More capital was invested; new machinery was acquired; the layout of the work was changed; lines of communication and degrees of responsibility were clarified; and record keeping, forecasting, and inventory control were introduced or improved. All this was in keeping with traditional management theory. They also instituted T-group sessions, involved management in decision making, reduced the incredible degree of centralization of authority, and treated the workers as human beings. Everything improved. The improvement in output and financial aspects was dramatic; the improvement in human relations and morale was less dramatic, but there was improvement in these areas, too.

Was this a demonstration of the effectiveness of System 4, as Likert holds? Or was it the result of more prosaic and traditional management techniques, the departure of some key people, and the correction of obvious human relations problems? Bowers and Seashore, with considerable ingenuity and detailed measurement, attempted to assess the reasons for the dramatic increase in productivity. Using the figure of a 30-percent gain in productivity, they conclude as follows: Over one third of the gain—11 percentage points—came from the "earnings development program." In this program, an engineer sat down with those employees who were producing at a rate much less than the federal minimum standard in their piecework output and attempted to improve their performance

---

through industrial engineering techniques. Next in order of importance, contributing a 5 percent increase in productivity, was the
"weeding out" of low earners. The training of supervisors and staff
in interpersonal relations also contributed about 5 percentage
points. The group consultation and problem resolution program
with the operators contributed about 3 percentage points. The remaining 6 percent came from miscellaneous sources.[80] Thus, the
showcase of System 4, the group consultation and problem resolution program, accounted for only 3 of the 30 percent increase in
productivity, and the training in interpersonal relations only 5. The
bulk of the change came from classical management theory—even
Taylorism—and simply involved the training of workers and the
firing of those who did not improve. The new machinery, layout,
etc., contributed also to increased productivity, but Bowers and
Seashore excluded gains from this source.

Another striking finding was that "dramatic changes in policy,
in work arrangements, in interpersonal relationships—and in work
performance and pay—were in Weldon accompanied by only
modest affective and motivational changes."[81] Thus, motivation and
morale may have had less to do with output than technical matters
such as job design, layout, and new machinery. Bowers and
Seashore rather reluctantly concluded that "basic gains in the 'output' of an organization with respect to satisfactions, motivations, and
positive feelings often may be harder to achieve than gains in cost
performance and work output." These gains in "achieving a more
trustful, open, cooperative, and self-determining organizational
system" may take place only over a long period of time.[82] Yet,
throughout the book, the authors of other chapters insisted that these
changes had already taken place.

Bowers and Seashore measured these attitudes in a variety of
ways to arrive at their unanticipated conclusion. If, however, they
had simply relied upon the rating scale that Likert used to measure
commitment to System 4, they would have seen a dramatic increase
in motivational and affective changes. Managers were asked to rate
their organization on forty-two counts—as the company stood prior
to the acquisition by Harwood, and as it was two years later. The
change in all items was dramatic. Apparently, Bowers and
Seashore were not willing to use this as a reliable instrument.

Another embarrassment crops up in a chapter by Bowers.
Though other chapters contained examples of workers exercising
more control over their jobs, participating in decisions, and feeling

---

[80]Ibid., pp. 181–182.
[81]Ibid., p. 200.
[82]Ibid., p. 201.

that control was no longer lodged in a remote headquarters, the measurement of this through the control graph technique (which we will discuss shortly) "shows that the control structure at Weldon did not change much. . . ."[83] Either the control graph is a poor instrument—a doubtful conclusion, as we shall see later—or large gains in productivity and satisfaction with work and pay can be made without giving groups more influence.

There is, indeed, some evidence that control remained centralized, though it is given little attention in the book. Bowers and Seashore note that: "Some of the demands placed upon Weldon managers by the new owners were, to put it mildly, preemptory and compelling," though they hasten to add that the demands were "always coupled with apparently limitless moral support and practical aid." Similarly, the enforcement of the absence and termination rules among the operators was "uncompromising," though applied only after much encouragement and personal aid.[84] Moreover, while the effect of group sessions on five of the top six members of the merchandising side of the business is described as dramatically successful in one chapter,[85] we learn much later that five of the six had to be replaced.[86] Such prosaic realities of organizational life as preemptory demands, uncompromising application of rules, and removal of top executives do intrude into this enthusiastic book, though they are only parenthetically and apologetically noted.

Finally, Bowers and Seashore make a very interesting and valuable point in their summary. Several people, they say, have argued that an organization is ready for change when it has a history of supportive management, good relations with the union, a fund of mutual trust and goodwill, and satisfied employees.[87] But, they remark, such a company hardly needs drastic change since it is likely to be flexible and adaptable. The case of Weldon, however, was one of "rescuing the destitute" and required "some coercive steps" by the new management.[88] This is perhaps the main point of the study. If an organization is destitute, almost any sensible effort will make a dramatic difference. Improving human relations is certainly one of the sensible efforts to make, but judging from their own assessment, sensible efforts in the form of classical management techniques had the most effect.[89]

---

[83]Ibid., pp. 213–214.

[84]Ibid., p. 240.

[85]Ibid., pp. 99–101.

[86]Ibid., p. 241.

[87]Ibid., p. 239.

[88]Ibid., p. 240.

[89]A close reading of other studies of dramatic changes suggests the important

The Control Graph

The last example of the second branch of human relations theory that we shall consider is the work of Tannenbaum and several associates in the area of the amount of influence, or, as they call it, "control," in organizations. One of the frequent imageries of the 1920s and 1930s in discussion of labor-management relations was the "pie." Commentators held that labor should stop worrying about getting a bigger slice at the expense of management, and management should stop worrying about the size of labor's slice. Instead, they should cooperate to produce a bigger pie. Then both would get a larger slice without worrying about changing the dividing points. We now formulate the issue in more abstruse but more exact terms. There are zero sum gains and variable or nonzero sum gains; that is, if one person gets more, but it has to be at the expense of another, that is a zero sum gain (subtracting what one gives up from what another gains produces a cipher). If, however, by combining forces in some way, and by maximizing the use of their resources or their ability to extract resources from the environment, both can get more, that is a nonzero sum gain (adding the two increments produces a total that is more than zero).

It is a tenet of the human relations school that things are not zero-sum (or, to use another popular expression, they are not "win-lose" situations; everyone can win). This is because better human relations improves efficiency and productivity, creating a larger pie. By allowing subordinates to participate in decision making, more resources are utilized and all will gain. The first "operationalization" of this idea in organizations (that is, developing ways of measuring the variables of interest) was performed by Arnold Tannenbaum and Robert L. Kahn. As elaborated and tested in

---

role of quite obvious factors which are not central to human relations theory. I explored this at length in the case of the reputed efficacy of milieu therapy in mental hospitals in "Hospitals: Technology, Structure and Goals," in *The Handbook of Organizations*, ed. James March (Chicago: Rand McNally & Company, 1965), chapter 22. Bowers and Seashore themselves, in a study of a packaging and printing firm, conclude that participative management theory should be applied within the general framework of classical management theory, and their evidence suggests that some structural changes had to precede changes in interpersonal relations. See their *Changing the Structure and Functioning of an Organization* (Ann Arbor: Institute for Social Research, University of Michigan, 1963). A classic study by Robert Guest can best be interpreted in terms of contracting the lines of authority and persistent interference of headquarters in the affairs of an automobile plant that lacked proper facilities, rather than merely as a case of the effect of leadership. See my discussion of this study in Charles Perrow, *Organizational Analysis, A Sociological View* (Belmont, Calif.: Wadsworth Publishing Co., 1970), chapter 1. The Guest study is Robert Guest, *Organizational Change* (Homewood, Ill.: Richard D. Irwin, Inc., 1962).

various types of organizations by Tannenbaum and others, it came to constitute "control graph" theory.[90]

The operationalization is very simple. Respondents in an organization are asked how much "say or influence" various levels of authority have in the organization. The levels might be higher management, plant managers, supervisors, and workers. The responses for each group are averaged and a graph is constructed. In a union, the levels might be president, board, bargaining committee, and members. Thus, in some unions the slope of the curve is "positive," that is, influence goes up as levels of authority go down. The president has the least influence, and the curve rises—with the executive board having more, the bargaining committee even more, and the members the most. (Unfortunately, in one particular case where a positive, or rising, slope was found, the question was ambiguous, asking about influence in *how* decisions are made, rather than, for example, influence over the content of decisions.[91])

In most of the extant studies of business and industrial organizations, the remotest group (e.g., the board of directors; headquarters) is seen as having only a fair amount of influence, but the head of the local unit (e.g., the plant manager) has a great deal, and the various levels under him have successively less influence, with the workers having the least. An example is given in Figure 1. In the League of Women Voters, a similar but far less marked pattern was found; the president and the board of directors were fairly close, with the membership dropping off somewhat. Thus, the measure is sensitive to differences in organizations; those differences make sense, and this increases our confidence in the measure.

More important than the slope of the curve, however, is its *height*, or more precisely, the amount of area under it. This indicates how much influence is perceived by respondents to exist in the total organization. Tannenbaum and his associates found that some organizations have significantly more total influence than others, and the greater the influence, the greater the effectiveness and member satisfaction. The *slope* of the curve is not related to effectiveness and morale. Furthermore, when asked how much influence each of the hierarchical levels should have, respondents almost invariably desire more influence not only for their own level, but for all other levels as well. For the respondents it is generally not a zero-sum, win-lose situation.

---

[90]The major publications dealing with the theory are included in Arnold S. Tannenbaum, *Control in Organizations* (New York: McGraw-Hill Book Company, 1968). A subsequent book reporting on the application of the technique in several nations is Tannenbaum et al., *Hierarchy in Organizations* (San Francisco: Jossey-Bass, Inc., 1974).

[91]Ibid., p. 35.

FIGURE 1   HYPOTHETICAL CONTROL GRAPH (INDUSTRIAL ORGANIZATION)

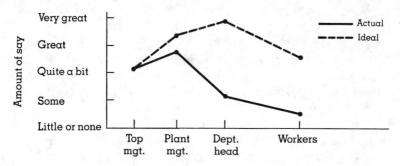

But, is there a relationship between the total amount of influence and organizational effectiveness and member satisfaction, or do effectiveness and satisfaction result in a perception of high influence? Tannenbaum says that the latter may be the case "in certain circumstances."[92] The effective organization has more rewards at its disposal, or more "organizational slack" to play with, and thus can allow all members to exercise more discretion, obtain more rewards, and feel that their influence is higher. Ephraim Yuchtman examined this problem by correlating influence scores from one date with performance factors obtained one year later.[93] The organizations were the life insurance agencies we encountered previously. He found that high influence in an agency was more likely to be associated with high performance a year later than it was with the performance scores for the same year. Yuchtman concludes as follows: "Thus, although control [influence] may be both a cause and an effect of performance, we feel reasonably confident that in these organizations it is at least a cause."[94]

In an extremely thoughtful summary, Tannenbaum makes the following points which indicate that neither the "traditional bureaucratic" arguments nor the "participative management" arguments have been able to carry the day: Organizations with an influential rank-and-file membership can be as effective as those where the workers are relatively uninfluential, in contrast to bureaucratic theory. On the other hand, organizations with influential officers can be as effective as those with less influential officers, in contrast to many contemporary arguments for democratic, participative organizations. Organizations in which *both* the leaders and members are judged high on influence will be more effective

---

[92]Ibid., pp. 58, 74.
[93]Ibid., chapter 8.
[94]Ibid., p. 127.

than those in which either or both are less influential. This contradicts both the traditional and the participative management schools. Finally, it is more important to maximize the total amount of influence than to try to equalize it to achieve "power equalization." Variations in influence among levels of the hierarchy—unless they are clearly extreme—are quite acceptable. But at the same time, there is no fixed sum of influence as traditional theories tend to assume.[95]

There are some problems with this theory.[96] By and large, however, it is superior to most of the human relations literature. It both recognizes and deals with different types of organizations, and the different findings make sense. It has been carefully tested in a number of organizations. It does not insist that there is one best way of organizing—the relative degree of influence of various groups can legitimately vary, with the slope declining sharply in some organizations but not in others. It generates and uses an *organizational* measure—total control—rather than aggregating morale scores or participation scores. Most important, however, it preserves the best insights of two hostile schools of thought while rejecting the more extreme claims of both, as the above commentary indicates.

A POSTSCRIPT

Even as the human relations school, in both its branches, has flourished and dominates organizational theory, so have criticisms of the school flourished. In addition to those already cited, Philip Selznick has written a penetrating section in a book on industrial

---

[95]Ibid., pp. 309–310.

[96]Among these are: (1) Whether "influence" is synonymous with control. The question concerns "say or influence"; Tannenbaum and his associates always speak of control. Would different results be obtained if the words "control" or "power" were used in the question? See the discussion of this issue in connection with measuring the reputed power of different functional departments in Charles Perrow, "Departmental Power and Perspectives in Industrial Firms," in *Power in Organizations*, ed. Mayer Zald (Nashville, Tenn.: Vanderbilt University Press, 1970), pp. 59–70. (2) No information is given regarding the standard deviations of responses. Are they highly consistent by level? If not, is the variation associated with morale and satisfaction questions, implying that this is what is really being measured instead of control? (3) In some organizations (auto dealers, Weldon Manufacturing Company) unexpected findings occur which should be more closely examined. (4) In some situations there seems to be a zero-sum effect present. In the delivery stations, the more influence the men have, the less overall influence there is in the station (ibid., pp. 154–159), and this may also be true of some of the other industrial organizations they studied. Unfortunately, in their subsequent study of organizations in several nations, these problems were again neglected (see Fn. 90).

justice in which he argues that there is a difference between foster-ing hygienic conditions and ability to participate on the one hand, and exercising legitimate self-assertion, which is a *political* re-source, on the other.[97] One may treat a slave humanely, and even ask his opinion regarding matters he is more familiar with than the master. But to transform his basic dependency and this presumption of his incompetence with regard to his own interests, there must be an institutional order or public process whereby the opportunity and capacity for legitimate self-assertion is guaranteed. Such a political process does not mean conflict and struggle as such, but a setting for ordered controversy and accommodation.

A different level of criticism, and the most penetrating and wide ranging to appear as yet, is provided in two articles by George Strauss.[98] (Strauss knows whereof he speaks, having been iden-tified with the school and having studied under McGregor, whose contribution he acknowledges.) Playing the role of a devil's advo-cate, he systematically questions such assumptions as harmony, need hierarchy, conflict resolution, and desire for participation that are found in the school.

Our own criticism in this chapter has been different still. We have tried to show that there is a little empirical support for the human relations theory or theories, that extensive efforts to find that support have resulted in increasing limitations and contingencies, and that the grand schemes such as Likert's appear to be methodologically unsound and theoretically biased. Underlying our criticism, however, has been a more basic level of analysis. One cannot explain organizations by explaining the attitudes and be-havior of individuals or even small groups within them. We learn a great deal about psychology and social psychology but little about organizations per se in this fashion.

In fact, what we are learning about psychology and social psychology from these studies may be an outmoded psychology and social psychology. These fields are no longer in agreement that such things as norms, values, and personality really exist or account for much; the concepts may only give a false sense of order to a world that both the academic and the person in the street desper-ately want to order. Sociology, too, is having some difficulty swal-lowing the simple, obvious proposition that attitudes predict be-

---

[97]Philip Selznick, *Law, Society, and Industrial Justice* (New York: Russell Sage Foundation, 1969).

[98]George Strauss, "Notes on Power Equalization," in *The Social Science of Organizations,* ed. Harold J. Leavitt (Englewood Cliffs, N.J.: Prentice-Hall, Inc., 1963); and idem, "Human Relations, 1968 Style," in *Industrial Relations 7,* no. 3 (May 1969): 262–276. Another good criticism is that of Sherman Krupp, *Patterns in Organizational Analysis* (New York: Holt, Rinehart & Winston, Inc., 1961).

havior (the proposition that morale predicts productivity is just one specification of this). Over the years, persistently trying to take the symbolic interaction position of Herbert Blumer seriously, when most were dismissing it as a philosophical canard, Irwin Deutscher has explored the problem of whether what we say predicts what we actually do.[99] The empirical evidence is surprisingly ambiguous. Attitudes often have little relationship to behavior. People who indicate prejudiced attitudes toward a minority group in a survey or interview do not necessarily act as they say in real-life situations, and, of course, those indicating no prejudice will often discriminate in their behavior. The research covers not only attitudes towards minorities, but also what we label as basic traits such as neatness, promptness, or honesty.

Following a line parallel with the leadership studies we considered earlier, researchers have tried to specify ever more narrowly the circumstances under which people's attitudes will predict their behavior. The circumstances are surprisingly few in number. The contingencies that must be controlled become enormous, and only in very specific, often trivial situations, can careful research find a sizable correlation between what we say and what we do. For example, the correlation between people's attitudes toward a candidate a few days before an election and the way they actually vote is high; the correlation between party preference and the candidate one selects is also high, but not as high.

Psychologists such as Walter Mischel and Albert Bandura have pushed the matter further criticizing the notion of personality, and the anthropologist Anthony Wallace has criticized the notion of cultural values.[100] It all has organizational application. Consider two people, A and his subordinate B. A is reputed to have an aggressive personality, B is reputed to be more accommodating, by people who are sympathetic to both. It is quite possible, though, that careful observation using measures of aggressiveness we could all agree upon would show that B exhibits more aggressive acts than A. But because B is in a subordinate role where aggressive behavior is not considered proper for an employee, his aggressive acts are reinterpreted by sympathetic observers as neutral, or accommodating, or even "creative." We expect certain kinds of behavior, given the power position of B, so we classify the behavior to fit the expectations and are confident that B does not have an aggressive person-

---

[99]Irwin Deutscher, *What We Say/What We Do* (Glenview, Ill.: Scott, Foresman & Co., 1973).

[100]Walter Mischel, "Toward a Cognitive Social Learning Reconceptualization of Personality," *Psychological Review* 80:4 (1973): 252–283; Albert Bandura, *Social Learning Theory* (New York: General Learning Press, 1971); Anthony Wallace, *Culture and Personality*, 2nd ed. (New York: Random House, Inc., 1970).

ality. (Were we unsympathetic to B, we might easily focus only on his aggressive acts which, though more frequent than those of A, might represent only a tiny fraction of his behavior.)

A, his boss, is expected to be aggressive; it gives us confidence that things are well in hand ("what organizations need is dynamic leadership"). He may exhibit far fewer aggressive acts than B, but when he does we nod knowingly and say, "Yes, he is an aggressive fellow." We may even reward him for aggressiveness, reinforcing his occasional aggressive acts and bringing out more of them. Then we are quite confident that he has an aggressive personality.[101] When this splendid quality is mentioned to his parents, they will confirm the diagnosis, saying, "He always knew what he wanted and how to get it." However, in another situation, he might appear quite different, and people could comment on how considerate and accommodating he is, and his parents (recalling items of behavior from the distant past that fitted this description) would say, quite honestly, "Yes, he has always been like that." Indeed, his behavior over the course of a few days or weeks or months probably will fluctuate far beyond what we would predict from our notions of "personality" as a stable set of responses. But because we attend to those things we expect him to do, and overlook the other types of behavior because it would damage the world we have constructed for ourselves and learned to live in, we ignore the fluctuation.

Though the link between the work on attitudes, behavior, and personality, and the work on organizations has not been made as yet, we can find leads in the disturbing views of Karl Weick, and James March and Johan Olsen.[102] Weick seems to be suggesting that organizations run backwards, so to speak. The thought is not necessarily the father to the deed; in fact, the deed may be father to the thought. Let me illustrate: For no particular reason, or at least none known to me, I may find that I never ordered the textbook that I usually use for next fall's classes. It might be that I simply forgot, or a misunderstanding occurred when I assumed the secretary knew it was a standing order for the fall, or I was out of town that week, or someone had made a disparaging remark about the book a month before which I didn't really recall, but which made the act of ordering it mildly distasteful. But now that the deadline has passed, I am forced to explain my behavior to myself and perhaps others. Almost

[101]For excellent organizational examples about sex typing that are consistent with this viewpoint see Rosabeth Kanter, *Men and Women of the Corporation* (New York, Basic Books, Inc., 1977). Here power relations are masked under the fictions of norms and personality traits that supposedly "explain" behavior.

[102]James G. March and Johan P. Olsen, *Ambiguity and Choice in Organizations* (Bergen, Norway: Universitetsforlaget, 1976); Karl Weick, *The Social Psychology of Organizing* (Reading, Mass.: Addison-Wesley Co., 1969).

any behavior can find its *post hoc* explanation; we are masters at ordering our worlds in this way. I may decide that the reason I never ordered it was probably that, good as the book is, I would learn more by assigning a number of articles, thus forcing me to read them carefully and integrate them; or that students are now more responsible and hard working so we can dispense with the crutch of a text; or that texts have gotten ridiculously expensive; or that I have been assigning too much reading.

During the idle chatter at a party at a colleague's home, I find myself taking one of these positions and arguing it with conviction. Come fall, I act upon that conviction (whichever one of the above I might have picked), and indeed, since they are all reasonable arguments and I sincerely believe in the one I thought explained my behavior, it will probably work out well and have a good effect upon my teaching. But the explanation was constructed after the behavior; the deed was father to the thought. There is not likely to be any way in which I would casually happen upon the "real" reason, which was far more trivial or accidental than my explanation.

Note that the idea that organizations may run backwards much of the time is not simply a matter of covering one's tracks, making excuses, lying or fabricating supporting data to justify what we want to do. Nor is it a matter of acting upon faulty information, or confusion created by someone not getting the message. Organizations are full of these events too. But events of this kind are much more a part of a planned world that we (often mistakenly) believe we can consciously direct or influence to some extent. The difficulty in making organizations work well cannot be overstressed. But in this postscript I am referring to the creation of new thoughts or meanings, to the social construction of a world we sincerely believe was there all along that is stimulated by accidents, random events, misinterpretations, memory failures, and so on. We do not cover our tracks, we unwittingly reconstruct the deed because we think that thought must have been behind it. To admit otherwise may be unnerving.

If our thoughts arise from our behavior, then what we take to be statements of organizational or group goals may merely be interpretations of where we have been, not where we particularly intended to go. Statements of goals, by individuals or organizations, serve to give meaning to what is probably a more random, disconnected, accidental, and stumbling process than we have thought. We cannot even state our goals clearly, or order them from the most important to the least important in any stable way (a view we shall encounter in the next chapter).

These possibilities are unsettling, and at first, second, and even third glance they defy our (carefully crafted) interpretations of our experience. We live with rationalizations for a long time without examining them. But when one starts fresh with a naive view, taking nothing for granted, and looks at social processes in a new way, it is often necessary to begin with the most apparently trivial events. This is perhaps why a school of thought that has explored the "social construction of reality" most carefully—the ethnomethodological school—has generally limited itself to the intensive study of trivial encounters such as greetings given at airports, the opening of phone conversations, and the gambits and expectations used in the employment interview. Perhaps only in the analysis of such encounters can we begin to rid ourselves of our everyday conceptions.

It is quite possible that our social theories in general, and organizational theory in particular, have been altogether too rational. The human relations tradition counters the extreme rationality of scientific management with a romantic rationality sometimes grounded in Freudian psychology wherein all sorts of unconscious needs are posited. But what if much of our world exhibits low coherence, accidental interactions and consequences, highly situational (rather than enduring or basic) determinants of behavior, and very specific rather than broad cultural reinforcements and demotivators? What we see as, say, sexual drives, may simply be a learning of social scripts about how we should feel and what we should desire, with different scripts for different groups, and with misread and changing scripts in addition.[103]

The prospects for such views are really quite startling. In addition to peeling away the myth of rationality we live by, such views might explain why the social sciences are poor at predicting behavior, and can find such weak support for their theories. There is less that can be explained than we thought. Not all our theories are directly derived from premises about human behavior and many of our findings are essentially unexplained correlations. But those theories that are derived from premises about behavior need expensive and painful dismantling; they are over-determined.

It is possible that the stabilities we assert are conjured up, and the disorderly universe pictured by novelists such as Thomas Pynchon (*Gravity's Rainbow*) or Joseph Heller (*Catch 22; Something Happened*) are far closer to the mark. (Both authors, incidentally, afford unusual insights into organizational behavior; the first part of *Something Happened*, in particular, is a remarkable description of behavior in a corporation office.) On the other hand, there are significant regularities in our world, such as the stable distribution of wealth in the U.S. over the last seventy years; the persistence of class and ethnic divisions; the persistence of discrimination and

---

[103]This theme is explored in John H. Gagnon and William Simon, *Sexual Conduct: The Social Sources of Human Sexuality* (Chicago: Aldine Publishing Co., 1973).

bigotry in an affluent, highly-educated society; the persistence of religious wars which continue in masked form even in indus-trialized, modernized Europe. The bridge between these perverse stabilities and the new view of human behavior remains to be made. It may be an example of what the Marxists consider as a dialectic process or the contradictions of capitalism. But at least we are less confident that explanations for these and other regularities reside in our usual formulations of "personality and social structure" or "the nature of man." In the next chapter we shall see that a "neo-Weberian" view of organizations has opened the door to the situational, limited rationality view of men and women.

4

The Neo-Weberian Model:
Decision Making, Conflict,
and Technology

DECISION MAKING

The human relations theorists sought to restore the individual, with
his needs and drives, to a central place in organizational theory, a
place denied to him by the classical management theory or by
Weberian bureaucratic theory. While the human relations theorists
focused upon the individual to an extent that Barnard would not
approve, they joined with Barnard by taking for granted what he
found necessary to insist upon, the moral and cooperative nature of
organizations. We have argued that their model is deficient in many
respects. It lacks empirical support and conceptual clarity, and it
fails to grapple with the realities of authoritarian control in organizations and the true status of the subordinate. But even if our critique
is valid, the question still remains: What do we do about the individual in organizations? Do we have to more or less ignore him, as
Weber did, because the alternative is to become mired in all his
complexities and contingencies? There is, obviously, cooperation in
organizations, and it is individuals who cooperate. There are such
things as good and bad leadership exercised by individuals and
identification with the goals of the organization on the part of individuals. Organizations are something more than the structural
categories of the Weberian model—the skeleton of hierarchy, rules,
offices, roles, careers, and so on. If we cannot accept the human

relations propositions as being adequate or plausible, must we ignore individuals?

Herbert Simon and James March have provided, somewhat unwittingly, the muscle and flesh for the Weberian skeleton, giving it more substance, complexity, and believability without reducing organizational theory to propositions about individual behavior. Or, to be more accurate, part of the work of March and Simon does this. Roughly half of their work, as laid out in two extremely important volumes, Simon's *Administrative Behavior*[1] and *Organizations* by March and Simon,[2] is concerned with the organization as a problem of social psychology. The other half uses a structural perspective; it speaks to *organizational* rather than to *individual* decision making.

Models of Man

Two different "models of man" are involved, and a discussion of them will serve to introduce the decision-making view of organizations. When individual decision making is under discussion, man is seen as able to make rational computations and rational decisions once he has decided upon his goals. "Two persons, given the same skills, the same objectives and values, the same knowledge and inclination, can rationally decide only upon the same course of action."[3] Goals depend in part upon group influences, but these can be mapped out. This is done extensively in Chapters Three and Four of *Organizations*, involving about 120 propositions with literally dozens of influences impinging upon, for example, the decision to

---

[1] Herbert A. Simon, *Administrative Behavior*, 2nd ed. (New York: The Macmillan Company, 1957). The first edition was published in 1947; the second edition contains a valuable new introduction. For a thoroughly unsympathetic and even outraged criticism of Simon's administrative theory see Herbert J. Storing, "The Science of Administration: Herbert A. Simon," in *Essays on the Scientific Study of Politics*, H. J. Storing, ed. (New York: Holt, Rinehart & Winston, Inc., 1962), pp. 63–105. I have reservations about some of Storing's points and miss any attempt to discuss the contributions that Simon has made, but nevertheless, it is an important critique. Probably no theorist would look well after such a detailed, relentless, and searching analysis. Another valuable and critical examination of Simon and organizational theory in general is Sherman Krupp's *Patterns in Organizational Analysis* (New York: Holt, Rinehart & Winston, Inc., 1961).

[2] James G. March and Herbert A. Simon, *Organizations* (New York: John Wiley & Sons, Inc., 1958). It will be impossible in this section to separate out the respective contributions of March and Simon when discussing this important book. Since the positions we are concerned with are also at least implicit in Simon's *Administrative Behavior* we will generally speak only of Simon, rather than of March and Simon. March himself will be discussed in the section on conflict.

[3] Simon, *Administrative Behavior*, pp. 13, 39. "Once the system of values which is to govern an administrative choice has been specified, there is one and only one 'best decision'. . . ." Ibid., p. 204.

stay with or leave the organization. Man also internalizes the goals of the organization and seeks affiliation with his group. He has a number of needs that require satisfaction. His social characteristics—age, sex, status, etc.—influence his decision. Finally, he has aspirations: if his aspirations are satisfied, his effort is relaxed, and if they are not, it is increased.

This portrait of man is, if anything, even more complex than the highly contingent human relations models, such as Fiedler's. Yet it is supposed to be the key to understanding organizations. Simon argues, first, that organizations are made up of individuals. "An organization is, after all, a collection of people, and what the organization does is done by people."[4] Therefore, understanding them is "a problem in social psychology."[5] Or, as March and Simon put it more decisively in a later volume, "propositions about organizations are statements about human behavior. . . ."[6]

There is another model of the individual in the writings of Simon and March, however. In the second model the complexity of individual wants, desires, and values and the multitude of the influences on his decisions are ignored. Instead, this model makes simplifying assumptions about the individual, so that we can get on with studying the organization rather than the individual. It assumes that the individual is not all that rational and that his behavior, within limits, can be deliberately controlled.

In this model, man is only "intendedly rational." He attempts to be rational but his limited capacities and the limited capacities of the organization prevent anything near complete rationality. For one thing, he does not have complete knowledge of the consequences of his act. There will be both unanticipated and unintended consequences of action. Second, he either does not have complete knowledge of the alternative courses of action available to him or he cannot afford to attain that knowledge. That is, he does not sit down and prepare an exhaustive list of alternatives before making every decision, and even if he tried to do so, the list could not be exhaustive. Therefore, he grossly simplifies the alternatives that are available and selects the first acceptable one. Third, even when he has several alternatives, he cannot accurately rank them in terms of their preference; he cannot be sure which is the most desirable and which is the least desirable.[7] These limitations on man conflict

---

[4]Ibid., p. 110.

[5]Ibid., pp. 1-2.

[6]March and Simon, *Organizations*, p. 26. This, presumably, would rule out of court a proposition such as "the higher the degree of specialization, the higher the centralization."

[7]Ibid., p. 138; Simon, *Administrative Behavior*, p. 81.

sharply with statements by Simon regarding rationality, efficiency, and the "one best decision."

It is important, before we go any further, to note the implications of this view and to distinguish it from Barnard's view of nonrational man and rational organization. In Barnard's model, man by himself is nonrational, but he achieves rationality through organizations. Simon's man is intendedly rational, but participation in the organization does not produce a more rational or superior man, nor does it produce an organizationally induced increment of rationality in the individual. Instead, the individual has his decisions made "subject to the influences of the organization group in which he participates."[8] This is done, Simon says, through the division of labor, standard practices, the authority system, channels of communication, and training and indoctrination. (He might have noted that these are the building blocks of the Weberian model, but March and Simon dismiss the Weberian model in a couple of paragraphs as too mechanical.[9]) The result is that members are made to "adapt their decisions to the organization's objectives" and they are provided with the information needed to make correct organizational decisions.[10] The organization gains, not the individual. It is organizational rationality that is enhanced through such devices as the division of labor. Simon, in his model of organizational decision making, is concerned with the organization as a tool, or with individuals as tools of the organization.[11] Barnard could not admit to this possibility, because organizations in his view are cooperative systems where the organizational and the individual objective must coincide. For Simon this is not the case; the individual satisfies his needs (for income, for example) through the organization, but his personal ends are not necessarily the ends of the organization.

Given the limits on rationality, what does the individual in fact do when confronted with a choice situation? He constructs a simplified model of the real situation. This "definition of the situation," as sociologists call it, is built out of past experience (it includes prejudices and stereotypes) and highly particularized, selective views of present stimuli. Most of his responses are "routine"; he invokes solutions he has used before. Sometimes he must engage in problem solving. When he does so, he conducts a *limited* search for alternatives along familiar and well-worn paths, selecting the first

---

[8]Simon, *Administrative Behavior*, p. 102. Simon veers more strongly to the view that man becomes rational only through organizations in his *Models of Man* (New York: John Wiley & Sons, 1956).

[9]March and Simon, *Organizations*, pp. 36–37.

[10]Simon, *Administrative Behavior*, p. 79.

[11]"The behavior of individuals is the tool with which organization achieves its purposes." Ibid., p. 108.

satisfactory one that comes along. He does not examine all possible alternatives nor does he keep searching for the optimum one. He "satisfices" instead of "optimizes." That is, he selects the first satisfactory solution rather than search for the optimum. His very standards for satisfactory solutions are a part of the definition of the situation. They go up and down with positive and negative experience. As solutions are easier to find, the standards are raised; as they are harder to find, the standards fall. *The organization can control these standards and it defines the situation;* only to a limited extent are they up to the individual.[12]

The importance of this assumption about human beings is that it gives to organizational variables (division of labor, communications system, etc.) the predominant control over individual behavior. This control is so extensive that we can neglect individual behavior (supposedly the real stuff of organizational life) in all its multiplicity and variability and deal with group or subunit behavior. It calls for simplifying models of *individual* behavior in order to capture the complexities of *organizational* behavior.

The Model of Organizations

What does the Simon model of organizations look like? First, we learn that goals are set by the leaders and then broken down into subgoals at each level of the organization. Each lower-order goal becomes a means to a higher-order goal. People do not accept these goals because they necessarily share them or believe in them, in contrast to the cooperative model, but because the organization

---

[12]This is one of the additional reasons beyond those noted in the chapter on Barnard that the equilibrium model of inducements and contributions, utilized in both *Administrative Behavior* and *Organizations* is so suspect—the organization sets the terms of the expectations and thus can manufacture the ratio of inducements to contributions in its own interests. This is noted by Storing, *Essays on the Scientific Study of Politics,* p. 106.

In an effort to defend the rational, economic man view, some critics have pointed out that "satisficing" behavior is really maximizing behavior when one takes into account the costs of search. That is, the person who selects the first acceptable alternative is saying "there may be a better one, but it will not be so much better as to make up for the cost of additional search." March and Simon illustrate their satisficing model with the example of looking for a needle in a haystack—you do not search for the sharpest needle, only one sharp enough to sew with. But the example is not apt; no economist (who is supposed to deal only with completely rational man) would argue that you search for the sharpest needle. The real reason why the Simon formulation is so useful is that the costs of search are usually unknown to the individual. He does not know if there is a sharper needle or how long it would take to find it. Therefore, he cannot take into account the cost of search in many cases. At any rate, Simon does not say that all behavior ignores cost of search, or does not seek maximum solutions, but only that it is impossible to do so all or most of the time.

has mechanisms to insure that working toward them meets the individual's own personal values. (These personal values, of course, influence the organizational goal to some extent.) In commercial, governmental, and voluntary organizations, the controlling group of top administrators identifies closely with the objectives of the organization;[13] the rest need not. Once established, the goals remain quite stable because of such things as the high cost of innovative activity, "sunk cost," and "sunk assets." These refer to capital investments which cannot easily be changed (e.g., single purpose machinery in a plant) and to the know-how or knowledge and the goodwill. Regardless of "wants, motives, and desires" or the dynamics of decision making in individuals, these nonpersonal aspects stabilize objectives and activities.[14]

Other sources of stability in the organization stem from the routinization of activity through the establishment of programs and standard operating procedures. Changes are introduced only when objectives are clearly not met, and even then the search for new programs follows well-worn paths, minimizing the disruption; the satisficing solution is to select the least disruptive alternatives. Even planning is difficult, for "daily routine drives out planning."[15] To plan—and thus change—routines, resources have to be allocated to units which have as their tasks innovation and planning. Another source of change is the deadlines that provoke crises in which programmed activity must be abandoned. March and Simon devote a chapter to planning and innovation, but it is clear that these are only adaptive responses of an organization, not ends in themselves. Innovation is designed to stabilize the organization and allow routine to be reestablished or to reappear.

The key to the Simon model of organizations is the concept of organizational structure. March and Simon define this as "those aspects of the pattern of behavior in the organization that are relatively stable and that change only slowly."[16] Clinging to their psychological predisposition, they argue that the basic features of the structure "derive from the characteristics of human problem-solving processes and rational human choice."[17] But once we have established that humans do not maximize, but only satisfice, can attend to only a few things at a time, and tend to factor problems into established and familiar dimensions, the attention to the charac-

---

[13]Simon, *Administrative Behavior*, pp. 120–121.

[14]Ibid., pp. 66, 95, 120. Simon treats sunk costs at one point as "mechanisms of behavior-persistence," thus retaining a psychological perspective (p. 95).

[15]March and Simon, *Organizations*, p. 185.

[16]Ibid., p. 170.

[17]Ibid., p. 169.

teristics of human behavior is not necessary. Because of these limits upon human capacities and the complexity of organizational problems, "rational behavior calls for simplified models that capture the main features of a problem without capturing all its complexities."[18]

The simplified model can be described as follows, drawing from the two volumes: it calls for satisficing behavior; sequential and limited search processes that are only mildly innovative; specialization of activities and roles so that attention is directed to "a particular restricted set of values"; "attention-directors that channelize behavior"; rules, programs, and repertories of action that limit choice in recurring situations and prevent an agonizing process of optimal decision making at each turn; a restricted range of stimuli and situations that narrow perception; training and indoctrination enabling the individual to "make decisions, by himself, as the organization would like him to decide"; and the factoring of goals and tasks into programs that are semi-independent of each other so as to reduce interdependencies. Most organizational activity takes most of the conditions as given; "only a few elements of the system are adaptive at any one time."[19]

The view of authority in this model departs from that of Barnard. In March and Simon's view, authority is not bottom-up, emphasizing the power of the subordinate to grant authority to the superior or emphasizing participation as in the human relations school. Instead, the superior has the power or tools to structure the environment and perceptions of the subordinate in such a way that he sees the proper things and in the proper light. The superior actually appears to give few orders (confirming my own observations in organizations). Instead, he sets priorities ("we had better take care of this first"; "this is getting out of hand and creating problems, so let's give it more attention until the problems are cleared up") and alters the flow of inputs and stimuli. The image of the order-barking boss is not there, but neither is the image of participative management or of

---

[18]Ibid.

[19]For the quoted passages, see Simon, *Administrative Behavior*, pp. 98–103, and March and Simon, *Organizations*, p. 169. One of the most widely cited sections of *Organizations* concerns the authors' models of the theories of Robert Merton, Philip Selznick, and Alvin Gouldner. I find that these models violate the originals in several respects. But more important, most of the factors that are supposed to be "pathological" processes contributing to the "dysfunctions" supposedly described by Merton, Gouldner, and Selznick reappear in the second part of the book as functional. The pathologies of limited perspectives and subgroup goals and identification turn out to be necessary for the division of labor and provide means of control. Inattention to the complexities of human actors and their wants and needs proves to be necessary. The surveillance and control features of rules and programs are no longer self-defeating, but functional and essential.

Barnard's soldier deciding whether or not to move forward into battle after receiving the command.

The term "communication" looms large in this model, but it is not the term that is associated with the platitudes regarding clarity of orders or the authoritativeness of the source or even mechanical discussions of "information overload" and "flow charts." Instead, communication strategies center around checkpoints in the channels, the specialization of channels, the widening and deepening of favored channels which may bypass key stations inadvertently, the development of organizational vocabularies which screen out some parts of reality and magnify other parts, and the attention-directing, cue-establishing nature of communication techniques.

For example, let us explore March and Simon's concept of "uncertainty absorption." An organization develops a set of concepts influenced by the technical vocabulary and classification schemes; this permits easy communication. Anything that does not fit into these concepts is not easily communicated. For the organization, "the particular categories and schemes of classification it employs are reified, and become, for members of the organization, attributes of the world rather than mere conventions."[20] This is especially apparent when a body of information must be edited and summarized in order to make it fit into the conceptual scheme—to make it understandable. The inferences from the material rather than the material itself are transmitted. The recipient can disbelieve the "facts" that are transmitted to him, but he can rarely check their accuracy unless he himself undertakes the summarization and assessment. This gives personnel who are in direct contact with the information considerable discretion and influence. They "absorb" quantities of "uncertainty."

The most significant examples of uncertainty absorption occur at the boundaries of organizations, where information about the environment is obtained. The selective perception, distortions, omissions, and so on that can occur in a marketing unit are numerous, and there is little that can be done to check this tendency for it is impossible to obtain complete and accurate information. Even the information obtained still leaves much uncertainty because consumer preferences, competitors' actions, disposable income, or the weather may change rapidly. The tendency to tell the boss only what he wants to hear, so well noted in the literature, is probably not as important as the tendency to see things only in terms of the concepts reflected in the organization's vocabulary. In this way, we can translate an explanation regarding personal predispositions (the subordinate fears to tell the truth) into an organizational expla-

---

[20]March and Simon, *Organizations*, p. 165.

nation ("truth" is an organizationally established frame of reference, independent of courageous or timid members).

Information sources and uncertainty absorption also have a good deal to do with the amount of consensus in organizations, according to the March and Simon model.[21] Consensus depends in part upon the number of sources of information that are utilized and the degree to which uncertainty absorption can be centralized into one unit. If there are few sources of information, or if there is only one processing unit, the possibility for divergent subgroup perspectives to develop is reduced. An industrial organization with only a few customers and a few products would be such an organization, as would a prison or a mental hospital with a steady supply of inmates and patients and little concern about what happens to them after discharge. But if the mental hospital began to develop extensive links with the environment through social workers, public relations personnel, legislative lobbying activities, and contacts with courts and law enforcement agencies—all in an attempt to improve its services and responsiveness to the community—it could expect divergent views to develop regarding the kind of services needed, the techniques to be used, and the goals to be pursued. Similarly, an industrial organization with active links to the environment of technological developments, multiple consumer demands, varied suppliers, and personnel sources—all developed to broaden its product base and keep up with changing markets, products, and competitors—could expect internal consensus to decline. This explanation has little to do with the process of choice in individuals, nor, we might add, with the typical explanations of the human relations school. With the decline in consensus, there may well be increased conflict or a decline in the quality of interpersonal relations and organizational good identification. But poor interpersonal relations and goal identification are not the causes of a decline in consensus or increased conflict; they are the result of multiple sources of communication and an increase in uncertainty absorption, which in turn reduces the chances for consensus.

One important implication of the March and Simon model is that to change individual behavior you do not have to change individuals, in the sense of altering their personalities or teaching them human relations skills. Instead, you change the premises of their decisions. March and Simon give few examples in their book of concrete problems or instances of organizational behavior, so it is necessary to fabricate one to illustrate this point. (Although the example is fabricated, the idea was suggested in a conversation with James March.) A common problem in organization is how does

---

[21]Ibid., p. 127.

one make a basic change in the perspectives and values of the organizational leaders. To change the perspectives of the individual leaders themselves, is, we know, very difficult. In large organizations it is often difficult to merely replace them since those with sufficient experience and knowledge of the organization at the next level are likely to share the very perspectives one wishes to change. Going outside the organization for top management personnel also has its difficulties.

One way, though a slow one, is to change the kinds of experiences that will be had by people who will have access to top management positions. Typically, we might find that the perspectives of top management were shaped by the experiences they had while in the lower echelons of the organization and that these experiences were embedded in conventional career lines. Promotion may have typically been from line rather than staff positions, sales rather than production, home office experience rather than field or overseas experience, combat unit assignments rather than political assignments, custodial rather than clinical experience, large rather than small chapters of a voluntary association. We should then start promoting rapidly people who have had deviant rather than conventional career lines. (This is the burden of a perceptive analysis of modern military careers by Morris Janowitz.[22])

There are costs involved in this strategy because, up to the time of the change, those with the most ambition and ability have probably been following conventional career lines, since that has been the quickest way to the top. Therefore, in the short run, some competence must be sacrificed in order to secure altered perspectives. Those with experiences that promote the proper perspective must be rapidly, and quite visibly, promoted, even though they are not the most competent. In time, the ambitious people with high competence and willingness to adopt organizational goals as their own will seek these kinds of assignments. In the long run, both proper values and competence will be found in top management.

Note that this kind of analysis is foreign to the view of leadership held by Barnard and by the human relations school, and it would find no place in Weber's theory of bureaucracy or that of the classical school of management. It is based upon the idea that to shape behavior, you have to shape the premises of decision making—in this case through the use of rewards and sanctions.

Thus, from Simon we learn that it is the premises of decisions that are important, rather than the decision-making capabilities of individuals—once it is established that they are not superhuman. The organization does not control the "process of decision making,"

---

[22]Morris Janowitz, *The Professional Soldier* (New York: The Free Press, 1960).

as he says at several points, but the premises for decision making, as he says only occasionally.[23] These premises are to be found in the "vocabulary" of the organization, the structure of communication, rules and regulations and standard programs, selection criteria for personnel, and so on—in short, in the structural aspects.

Unobtrusive Control

But March and Simon are not merely "structuralists"; their view of organizations is superior to most sociological views in two respects. First, in the second part of their book, they strew about insights that have not often been surpassed in organizational theory. Second, by providing a vocabulary or conceptual scheme for discussing control in organizations without relying upon simple-minded views of control, they have enriched analysis. This second point will take some elaboration.

The conventional, structural viewpoint says that rules direct or control behavior. You tell a man what the rule is and he follows it or is punished. Or, we say that authority is vested in the office, and the commands that issue forth tell people what to do. Coordination is achieved by having one person or group find out what two other groups are doing and direct them to do it in such a way as to make their efforts fit together. Yet, the vast proportion of the activity in organizations goes on without personal directives and supervision—and even without written rules—and sometimes in permitted violation of the rules. We tend to deal with this "residue," which constitutes perhaps 80 percent of the behavior, by invoking general concepts such as habit, training, socialization, or routine.

March and Simon, however, fill in a good part of that residue by pointing to mechanisms that do not seem to be activated by directives or rules and by describing what these mechanisms do. Involved are such things as uncertainty absorption, organizational vocabularies, programmed tasks, procedural and substantive programs, standardization of raw materials, frequency of communication channel usage, interdependencies of units and programs. Such mechanisms affect organizational behavior in the following ways: they limit information content and flow, thus controlling the premises available for decisions; they set up expectations so as to highlight some aspects of the situation and play down others; they limit the search for alternatives when problems are confronted, thus insuring more predictable and consistent solutions; they indicate the threshold levels as to when a danger signal is being emitted (thus reducing the occasions for decision making and promoting satisfic-

---

[23]Simon, *Administrative Behavior*, pp. xii, 79.

ing rather than optimizing behavior); they achieve coordination of effort by selecting certain kinds of work techniques and schedules.

Note the extent to which behavior is shaped, or controlled, without reference to conventional items of rules and commands. In most organizational theory, the discussion of such "latent" or unobtrusive means of control of behavior applies primarily to professional roles and their reliance upon professional training, standards, and expectations and to informal group pressures. March and Simon make it very clear that the informal group and the characteristics of professionals are not the only sources of unobtrusive control in organizations. Most of us have neglected to locate and describe these unobtrusive controls, either taking them for granted or relying instead upon very general concepts, such as the division of labor or socialization, or relatively obtrusive devices, such as rules or job specifications. By moving back from the actual process of decision making to the premises of decision making, March and Simon have begun to fill in a significant gap surrounding organizational behavior. I suspect that their social-psychological preoccupation enabled them to do this more easily, but the level of analysis remains a sociological, or structural, one.

Thus, March and Simon join the mainstream of the classical theorists, especially Weber, and augment that stream significantly. The problem with humans in organizations is not just that they may go their own, selfish way, and thus need to be kept in line through such devices as hierarchical control, division of labor, job specifications, impartial and impersonal rules and standards, and so on; the problem is also that there are real limits to human rationality, and thus the premises of decisions and the flow of information upon which decisions are based must be controlled. As a result, organizations need not only the familiar appurtenances of bureaucracy, but also the more subtle and unobtrusive controls of communication channels, organizational vocabulary, and so on. The prospects for spontaneous cooperative activity are dim in this view; what "cooperation" there is, in Barnard's sense, is engineered. The prospects for participative management are also dim; they are reduced to minor innovations within a complex network of established premises for action. The organization is not static, by any means, but change is incremental, partial, hit-or-miss, and channeled in the well-worn grooves of established adaptations.

At this writing, twenty years after the appearance of March and Simon's *Organizations*, we can push the notion of what I have labeled as unobtrusive controls a bit further. Think of three types of controls—direct, fully obtrusive ones such as giving orders, direct surveillance, and rules and regulations; bureaucratic ones such as specialization and standardization and hierarchy, which are fairly unobtrusive; and fully unobtrusive ones, namely the control of the cognitive premises underlying action. Direct controls are expensive and reactive. They are often necessary in times of change and crisis, and always exist, but they do not draw upon the accumulated experience or the training or intelligence of the subordinate. Rules are ineffective when situations change frequently, and direct surveillance and orders require continual management effort and time. Bureaucratic controls, principally specialization and standardization (the matter of hierarchy is too complicated to deal with here), are far more efficient. Because the range of stimuli is greatly reduced by standardization and specializing in one activity, the subordinate has fewer opportunities to make decisions that maximize his own interests rather than the organization's interests. There are also gains in having steeper learning curves, limiting information flow, and so on. But the control of premises, while far more difficult to achieve, is even more effective. Here the subordinate *voluntarily* restricts the range of stimuli that will be attended to ("Those sorts of things are irrelevant," or "What has that got to do with the matter?") and the range of alternatives that would be considered ("It would never occur to me to do that"). Direct sanctions operate in the first type, direct control; remote controls operate in the second—one is simply assigned to a kind of job with more or less standard inputs, methods, and expected outputs; internalized premises for behavior are operating in the third.

Now we can better understand the paradoxical finding referred to in Chapter 1—the greater the degree of bureaucratization, the greater the delegation of decision making. Because the employee is well controlled, he or she can be trusted to make more of his or her own decisions. In the case of the actual research by the Blau and Aston groups, however, the decisions studied were either-or in nature, could be clearly specified in advance, and had quite visible consequences once they had been made. Such decisions are subject to fairly obtrusive controls. Rules are promulgated in advance, and their violation is apparent; furthermore, they are restricted to quite specialized and standardized matters. Not a great deal is being delegated here, and (unmeasured) controls are firmly in place.

It is in management's interest to delegate as many of these "either-or" decisions as possible, since such delegation reduces the cost to management of giving direct orders. (Otherwise, they may as well be making the analysis and the decision themselves.) Direct surveillance of behavior is reflected by checking outcomes, which is cheaper. Finally, delegation ensures that the decision is made by the person with the most knowledge of the situation.

But in the measurement of centralization of authority Blau and the Aston group have not included measures of specialization, standardization, or even formal rules, because these are considered parts of structure. Thus while delegation has taken place, it is only because another kind of centralization of authority preceded it, an unmeasured kind.

Nor do we measure the more powerful and subtle form of control found in premise setting. (It is, by its very nature, extremely difficult to measure.) We are content to speak of socialization, or culture, or community norms, thus making it both sanitary and somehow independent of the organization. But we could just as well label premise setting as indoctrination, brainwashing, manipulation, or false consciousness.

Premise controls are most important when work is nonroutine (since such work by definition cannot have standardized inputs, throughputs, and outputs, and cannot be specialized, nor governed by rules), and this is one reason scientists and other professionals have such latitude in organizations. Their premises are well set in their training institutions and professional associations. Premise controls are also most important near the top of organizations because managerial work there is less routine, the consequences of decisions are hard to assess immediately, and access to company resources is greatest, providing more opportunities to use company property and power for one's own ends. This is why social class, ethnic origins, and social networks are so important—they make it more likely that certain kinds of premises will exist. Further down the hierarchy, bureaucratic and direct controls increase in importance. But fully unobtrusive premise controls exist at all levels, created and reinforced by schools, the mass media, and cultural institutions in general.

The question that Bendix posed (see Chapter 2): why are some given the right to command and others the duty to obey in organizations, can only be asked once the premises of the economic order are held in abeyance. This is why it is rarely asked, even by social scientists. For most people it is not a meaningful question; it is just the way things are and presumably have always been. In the U.S., workers would have to violate the everyday premises that their organizations and the institutions outside of them constantly reinforce and reproduce if they were to demand, say, that occupants of all managerial positions be subject to direct election by their subordinates and required to run on announced policy platforms (e.g., no speedup, no in-plant pollution or dangerous chemicals, less pay for managers and more for workers). When we measure controls, or centralization and decentralization in organizations, we do not include the control of basic premises such as this.

In fact, we do worse. We reinforce these premises in our own work. For example, most effectiveness studies now assume that high morale is an indicator of one aspect of organizational effectiveness. But these morale studies ask how satisfied people are with their jobs, supervisors, career prospects, working conditions, and pay. It goes unremarked and unnoticed that the definition of morale is in terms of what the company assumes would be good for it. The unstated premise is that high morale means that people find it gratifying to do what the organization wants them to do. So thoroughly grounded is this premise that at first glance it seems absurd to recommend a morale measure that would assume that the happy employee is happy doing what he or she wants, rather than what the company wants. But I would recommend that future morale studies ask such questions as the following:

Is this the kind of organization where you can . . .

Have pleasant chats with others about things that interest you?
Daydream or relax from time to time without being bothered?
Use the organization's facilities for your own personal needs (the telephone, typists, office supplies, machine shop, personnel department, auto maintenance shop, travel facilities, etc.)?
Control the work pace so that if you are depressed or upset you don't have to work too hard?
Hide your mistakes and advertise your successes?
Pick up interesting tidbits about the world by working here, or be more interesting at social gatherings because of what you do here or learn here?
Make use of tediously acquired skills and knowledge so that you have some sense that what you are doing is meaningful and related to your abilities?
Get a friend or relative a job here?
Expect to have a job here as long as you need it?[24]

So thoroughly have researchers adopted the premises of management that it would be heretical to consider the above questions as valid measures of organizational effectiveness. But why not?

CONFLICT

Even the expanded bureaucratic model of March and Simon fails to deal with an obvious and pervasive aspect of organizations—conflict among groups. Of course, theorists and researchers, and cer-

---

[24]Charles Perrow, "Three Types of Effectiveness Studies" in Paul S. Goodman, Johannes M. Pennings and Associates, *New Perspectives on Organizational Effectiveness* (San Francisco: Jossey-Bass, Inc., 1977), pp. 96–105.

tainly members of organizations, are aware that conflicts go on continuously between departments and divisions, and among groups within them. To Barnard, who seldom referred to it, conflict was possibly a melancholy failure of leadership. To Weber, who describes it impatiently and in some detail as it is found in government and political bureaucracies,[25] it sometimes appears to be only a result of human shortcomings such as cowardice, stupidity, and greed. To the classical management theorists it is a failure of adequate control, planning, and execution. For the human relations theorists it is variously a failure of leadership, lack of participative management, or something that is constructive in passing, because it shows up areas where more work needs to be done. Elimination of conflict is always the goal, even if it is seen as constructive in the short run. For March and Simon, as with the human relations theorists, it is primarily an interpersonal problem, even though the two men deal briefly with intergroup conflict. For all, from Weber to Likert, intergroup conflict is a fact of organizational life but not a fact that is built into their models, except as evidence of a failure to utilize the model.

While much conflict in organizations is undoubtedly an interpersonal phenomenon—two men in competition, or with incompatible personalities, or lacking in ability to empathize with one another—a theory of organizations, rather than one of individual interaction, should be able to accommodate group conflict. Theory should see conflict as an inevitable part of organizational life stemming from organizational characteristics rather than from the characteristics of individuals. Why are sales and production in conflict in all firms—though to greatly varying degrees? Or faculty and the administration in colleges, doctors and nurses and administrators in hospitals, the treatment and custodial staffs in prisons? Why can one generally assume that even within departments there is a good chance of conflict between representatives of different product lines, different treatment technologies (such as social workers and psychiatrists), or different disciplines, such as the social sciences and the engineering school?

One answer is obvious enough: there is a never-ending struggle for values that are dear to participants—security, power, survival, discretion, and autonomy—and a host of rewards. Because organizations do not consist of people sharing the same goals, since the members bring with them all sorts of needs and interests, and because control is far from complete, people will struggle for these kinds of values. To reduce, contain, or use these conflicts is the job of

---

[25]Max Weber, *Economy and Society*, ed. Guenther Roth and Claus Wittich (New York: Irvington Publications, 1968), 3: 1381–1462.

the administrator. The most important conflicts are those that involve groups, since groups can mobilize more resources, extract loyalty, and shape perceptions.

The matter has been little studied beyond anecdotal or descriptive case studies. Some time ago, Philip Selznick pointed out the prevalence and the positive and negative functions of group conflict within organizations.[26] Dalton deals with conflict in a descriptive and rather social-psychological, but still valuable, manner in his *Men Who Manage.*[27] The sociological literature on hospitals and prisons has dealt with conflict since it is so obviously a fact of life in these organizations.[28] The general area of labor-management conflict has been well studied, of course, but will not be reviewed here.[29] Recently, some attempts have appeared to conceptualize types of conflicts, where they are likely to occur, and so on.[30] Some researchers in the field emphasize formal groups and rather obvious clashes of interest,[31] and some emphasize a confused, fluid, and "negotiated" order.[32] Others have attempted to build systematic models containing the observed bases of conflict and power.[33] Most of these efforts appear to be consistent with the neo-Weberian model we have described in this chapter.

However, the most interesting speculation on internal conflict in organizations revolves around the question of conflict over goals and, in the process, challenges a number of assumptions about goals in organizations.

---

[26]Philip Selznick, *TVA and the Grass Roots* (Berkeley and Los Angeles: University of California Press, 1949). For a more systematic view, see his *Leadership in Administration* (New York: Harper & Row, Inc., 1957).

[27]Melville Dalton, *Men Who Manage* (New York: John Wiley & Sons, Inc., 1959).

[28]Mayer Zald, "Power Balance and Staff Conflict in Correctional Institutions," *Administrative Science Quarterly* 7 (June 1962): 22–49; David Street, Robert Vinter, and Charles Perrow, *Organizations for Treatment* (New York: The Free Press, 1966); H. L. Smith, "Two Lines of Authority: The Hospital's Dilemma," in *Patients, Physicians and Illness: Source Book in Behavioral Science and Medicine*, 2nd ed., ed. E. G. Jaco (New York: The Free Press, 1972); Charles Perrow, "Hospitals: Technology, Structure, and Goals," in *Handbook of Organizations*, ed. James G. March (Chicago: Rand McNally & Company, 1965), 910–971.

[29]A. Kornhauser, R. Dubin, and A. Ross, *Industrial Conflict* (New York: McGraw-Hill Book Company, 1954).

[30]Mayer Zald, ed., *Power in Organizations* (Nashville, Tenn.: Vanderbilt University Press, 1970); entire issue of *Administrative Science Quarterly* 14, no. 4 (December 1969).

[31]Charles Perrow, "Departmental Power and Perspective in Industrial Firms," in Zald, *Power in Organizations*, pp. 59–89.

[32]Rue Bucher, "Social Process and Power in a Medical School," in ibid., pp. 3–48; Fred H. Goldner, "The Division of Labor: Process and Power," in ibid., pp. 97–143.

[33]David Hickson et al., "A Strategic Contingencies Theory of Intra-Organizational Power," *Administrative Science Quarterly* 16, no. 2 (June 1971): 216–229.

The first such challenged assumption is that organizations are oriented toward a specific goal. Almost all definitions of organizations make this assumption. Yet the goals pursued by organizations are multiple, and they are generally in conflict. As Richard Cyert and James March point out in a brilliant discussion which we shall follow closely,[34] those objectives that are agreed upon—reforming delinquents, making a satisfactory profit—are highly ambiguous and not "operational." That is, they do not indicate the specific operations or steps that must be taken to achieve them, so there can be many routes to these goals. Further, one is not even sure when they are achieved adequately. Satisfactory profits this year may be at the expense of satisfactory profits three years from now. Thus, to describe the single, specific goal of an organization is to say very little about it. Actual goals are discovered only when the public or official goal is factored into operational goals—those for which specific operations can be discovered.[35] Once this is done, it turns out that there are several goals involved, and maximizing one will usually be at the expense of another.

If goals are, in fact, multiple, then another assumption held by some schools of thought (including the bureaucratic and the expanded bureaucratic models) must be abandoned. That is to say, it is not possible for the head of an organization to fully establish the "preference ordering" of goals. There may be such an ordering, and it may actually reflect the operative goals, but we cannot count on it. Instead, we have to assume that goals should be viewed as emerging from a bargaining process among groups. Furthermore, they are subject to a learning process, say Cyert and March. Aspirations of groups rise depending upon the success or failure of group strategies. Therefore, we cannot assume that even the masters of an organization are completely free to rank specific goals in terms of their preference. Organizations are tools in the hands of their masters, but they are imperfect, not completely controlled, tools, and it is a struggle to maintain control over them. (In his later work, reviewed on page 158, March goes further and views goals as rationalizations of past events, many of which were not intended or anticipated.)

This implies that if we accept the idea of multiple and conflicting goals, which are the result of a continuous bargaining learning process, we must go one step further. Contrary to the theories behind most models of organizations, conflicting goals can be met.

---

[34]Richard M. Cyert and James G. March, *A Behavioral Theory of the Firm* (Englewood Cliffs, N.J.: Prentice-Hall, Inc., 1963), chapters 1, 2, 3, 6.

[35]Charles Perrow, "Goals in Complex Organizations," *American Sociological Review* 26, no. 6 (December 1961): 854–865.

Organizations, Cyert and March note, can pursue goals in a sequence; it is not necessary that they all be pursued at once. If pursued in a sequence, growth, for example, may take precedence over profit for a time, and then profit over growth. Both may be pursued and met at the same time, too. The goals of treatment and custody are in some conflict in prisons and mental hospitals, but if the organization is large and complex enough, some units may be providing mostly treatment for their clients, others mostly custody. This is obvious, but it rarely is given much attention, and the problems it raises for characterizing the organization are numerous.[36] More commonly, many goals are not in conflict in the short run; for example, increased market share or sales volume may, but may not, conflict with profit goals.

Pursuing different goals in sequence, or simultaneously, even if they are in short-run conflict, can take place if the environment is "benign"—poses few threats to the organization, has adequate resources, etc. —or if the organization has a lot of "slack." Slack simply means an excess of resources (money, time, personnel, equipment, ideas). When slack is high, several conflicting goals can be pursued if there are sufficient funds. Sociology departments generally resist teaching Marriage and the Family, a very popular service course for nonsociology majors, but as long as they can continue to recruit new assistant professors or instructors in sufficient volume, they can stick à few of them with this task. When departmental growth slows or stops, however, and manning this course means cutting some "true" sociology courses, the goals conflict. Obvious enough, but the degree of fat in organizations is rarely taken into account in a systematic fashion in research, even in research on goals.

Cyert and March point out that people have a disorganized file drawer of goals at hand, ready to pull out when situations warrant. There may be more ample resources, or a political payoff is due for joining a coalition of groups to support some other goal, or there may be a trade-off for a defeat in some other area. Goals may emerge, thus, in a rather fortuitous fashion, as when the organization seems to back into a new line of activity or into an external alliance in a fit of absentmindedness. Goals of a rather low level,

---

[36]One promising characterization is offered by Karl Weick in "Educational Organizations as Loosely Coupled Systems," *Administrative Science Quarterly* 21:1 (March 1976): 1–19. For a somewhat extreme emphasis upon the largely symbolic character of goals, see John W. Meyer and Brian Rowan, "Institutionalized Organizations: Formal Structure as Myth and Ceremony," *American Journal of Sociology* 83:2 (September 1977): 340–363. For an argument that official goals are generally one of the least important constraints upon behavior, see Charles Perrow, "Demystifying Organizations" in Rosemary Sarri and Yeheskel Hasenfeld, eds. *The Management of Human Services* (New York: Columbia University Press, 1978).

but still with consequences for the organization, also emerge as a secondary consequence of a primary function. For example, if personnel turnover or increased recruitment is sufficient to warrant enlarging the personnel department, the organization may find itself devoting substantial attention to personnel goals by running training programs, doing counseling and testing, setting up elaborate retirement counseling schemes, and establishing or revising pension plans. These emerge not because they are necessarily pressing problems for the organization, "but because the subunit keeps generating solutions that remind other members of the organization of particular sets of objectives they profess."[37] Solutions are looking for problems, in this case, rather than problems looking for solutions.

In a striking extension of these ideas, James March and his associates have formulated a "garbage can" model of organizations wherein problems are convenient receptacles for people to toss in solutions that happen to interest them, or for interests that are not being met at the time. The can, with its problems, becomes an opportunity or resource. Depending upon the number of cans around, the mixes of problems in them, and the amount of time people have, they stay with the particular can or leave it for another. The problem, then, gets detached from those that originally posed it, may develop a life of its own, or get transformed into quite another problem. Solutions no one originally intended or even expected may be generated, or no solutions at all. Some problems simply waste away. In this view, the problem or the opportunity is conceptually dislodged from the people in the organization and can be analyzed independently of them. In one striking example, the problem of rewarding a particularly valuable secretary gets mixed up with a stream of quite unrelated and quite unpredictable other problems and interests and opportunities (and some sheer accidents) and some years later the consequences are the restructuring of a number of university departments. The process is then reinterpreted in a rationalistic account as the inevitable modernization of the university due to forces in the environment, when it was manifestly not that at all. No coherent, stable goal guided the total process, but after the fact a coherent stable goal was presumed to have been present. It would be unsettling to see it otherwise.[38]

---

[37]Cyert and March, *Behavioral Theory of the Firm*, p. 35.

[38]A short statement of the model appears in Michael D. Cohen, James C. March and Johan P. Olsen, "A Garbage Can Model of Organizational Choice," *Administrative Science Quarterly* 17:1 (March 1972): 1–25. An extended one, with the example given above appearing in Chapter 14 is in James C. March and Johan P. Olsen, *Ambiguity and Choice in Organizations* (Bergen, Norway: Universitetsforlaget, 1976). See the useful reviews of this important but aggravating book in *Contemporary*

By this time, one may wonder if organizational goals can really be that fluid and random, the outgrowth of political bargaining, accident, unintended consequences, and so on. Many are, but the process is not as unstable as this description might indicate. Cyert and March themselves outline some mechanisms which stabilize the goal-setting process considerably. One key one is the budget. Rather than viewing the budget as a rational plan developed by the central authority to maximize the goals of the leader, they describe it as "an explicit elaboration of previous commitments."[39] It stabilizes bargainings and expectations for a year or longer. Continual renegotiation of major items is prevented in this fashion, and groups agree to abide, in general, by the rules of the game until they can try to further their own goals in the next budget.

Reference to precedent, usually in the form of rules, standing operating procedures, or informal understandings and traditions, is another stabilizing factor. These precedents "remove from conscious consideration many agreements, decisions, and commitments that might well be subject to renegotiation in an organization without a memory."[40] This is one of the functions of record keeping, files, and men with long seniority. While the organization is, as Anselm Strauss and his associates have stressed, a "negotiated environment,"[41] most of the negotiations have been consummated in the past. Only a few items are under negotiation at any one point in time.

Finally, despite the existence of conflicting groups, changing coalitions, and multiple goals pursued in sequence or simultaneously, it is clear that the vast majority of organizations have interpretable goal structures. The people at the top are in a position to win most of the battles and to shape the nature of the contest that goes on below them. We would be wrong to assume a specific goal with specific means attached to it, and the conflict model of organizations is essential in this respect. But organizations are not such open systems that goals fluctuate continually and rulers never get their way—or at least the issue is in doubt. In the next chapter, we will present the most persuasive extant argument for the view that leaders themselves are captives of their organizations: in the view of the institutional school, organizations are organic entities with a life

---

Society 6:3 (May 1977): 294–298; and *Administrative Science Quarterly* 22:2 (June 1977): 351–361.

[39]Ibid., p. 33. See also Aaron Wildavsky, *Politics of the Budgetary Process*, 2nd ed. (Boston: Little Brown and Company, 1974).

[40]Cyert and March, *Behavioral Theory of the Firm*, p. 33.

[41]Anselm L. Strauss et al., *Psychiatric Ideologies and Institutions* (New York: The Free Press, 1964).

of their own, and leadership can only try to stay on top of the evolving process, rather than bend it completely to their will.

The formulation of Cyert and March is consistent with the neo-Weberian model of organizations that we have abstracted from the decision-making model of March and Simon, and it extends that model to include goals and conflicts over the goals. In the remainder of this volume, we shall continue to use that model, attempting to extend it further by examining two major contingencies of all theory, technology and the environment.

TECHNOLOGY

Until now, we have usually treated all complex organizations as being alike. We have done so because most of the theoretical schools have done so. Weber would, of course, admit that organizations are only more or less bureaucratized, since he saw it as an irregular historical process and was avowedly constructing an "ideal type" with his model. Barnard noted some differences among organizations upon commonplace dimensions—business, government, voluntary associations. We noted that the human relations school has moved toward various forms of differentiation—group climate, size, task—in explaining groups, and that Likert acknowledged that things might be different in organizations with routine tasks from things in organizations with varied tasks, but he abandoned the idea in favor of System 4 for all organizations. Finally, March and Simon made a more penetrating stab when they distinguished programmed from nonprogrammed tasks in organizations and briefly examined some consequences of this.[42]

But by and large, organizational theory has not until recently attempted to build into its models any systematic consideration of different types of organizations. The ideas that have been put forth, by Peter Blau and Richard Scott, Alvin Gouldner, Talcott Parsons, and Amitai Etzioni, have not proved very useful.[43] We desire typologies that will order the diversity of organizations in such a way that we can explain differences in structure and/or goals. Organizations of the same type should have similar structures and/or

---

[42]March and Simon, *Organizations*, pp. 141–148 and *passim*.

[43]Peter Blau and W. Richard Scott, *Formal Organizations* (San Francisco: Chandler, 1962), pp. 42–45; Amitai Etzioni, *A Comparative Analysis of Complex Organizations*, rev. ed. (New York: The Free Press, 1975); Talcott Parsons, *Structure and Process in Modern Societies* (New York: The Free Press, 1960), pp. 44–47; Alvin Gouldner, *Patterns of Industrial Bureaucracy* (New York: The Free Press, 1954).

goals. But if the typology is based upon either structure or goals, we risk tautologies.

For example, Etzioni bases his typology upon the type of power utilized in the organization to gain compliance of participants, a structural characteristic. This leads him to predict that such organizations as prisons, which use "coercive" power, will have the structural attribute of alienated participant involvement, will exhibit goals of internal order, and will represent a type of organization he calls "coercive." We have not learned much about prisons from this exercise that we did not already know. Prisoners are coerced in coercive organizations by coercive power and do not like it. The economic gain type of organization (e.g., a factory) has economic goals and calculative participant involvement (the members calculate whether the wages are worth it), and uses remunerative power (wages) to gain compliance. Again, we appear to have only described various aspects of the organization with similar terms. The case is similar with the normative organizations, such as churches—they have the goal of cultural (normative) outputs, members are normatively involved, and normative power is used. Equally as serious as the tautology involved is the neglect of wide ranges of differences within the types. Some churches and schools, for example, are run like factories; some like prisons.

Etzioni's book has the merit of systematically using his typology to explore structural and other properties. But the value of his discussions does not appear to reside in the typology. This is also true of the volume by Blau and Scott, where the typology is quickly abandoned and does not inform the rest of the book. The two authors distinguish organizations on the basis of who benefits from them and they come up with a familiar typology: voluntary associations (members benefit), welfare agencies (clients benefit), business (owners), and government (the public). Vast differences in structure within each type are ignored. Parsons' scheme is a bit more unusual since he distinguishes economic organizations, pattern maintenance organizations (e.g., universities, churches), integrative organizations (hospitals, courts, law firms, political parties), and political organizations (the military, government, some aspects of banking). His highly general comments—e.g., that the military is the most authoritarian, universities the least, and business in between—hardly enlighten us, and the variations in structure within types are, again, enormous. The typology by Gouldner is a replay of the simple distinction between democratic, authoritarian, and laissez-faire leadership.

This suggests that an adequate typology should be based upon organizational characteristics that are conceptually independent of either goals or structure. Size might be one, but it has not proved to have much of an analytical cutting edge, nor has geographic location, age, or physical resources. Organizations have two other characteristics which might provide a basis for a typology: raw materials (things, symbols, or people) which are transformed into outputs through the application of energy; and tasks, or techniques of effecting the transformation. Raw materials vary in a number of ways, such as their uniformity and their stability. Tasks also vary in a number of ways, including the difficulty of learning them or executing them, their simplicity or complexity, whether they are repetitive or not, and whether they are well structured or ill defined.

It is one of the merits of the "technological school," or contingency theory as it has come to be called, that it provides for some independent leverage in constructing typologies because it focuses upon something more or less analytically independent of structure and goals—the tasks or techniques utilized in organizations. ("Technology" is not used here in its commonplace sense of machines or sophisticated devices for achieving high efficiency, as in the term "technologically advanced society," but in its generic sense of the study of techniques or tasks.) Organizations are classified in terms of the kinds of tasks that are performed in them, and this is presumed to affect the structure of the organization (the arrangements of roles for carrying out these tasks) and, to some extent at least, the range of goals that can be achieved. There is no agreement in this rather new school of thought as to how to define technology in any precise way or how to measure it, but the general outlines of a theory are present.

The Basic Argument

In its simplest form, the argument goes like this: When the tasks people perform are well understood, predictable, routine, and repetitive, a bureaucractic structure is the most efficient. Things can be "programmed," in March and Simon's term. Where tasks are not well understood, generally because the "raw material" that each person works on is poorly understood and possibly reactive, recalcitrant, or self-activating, the tasks are nonroutine. Such units or organizations are difficult to bureaucratize. More discretion must be given to lower-level personnel; more interaction is required among personnel at the same level; there must be more emphasis upon experience, "feel," or professionalization. If so, it is difficult to have clear lines of authority, a high degree of division of labor, rules and procedures for everything, exact specification of duties and responsibilities, and so on. There is more craft, or art, or esoteric skills (in the case of professionals) involved.

Organizations, it is assumed, vary considerably in their degree of routinization. One steel mill may be making exotic metals for aerospace purposes; this mill may have high scrap rates because the materials it is working with are poorly understood. Another mill may be turning out galvanized steel for garbage cans with little unpredictability and low scrap rates. One school in a wealthy suburb will try to mold the whole personality; another in the ghetto will try only to maintain order or teach shop. The custodial mental hospital can be routinized; the treatment-oriented one cannot. In all these cases, the advantages of bureaucracy can be realized in the routine situation; the nonroutine organization must pay the considerable price of long periods of personnel training, professional employees, confusion, wasted materials, hit-or-miss efforts, unpredictable outputs, and so on. They charge more.

This is the simplest form of the argument. Actually a number of versions have appeared, stressing different things and constructing more elaborate classification schemes than merely routine and nonroutine.[44] The Woodward scheme proposes three basic models—for

---

[44]A discussion of the work done in this area up through 1966 can be found in the bibliographic essay at the end of Charles Perrow, "A Framework for Comparative Organizational Analysis," *American Sociological Review* 32, no. 2 (April 1967): 194–208. The same issue of that journal contains a sympathetic review and brief summary of the pioneering work of Joan Woodward; see her *Industrial Organization: Theory and Practice* (Oxford, England: Oxford University Press, 1965). Since that article, an important book by Paul Lawrence and Jay Lorsch, *Organization and Environment* (Cambridge, Mass.: Harvard University Press, 1967), has appeared, which deals with the problem of integrating various technologies within a firm. The general theory has been found useful in explaining some findings in welfare organizations in Jerald Hage and Michael Aiken, "Routine Technology, Social Structure, and Organizational Goals," *Administrative Science Quarterly* 14, no. 3 (September 1969): 366–377; and public health departments in Dennis J. Palumbo, "Power and Role Specificity in Organization Theory," *Public Administration Review* 29, no. 3 (May/June 1969): 237–248; Peggy Overton, Rodney Schneck, and C. B. Hazlett, "An Empirical Study of the Technology of Nursing Subunits," *Administrative Science Quarterly* 22:2 (June 1977): 203–219; and industry in general in W. A. Rushing, "Hardness of Material as Related to Division of Labor in Manufacturing Industries," *Administrative Science Quarterly* 13:2 (September 1968): 229–245. James Thompson, a pioneer in this area, has elaborated his early scheme in *Organizations in Action* (New York: McGraw-Hill Book Company, 1967). Measurement and conceptualization problems are examined carefully in Beverly P. Lynch, "An Empirical Assessment of Perrow's Technology Construct," *Administrative Science Quarterly* 19:3 (September 1974): 338–356, as well as in Overton et al., cited above. Some readers have appeared, e.g., Fremont Kast and James Rosenzweig, *Contingency Views of Organization and Management* (Palo Alto: Science Research Associates, 1973). There has been considerable discussion of the issue in connection with the research of the Aston group, mentioned below, but the most serious empirical refutation is found in Lawrence B. Mohr, "Organizational Technology and Organizational Structure," *Administrative Science Quarterly* 16:4 (December 1971): 444–459. Mohr took considerable pains with operationalizing the concept, and while there are problems with the study, it is one of the most careful in the literature, and the most damaging to this viewpoint. It would appear that for

unit and small-batch production processes (custom suits, engineering prototypes), for large-batch, mass, and assembly processes (autos, metal industries), and for continuous process industries (oil, chemicals, candy). The present author has proposed a four-fold typology, later expanded to include other "clusters" of technological types[45] based upon two independent dimensions, the degree of variability and the degree of uncertainty in search procedures. Other versions will no doubt come along.

Unresolved Problems

There are many problems with this recent development in organizational theory. The foremost has been the measurement (and thus the definition) of technology itself. To be pure, and to keep the concept independent of structure, we should focus upon characteristics that are measured independently of human behavior—perhaps the number of items produced per minute, the number of design changes over a period of time, the number of occupational specializations, or the scrap rate. For a number of reasons, this has not proved feasible; organizations vary in these terms independently of what we vaguely mean by technology. Failing here, we should try to focus upon actual human behavior—detailed observations of what is actually done. This, too, has thus far been rather unproductive and prohibitively expensive.[46] A "quick and dirty" method is to ask people about the frequency with which they come across problems for which there is no solution ready at hand, and about which no one else is likely to know much. This has the virtue of being an easy method, and it is applicable to all personnel at all levels in all kinds of organizations (and not just the basic work-flow level such as the production line in industry). But it is rather unreliable since people cannot, or choose not to, give "accurate" answers.[47] It also

---

many public service organizations there are more important things to do than to maximize the fit between technology and structure in the interests of effective goal achievement. See Perrow, "Demystifying Organizations," op. cit.

[45]Perrow, "A Framework for Comparative Organizational Analysis"; Charles Perrow, "The Effect of Technological Change on the Structure of Business Firms," in *Industrial Relations: Contemporary Issues*, B. C. Roberts, ed. (London: The Macmillan Company, 1968), pp. 205–219; and *Organizational Analysis* (Belmont, Calif.: Wadsworth Publishing Co., 1972), chapter 3.

[46]For a detailed and sobering discussion of intensive efforts in both these directions, see Joan Woodward, ed., *Industrial Organization: Behavior and Control* (Oxford, England: Oxford University Press, 1970).

[47]I have used this method in a study of industrial corporations; for a very preliminary report on one aspect of organizations, see Perrow, "Departmental Power and

has a more serious limitation: the measure of technology is confused by the effects of structure. For example, the structure of an organization can generate nonroutineness of tasks, as in one firm where tasks *might* have been highly routinized, but the head of the firm did not allow them to be. He deliberately did not use a bureaucratic model (apparently so as to increase his control by requiring that everything come to him for review), and people experienced much uncertainty in what would normally be routine tasks.[48]

There is also disagreement at present as to whether the technological model should be restricted to the basic work-flow process, allowing us to measure it through fairly "pure" indices such as the proportion of single purpose machines, or whether other aspects of the organization should be included—e.g., sales, personnel, accounting, research and development, industrial relations, and so on.[49] These debates will go on for some time.

But the most serious problem with the current state of the technological view is that it reverts to the old dichotomies, putting the new wine into the same old bottles. By clinging to a routine-non-routine distinction, the technological theories too often place a caricature of Weber in the former and the human relations model in the latter type of organization, and we have a replay of the old social-psychological distinction between initiating structure and consideration. What promises to be a way out of these oversimple dichotomies is in danger of becoming trapped by them. Neither the simple bureaucratic model nor the human relations model is adequate, so a theory which tells us which to use is not all that useful. The work of Joan Woodward does not make this mistake; her insights into such diverse areas as types and degrees of conflict, the role of boards of directors, the conditions under which either research and development, production, or marketing will be the critical function in an organization, and the insightful way she uses the

---

Perspective in Industrial Firms," op. cit., pp. 59–89. Despite problems, the two sets of questions finally used discriminated well among organizations and within organizations.

[48]For a more extensive argument along this important line see John Child, "Organizational Structure, Environment, and Performance: The Role of Strategic Choice," *Sociology* 6:1 (January 1972): 1–22.

[49]David J. Hickson, D. S. Pugh, and Diana C. Pheysey, "Operations Technology and Organizational Structure: An Empirical Reappraisal," *Administrative Science Quarterly* 14, no. 3 (September 1969): 378–397. They restrict the meaning of technology to the work-flow load and, not surprisingly, find that their measure has little to do with other aspects of the organization. Unfortunately this has been cited as evidence that technology has little impact upon structure when only a very narrow definition of technology is applied to only one part of the organization.

distinction between lower and middle management—all these and others suggest the possibility of developing new models as a result of using technology as an independent variable, rather than just trying to find room for old models.[50]

Hopefully, more subtle models of types of organizations will emerge from this effort. The neo-Weberian model we have been discussing, for example, has enough dimensions and room for variations to suggest that there could be more than one variety of routineness. The flavor of improvisation and uncertainty that Burns and Stalker describe for their electronic firms[51] is one kind of nonroutineness that does not have to piggyback all the tenets of the human relations school. Gouldner's description of the organization of gypsum miners sounds like quite another variant of nonroutineness.[52] We may also be able to find systematic differences among organizations in the extent to which levels of the organizations vary in technology. It is possible for lower management, for example, to be quite nonroutine while middle management is routine; the reverse could also hold. Furthermore, while something like research and development is always likely to be more nonroutine than production, there may be large degrees of difference in some firms and only small degrees in others. As Lawrence and Lorsch point out, the communication problems between units with quite dissimilar technologies (or environment, as they call it) can be substantial,[53] and the organizational structure is likely to reflect this.

We still do not have a good model of political organizations at the higher levels of government. For example, the descriptions of the way that President Franklin D. Roosevelt worked suggest a combination of nonroutine tasks and a traditional form of organization that emphasizes loyalty, assigning several people to the same tasks, spying, and so on.[54] This is a reasonably common style of leadership in administrative units with political tasks, and while it is somewhat illuminating to say that these tasks are nonroutine, and that loyalty rather than efficiency takes precedence where political tasks dominate, we still need a more carefully considered model of such types of administration or types of organizations.

---

[50]One reviewer of her book complained that she appeared unaware of the U.S. literature on organizations. It may have been her greatest strength; otherwise, she might have just searched for evidence for bureaucracy and cooperation.

[51]T. Burns and G. M. Stalker, *The Management of Innovation* (New York: Barnes & Noble, 1961).

[52]Gouldner, *Patterns of Industrial Bureaucracy.*

[53]Lawrence and Lorsch, *Organization and Environment,* op. cit.

[54]For a lively summary description of this, see Harold Wilensky, *Organizational Intelligence* (New York: Basic Books, Inc., 1969), pp. 50–53.

"Beyond Bureaucracy"

We should briefly consider two dissents from the view that there are
a variety of technologies and thus a variety of structures appropriate
to the technologies. An extreme one, which seems to have faded in
recent years, argues that routinization is proceeding so fast that
workers will be thrown out of work and we will be left with fully
automated factories and offices, run by a handful of technicians and
scientists. The prediction, so widespread in the early 1960s, proved
to have been premature. Even at the time, responsible journalists
were dissenting from the views of the academics.[55] Management, it
seems clear, is still learning to grapple with the most simple aspects
of the industrial revolution. For example, when General Motors designed a totally new car, the Vega, it built a new plant at Lordstown,
Ohio, to manufacture it. If automation was ever to strike, it should
have struck there, where the gigantic resources of a company richer
than the vast majority of nations on the earth could be utilized.
Indeed, it was heralded as "the very model of automation" at the
time.[56] But aside from a few complex machines, some of which often
broke down, most of the economies in this "breakthrough" consisted
of fuller use of practices pioneered by Henry Ford in the 1920s and
1930s! There were more interchangeable parts for all models, a
reduction in the number of parts, more subassemblies, more
simplified assemblies, a one-piece roof, and finally a basic model
life of five years rather than three. Much of the increased output, to
drive the point home, was the result of a speedup of the assembly
line, not advanced technology, and this provoked a long strike.
There are still no fully automated factories in existence, and the
productivity of American industry continues to rise at the same rate
it has since the beginning of the century, rather than doubling or
trebling its rate as it should if technological change were rapidly
eliminating routine work. Indeed, the proportion of the male
employed work force that is classified as blue collar has declined by
only 13 percent during the long period of technological revolutions
from 1900 to 1969 (from 70 to 57 percent). We are a white-collar
nation largely because of heavy employment of women in lower
white-collar positions and their concentration in education and

---

[55]See the partisan discussion of this issue in Charles E. Silberman, "The Comeback of the Blue-Collar Worker," *Fortune*, February 1965, pp. 153–155ff. and "The
Truth About Automation," *Fortune*, January 1965, pp. 125–127ff. See also, for a very
sobering study of the use and value of computers, Tom Alexander, "Computers Can't
Solve Everything," *Fortune*, October 1969, pp. 126–129ff.

[56]"GM's Mini: The Very Model of Automation," *Business Week*, August 8, 1970, p.
26.

nursing, while it is in industry that the rapid change is supposedly taking place.[57]

A less extreme position is that of those who have heralded the age of nonroutine, "organic," decentralized, professionalized, and democratic organizations designed to withstand extremely rapid technological and environmental changes. This school of thought takes very seriously the technological view that changing tasks have necessitated new structures.

The foremost proponent of this view of increasing nonroutineness in organizations is Warren Bennis.[58] The argument is that organizations, if they are to survive, *must* become decentralized, practice participative management, and be adaptive and responsive to their members. This is not a desideratum, as with some arguments in the human relations school; it is not even the route to increased efficiency and productivity, as with the tenets of that school. It is an absolute imperative for survival, at least for a large number of organizations, and especially the big, glamorous ones on the forefront of scientific and engineering technology.

The imperative stems from (1) the increasing professionalization of management—these men demand responsibility, and bureaucracy is supposed to deny it. But one can have a great deal of responsibility and make a great many decisions without reducing the extent to which the important powers remain in the hands of the top men. General Motors is celebrated in a number of books as a highly decentralized organization, yet decisions as trivial as leg room, and as important as basic styling, body design, advertising, pricing, capital investment, pollution control, and scheduling in factories that assemble cars for several divisions, are not in the division manager's hands. They are made at the top.[59] The division

---

[57]Charles Perrow, "Is Business Really Changing?" *Organizational Dynamics* (Spring 1974): 31–44.

[58]See Warren G. Bennis, *Changing Organizations* (New York: McGraw-Hill Book Company, 1966); Warren G. Bennis and Philip E. Slater, *The Temporary Society* (New York: Harper & Row, Inc., 1968); Warren G. Bennis, "Post-Bureaucratic Leadership," *Trans-action* 6 (July/August 1969): 45–51ff; Victor A. Thompson, *Modern Organizations*, 2nd ed. (University, Ala.: Univ. of Ala. Press, 1977); and Jong S. Jun and William B. Storm, *Tomorrow's Organizations* (Glenview, Ill.: Scott, Foresman & Co., 1973).

[59]The view that General Motors is decentralized is put forth by Peter Drucker, *Concept of the Corporation* (New York: John Day Company, 1972); Alfred A. Chandler, *Strategy and Structure* (Cambridge, Mass.: M.I.T. Press, 1969); Ernest Dale, *The Great Organizers* (New York: McGraw-Hill Book Company, 1971); and of course, Alfred P. Sloan, *My Years with General Motors* (New York: Doubleday & Co., 1972). A close reading of these sources, especially Chandler and Sloan, but also Drucker, will disclose how more and more decisions were removed from the divisions to the corporate headquarters throughout the history of the organization. An unpublished paper by Arthur Kuhn, "Centralization-Decentralization and Control Theory," prepared at

manager is not thereby reduced to the status of a clerk; in an enterprise as large as, say, the Chevrolet division, he has a great deal to do, and the decisions he makes are important ones indeed. But he is not influencing the goals of the organization in any very meaningful sense. General Motors is a highly centralized organization; it just happens to be big and produce a variety of cars, weapons, trucks, locomotives, and so on, so that the density of decision making is correspondingly greater.

(2) Another predicted source of debureaucratization is the increasingly "turbulent" environment,[60] where the very ground is shifting under one's feet because of rapid change and increasing interdependency. Granted that technological and social changes are vastly more frequent today than twenty years ago, it also seems apparent that large organizations are increasingly able to cope with these changes. Through mergers, administered prices, price fixing, cost-plus government contracts, forward integration (where they can go from manufacturing a product to retailing it), backward integration (owning and producing the raw materials and supplies, rather than buying them from an independent organization), domination of foreign markets and sources of raw material, and so on—through all this, business organizations appear to have risen to the challenge.[61] In some respects, the large corporations are more able to deal with a rapidly changing environment today than they were in the past. In the voluntary and welfare sector, there has been much less ability to cope with change, but this is not the showpiece area of the "beyond bureaucracy" viewpoint.

(3) Finally, rapid technological change by itself is supposed to produce new-style democratic organizations. Such changes give more power to the "technostructure" or the middle- and upper-middle-level professionals such as scientists and engineers.[62] We have

---

the School of Business Administration, University of California, Berkeley, California, documents the centralization extensively. The myth of decentralization is, of course, a valuable public relations device for this most giant of all corporations, and academics have embraced it willingly.

[60]F. E. Emery and E. L. Trist, "The Causal Texture of Organizational Environments," in *Readings in Organization Theory—A Behavioral Approach*, ed. Walter A. Hill and Douglas Egan (Boston: Allyn and Bacon, 1966), pp. 435–447. As Bennis says, "The real *coup de grace* to bureaucracy has come as much from the turbulent environment as from its incorrect assumptions about human beings." Bennis and Slater, *The Temporary Society*, p. 67.

[61]For a melancholy assessment of this ability see Walter Adams, "Competition, Monopoly, and Planning" in *American Society, Inc.*, ed. Maurice Zeitlin (Chicago: Markham Publishing Company, 1970), pp. 241–248; and Staff Report of the Federal Trade Commission, *Economic Report on Corporate Mergers* (Washington, D.C.: U.S. Government Printing Office, 1969).

[62]These professionals will join with the managers, *and* with academicians, ar-

already argued, in Chapter 1, that the distinction between the professional and the lowly manager is suspect, and that both readily embrace the goals of the organization. I know of no evidence that they are creating any revolutions within organizations. The heady talk in the late 1960s about relevancy, responsiveness, and public interest work has not perceptibly changed organizations. What changes there have been seem to have come from isolated "whistle-blowers" such as A. Ernest Fitzgerald who refused to knuckle under to his Pentagon bosses in the matter of massive overruns, from new organizations such as Common Cause and new environmental groups, and from new legislation, such as the incredibly important Freedom of Information Act.

Perhaps the most convincing grounds upon which to question this new view of organizations is the matter of "after problem solving, what?" The evidence for the new view comes from the increasing use of project groups in industrial organizations. These are, it is quite true, often forced upon the organization by the need to respond much more quickly to the turbulent environment (and thus control it). They consist of temporary groups of people drawn from different departments and different levels in the organization according to their relevance to the problem at hand—for example, designing a new steel, as we described in Chapter 1. Once the problem is solved, the group dissolves and new groups are formed around new problems. Bureaucracy, with its hierarchy, rules, routine, and departmental base, is foreign to this form of operation.

But once the problem is solved, what then? Is the production, sales, or accounting task then turned over to a robot or a fully automated assembly line? Hardly. The production process is altered to accommodate the new decisions and knowledge, and then it resumes its routine function; all the people manning it—including

---

gues Bennis. "The intellectual and the manager have only recently come out of hiding and recognized the enormous possibilities of joint ventures." Bennis and Slater, *The Temporary Society*, p. 62. Bennis does admit at one point that the bureaucratic structure was "an eminently suitable social arrangement for routinized tasks" (Ibid., p. 9), but all that is changed now, and he never returns to this possibility. Note the new ethic of work that goes beyond the last stage of cooperation described by Bendix and discussed in Chapter Two of ibid., p. 14: "For now we require organic-adaptive systems as structures of freedom to permit the expression of play and imagination and to exploit the new pleasure of work." In a more recent article Bennis has substantially revised his optimistic predictions. However, his pessimism stems from different sources than our analysis. Rather than viewing the issue as one of control by leaders who can shape environments, he sees the chance of democratic organizations fading because of insurgency in society and the breakdown in established (and thus elitist) values. See Warren Bennis, "A Funny Thing Happened on the Way to the Future," *American Psychologist* 25 (June 1970): pp. 595–608.

some of the members of this temporary group—continue their appointed rounds. A few engineers and scientists or computer experts may, in fact, be floating pools of expertise responsible for setting up new routines, but that is just what they do—set up new routines for the mass of employees to follow.

I think that it is the resurrection of the viability of the bureaucratic model, afforded by the work of March and Simon, among others, and further extended by the development of the technological school, that makes it possible to see the problem in this light. Bennis, Victor Thompson, and others do admit, of course, that some organizations will best remain bureaucratized; but they do not see the extent to which routine pervades all organizations and thus makes a considerable degree of bureaucracy necessary even in the space-age organizations that are supposed to save us from authoritarianism. The "beyond bureaucracy" school is still the science-fiction wing of organizational theory, and like all science-fiction literature, it is highly moralistic. In contrast to the science-fiction novelists though, these men are vastly more optimistic and committed to the idea that in organizations men will find themselves and their freedom.

In my judgment, most organizations are, and will continue to be, moderately routine in terms of the tasks of most of the salaried and hourly work force. They are neither so routine as to permit full automation, nor so nonroutine as to permit the decentralization of ends and democracy.[63] As the service sector expands as disposable income and environmental ravage goes up, service organizations will also become more and more rationalized and routinized. If moderate routineness continues to characterize almost all large organizations in our society and most of the small ones, bureaucracy, with its centralized power in the hands of a few, will remain the dominant mode of organization. The only change will be that those few will command ever greater resources and increasing political, social, and economic power. If we should fear large, bureaucratic organizations, as I shall argue in the next chapter, we will not be saved from their selfish ravages by believing that they are disappearing, to be replaced by highly decentralized, problem-solving, profession-loaded organizations concerned with a responsible approach to society's multiplying social problems.

---

[63]I have argued elsewhere that the issue of democracy does not arise in organizations, even voluntary associations, except for small expressive groups. Charles Perrow, "Members as a Resource in Voluntary Associations," in *Organizations and Clients*, ed. William Rosengren and Mark Lefton (Columbus, Ohio: Charles E. Merrill Publishing Co., 1970), pp. 93–116.

SUMMARY

This chapter has sought to bring the bureaucratic model up-to-date. It does not contradict the description we gave in the first chapter, but it has sought to lay out more systematically some of the aspects of bureaucracy that Weber neglected or assumed. The contribution of the structural half of March and Simon's *Organizations* and parts of Simon's *Administrative Behavior* has not been to understand the organization as a problem in social psychology but as a problem in unobtrusive control through recognizing the importance of shaping the premises of decisions. The Weberian model, with its simple reliance upon a few formal properties, gains in both strength and complexity thereby. The contribution of Cyert and March, in their *Behavioral Theory of the Firm*, initially presented in March's article on the organization as a political coalition,[64] was to accommodate the reality of group conflict to the neo-Weberian model. It complicates things further. Although it does not deny the reality of control from the top, it does recognize the difficulty of that control more than Weber was wont to do.

Finally, the technological school has argued for the reality and the efficiency of the bureaucratic model by distinguishing it from other models. Organizational structure varies with the type of work done. A fundamental fact about organizations is that they do work; they transform raw materials into acceptable outputs. The characteristics of this work process will tell us more about the structure and function of the organization than the psychological characteristics of the members, their wants, motives, and drives. And it will tell us more than we can learn from the type of output produced (ashtrays, education, rehabilitation of delinquents). It will predict to structure. Not completely, and certainly not always. Goals can influence structure, which can then influence the type of technology that will be adapted. An executive may choose to organize nonroutine work as if it were routine, or routine work as if it were nonroutine. In people-changing organizations, he may define the way the raw material is to be perceived, and thus select the technology.[65] But in the long run and over a sample of a large number of organizations, these and other sources of variability should wash out. By and large, it is assumed the technology must fit the structure, or the organization will pay a heavy price in terms of efficiency.

But in all this, while we have extended and complicated the simple bureaucratic model, we still have not addressed ourselves to

---

[64]James G. March, "The Business Firm as a Political Coalition," *Journal of Politics* 24 (1962): 662–678.

[65]Child, "Strategic Choice," op. cit.

the dominant preoccupation of organizational theory in the late 1960s—the environment. With a few exceptions, we have treated the environment as "given" and unproblematical. Furthermore, we have still not given adequate consideration to the possibility that organizations may not be the products of technology and a structure adapted to it, ruled over by a few men who use them as tools. They may be things that take on a life of their own—organic entities or "natural systems" in their own right, going their own way and generating leaders who will follow that way. Here we confront a still more serious challenge to the tool view and the bureaucratic model, with which even a neo-Weberian version cannot easily cope. We turn to it in the next chapter.

5

The Institutional School

ELEMENTS OF THE MODEL

Of all the schools of thought considered in this book, the institutional school is the closest to a truly sociological view of organizations. It combines much of the best, and some of the worst, of sociology as it existed in the 1950s and the 1960s. Its major conceptual framework is that of structural-functionalism, indicating that functions determine the structure of organizations and that structures can be understood by analyzing their functions. A great deal has been written about the structural-functional school,[1] the dominant one in sociology. We will only highlight a few points as they apply to organizational theory. (Though not exclusively derived from the writings of Philip Selznick, the school is best represented by his works; his essay *Leadership in Administration*, will be referred to without specific page citations in this section.[2])

---

[1] N. J. Demerath, III and Richard A. Peterson, eds., *Systems Change and Conflict* (New York: The Free Press, 1967).

[2] Selznick's first two articles present the major preoccupations that the later books revolve about. See "An Approach to a Theory of Bureaucracy," *American Sociological Review* 8 (1943): 47–54; and "Foundations of a Theory of Organizations," *American Sociological Review* 13 (1948): 25–35. This was followed by an impressive case study, *TVA and the Grass Roots* (Berkeley and Los Angeles: University of California Press, 1949; New York: Harper & Row, Inc., 1965), that still remains a classic in that tradition. (The newer edition has a valuable preface.) Subsequently, he analyzed the Communist party under the apt title, *The Organizational Weapon: A Study of Bolshevik Strategy and Tactics* (New York: McGraw-Hill Book Company, 1952). Though the political stance of Chapter Seven of this book is dated today, this volume has not received the recognition it deserves. Organizations are, or can be, weapons. This

Natural and Organic Systems

For institutional analysis, the injunction is to analyze the whole organization. To see it as a whole is to do justice to its "organic" character. Specific processes are, of course, analyzed in detail, but it is the nesting of these processes into the whole that gives them meaning. To wrench a process such as leadership or communication free of a specific organization without considering how it is organically linked to the rest of the organization is to drain it of meaning.

The emphasis upon wholes implies considerable uniqueness about organizations, limiting our ability to focus only upon specific processes or to survey a large number of organizations searching, say, for evidence regarding propositions on hierarchy or control. The implied injunction, then, is to do case studies. This is the forte of the institutional school—the carefully documented and analyzed case study. Comparative analysis is generally restricted to comparisons of case studies.

Because the interchange of structure and function goes on over time, a "natural history" of an organization is needed. We cannot understand current crises or competencies without seeing how they were shaped. The present is rooted in the past; no organization (and no man) is free to act as if the situation were *de novo* and the world a set of discrete opportunities ready to be seized upon at will. All kinds of structural restraints embedded in the past limit freedom. A "natural history" implies natural forces: organizations as living entities grow in natural ways. The discovery of these forces, as in biology or psychoanalysis, will yield understanding.

Thus, the evolving accommodations and dependencies of an adult education program to the demands of its clients eventually deny it freedom to control standards.[3] The lack of standards leads to trivial programs of flower arrangements and fly tying. They become the mode of survival, not because anyone planned them, but because of the "drift" of the organization responding to enrollment pressures.

The idea of an organic, growing, declining, evolving whole, with a natural history, points up the importance (and danger) of

---

was followed by a short work, *Leadership in Administration* (New York: Harper & Row, Inc., 1957). This rewarding work was written for businessmen as much as anyone, but it provides a highly literate statement of his major themes and good summaries of his earlier books. His most recent volume, continuing his line of analysis but turning toward the role of law in society, is *Law, Society and Industrial Justice* (New York: Russell Sage Foundation, 1970).

[3]Burton Clark, *Adult Education in Transition* (Berkeley: University of California Press, 1956).

unplanned adaptations and changes. Unplanned aspects of organizations are those which are subject to little administrative control and are often not even noticed until their effects are quite evident, if even then. They are revealed by analyzing how the structure responded to certain processes that were dictated by basic "needs" or functions. Natural forces work their ways quietly, and it is often not until too late that the organization discovers, for example, that its social base in the community—the groups that supply its personnel, receive its services, provide its legitimacy—is "eroded."

A church may be aware that its neighborhood is "deteriorating" and that it must acquire land for larger parking lots so that the constituents can drive to religious services. But the implications are only slowly grasped because normal activities continue as before. On the one hand, the church does nothing to stem the transition; on the other hand, it fails to adapt to the new social base by changing its religious services, its pastoral counseling, and its source of funds.

The rise of administrative tasks and coordination of complex specialties leads the hospital to search for a new director among those with training in hospital administration. It does not fully anticipate that this will challenge the authority of the medical staff and perhaps reshape the hospital's goals and "character"—for example, the types of patients it will receive, sources of funds, involvement with other health programs, building programs, and medical specialties.[4]

As corporations grow ever larger and seek security and profits through mergers and expansion, the financial problems become more visible. The route to the top changes: it is less through sales and more often through finance—reached by someone who can master the complexities of funding, mergers, and capital improvements. But then the corporation is likely to lose its ability to search out new markets and make rapid internal adjustments to new technology and markets; it is also less likely to allow waste and inefficiency in the transition periods so as to insure adaptability. Instead, cost accounting, rationalization, predictability, and the careful husbanding of resources take over. All this was not planned; it was a consequence of changing the line of succession.

The hospital allows rates to rise so that it can finance expensive treatments for a few exotic cases and care for improverished patients and for long-term illnesses. But proprietary hospitals (those that operate for a profit, and are usually owned by a group of physicians or a franchising chain) spring up and take the profitable cases, charging less. The profit-making nursing homes skim off the

---

[4]Charles Perrow, "Goals and Power Structures," in *The Hospital in Modern Society*, ed. Eliot Freidson (New York: The Free Press, 1963), pp. 112–146.

long-term cases that need little care. The voluntary hospital is left with the complex, expensive cases that need expensive stand-by facilities, the charity cases, and the long-term patients who require expensive care. The voluntary hospitals did not plan it that way; they were using the routine cases to subsidize the others, and after a time their situation became impossible.[5] In these examples, the un-planned nature of organizational life and the importance of its natural history is revealed.

The Exposé Tradition

Finally, this school is of the "exposé" variety. In keeping with a general sociological tradition, it shows that "things are not as they seem." The sociologist, according to this view, looks beneath the obvious surface that preoccupies the other social sciences. He looks at the nonpolitical aspects of political behavior, the noneconomic aspects of economic behavior, and so on. The explanation for politi-cal behavior is not in the formalities of constitutions and elections, but in the submerged part of the iceberg—ethnic identity, social class, generational experiences, and population changes. The explanation for organizational behavior is not primarily in the for-mal structure of the organization, the announcements of goals and purposes, the output of goods and services. It lies also in the myriad of subterranean processes of informal groups, conflicts between groups, recruitment policies, dependencies upon outside groups and constituencies, the striving for prestige, community values, the local community power structure, and legal institutions.

In the process of uncovering these realities of social systems, an institutional analysis exposes to scrutiny all sorts of deviations from the "obvious." Dalton belongs here, with his contrast of the formal and informal chart, as does Gouldner with his description of the interdependencies of the gypsum plant and the local community with its insular values (see Chapter 1). But even more representative than this is the exposure of policy matters. The organization is tan-gled in a web of relationships that prevent it from fulfilling its real goals, and we can see how it deviates by examining this web. The institutional school is preoccupied with values, and especially the way values are weakened or subverted through organizational pro-cesses. Let us look at some examples from the literature.

The Tennessee Valley Authority (TVA), the first (and only) exten-sive flirtation in recent times with socialist programs in the United

---

[5]For two discussions of these kinds of problems, see Arthur Owens, "Can the Profit Motive Save Our Hospitals?" *Medical Economics* (March 30, 1970): 77–111; and "Power to the Coalitions," *Modern Hospital* (April 1970): 39–40d.

States, was established in the late 1930s to produce power, manufacture fertilizer, control flooding, increase the utility of waterways
(by building ports and widening channels), and build dams. Aside
from these commercial activities, it was also to preserve forests and
carry out reforestation, help farmers (especially the poor ones), and
develop recreation areas. Philip Selznick's study of the TVA[6] found
that its doctrine of grass-roots involvement and control in the recreation, forestation, and farming programs led to powerful local and
national interests achieving control of the agency and subverting
these goals. The U.S. Department of Agriculture, the Farm Bureau
Federation, the local land grant colleges and universities, the ag-
ricultural extension workers and county agents, and the local political and business leaders "co-opted" the program.[7] They took it over
by placing their representatives within the relevant branches of the
TVA so as to control policy. As a consequence, all the programs
suffered. The poor farmers did not get aid or services, only the
better-off ones; some recreation areas were given over to private
business which destroyed their natural beauty; forests could not be
saved from the lumber industry; and so on. By paying this price at
the local level, the TVA was able, presumably, to forestall more
intense attacks and opposition to the economic program (flood control, power, fertilizer, etc.) at the national level. The organization
adjusted to its environment and was changed in the process.
Selznick implies that such an accommodation was the only feasible
one; it helped save the major programs.

In Sheldon Messinger's analysis of an old-age pressure group
formed in the 1930s, the Townsend organization, he shows how the
organization managed to stay alive by transforming its political goal
of increased support for the aged through a radical economic plan
into social goals of fellowship and card playing and fiscal goals of
selling vitamins and patent medicines to its members.[8] The unanticipated consequence of fund-raising techniques based upon selling items, rather than political programs, was to turn the organization into a social club. The changing social and political scene also,
of course, produced a change in goals. In a somewhat similar vein,
Joseph Gusfield shows how the Women's Christian Temperance
Union (WCTU) had to abandon its attack upon drinking, per se, after
prohibition was repealed and change to an attack upon middle-

---

[6]Selznick, *TVA and the Grass Roots.*

[7]On the ambiguity of the concept of co-optation, see James L. Price, "Continuity
in Social Research: TVA and the Grass Roots," *Pacific Sociological Review* 1, no. 2
(Fall 1958): 63–68.

[8]Sheldon L. Messinger, "Organizational Transformation: A Case Study of Declining Social Movement," *American Sociological Review* 20 (1955): 3–10.

class mores and life-styles in general, in order to serve the needs of its members.[9] Mayer Zald outlines how the Young Men's Christian Association (YMCA) changed from helping poor migrants from the farm or from abroad, who found the city a fearsome experience, to providing recreation for middle-class suburban youths.[10] The Christian ethics of the early period, designed to sustain the faith of helpless people, gave way to a bland ethic of the American way of life; the practical help and training changed from information and techniques for survival in the urban jungle to physical culture and recreation for youths and adults with leisure time on their hands. In both cases, the organization survived the environmental changes and found a new mission.

Burton Clark's study of a junior college shows that because of the low ability of the students, the college in question was designed to actually provide a repeat of the eleventh and twelfth grades of high school and some vocational training.[11] But the students saw success in terms of academic programs which would allow them to transfer, after two years, to a regular four-year college. Neither teachers (who were drawn largely from high schools and local businesses and industry) nor students were equipped to deal with academic programs, so devices were developed to "cool out the mark"—underworld jargon for techniques to convince the victim of a con game that he has not been conned, or at least that he had better not report it. Extensive regulations and counseling devices had to be provided to convince the students that they should take remedial English and sheet metal work. Clark also shows how the remedial and vocational nature of the college—in San Jose, California—was guaranteed by the web of organizations in the community that set up and controlled it.

The Community Chest of Indianapolis, ostensibly rationalizing fund-raising activities by minimizing the inconvenience of multiple fund drives and increasing their efficiency, is analyzed as an occupying army by John Seeley et al.[12] According to this view, it dictated agency goals on the basis of fund-raising ability; established fund-raising devices which resulted in the working class

---

[9]Joseph R. Gusfield, "Social Structure and Moral Reform: A Study of the Women's Christian Temperance Union," *American Journal of Sociology* 61 (1955): 221–232.

[10]Mayer N. Zald and Robert Ash, "Social Movement Organizations: Growth, Decay and Change," *Social Forces* 44, no. 3 (March 1966): 327–341; Mayer N. Zald and Patricia Denton, "From Evangelism to General Service: The Transformation of the YMCA," *Administrative Science Quarterly* 8, no. 2 (September 1963): 214–234.

[11]Burton R. Clark, *The Open Door College: A Case Study* (New York: McGraw-Hill Book Company, 1960).

[12]John R. Seeley, Bulford H. Junker, and R. Wallace Jones, Jr., *Community Chest* (Toronto: University of Toronto Press, 1957).

making heavy contributions to support essentially middle-class agencies (the Y's, Scouts) rather than the poor; and used the agency as a testing and training ground for middle-level executives in business.

Charles Perrow shows how the research efforts of a private, voluntary hospital were subverted by the demands of the board of directors and other donors for publicity about the research.[13] As the director of the hospital indicated, the donors gave the money for the fancy, elaborate electronic gadgetry in order to see it well publicized in national magazines. The researchers, however, resisted such publicity because it was not accurate, would alienate the federal agencies that were providing the bulk of the enormous sums of research money, and would swamp the unit, designed only to do research, with requests for treatment. In another example, the writer shows how the outpatient department of the hospital existed largely as a device for giving evidence of the extensive charity activities of the hospital while actually it suffered from administrative neglect, inadequate staffing, poor quarters and facilities, and a highly selective intake system.[14]

Robert Scott analyzed agencies that seek to rehabilitate the blind.[15] He found that while the vast majority of the blind are the aged or those severely handicapped in other ways, the agencies pay little attention to these. Instead, they prefer the "desirable" blind—young people who have some employment prospects—because it is easier to raise money for these. They touch the hearts of the softhearted and promise economic returns for the hardhearted. However, there are not enough desirable blind to go around, so agencies have to compete with one another to get clients. They then attempt to keep the blind dependent upon the agency rather than make them independent, self-supporting members of society—the professed goal.

David Sudnow took a look at the court procedures in a large metropolitan area on the West Coast and found that hearing and sentencing procedures for persons accused of crimes resembled a mass-production line.[16] The prosecutor and the defense lawyer (court appointed) routinely classified defendants on the basis of superficial evidence, convinced the defendants that they should plead guilty to charges less severe than the ones they had been arrested

---

[13]Charles Perrow, "Organizational Prestige: Some Functions and Dysfunctions," *American Journal of Sociology* 66, no. 4 (January 1961): 335–341.

[14]Perrow, "Goals and Power Structures."

[15]Robert A. Scott, "The Selection of Clients by Social Welfare Agencies: The Case of the Blind," *Social Problems* 14, no. 3 (Winter 1967): 248–257.

[16]David Sudnow, "Normal Crimes," *Social Problems* 12, no. 3 (Winter 1964): 255–275.

for, and had an understanding with the judge for the routine and expeditious processing of these pleas. Each defendant was passed from defense attorney to defense attorney as he traveled from station to station in the procedure; the truth of the charge was not examined or even considered very relevant. If a defendant objected and wanted to plead not guilty, he was shunted off to a special track where a special group of prosecutors took over the case with vengeance. In this way, the interests of efficiency and routinization were served, though the connection with "justice" was remote. Similar analyses have been made of prisons, reform schools, and, of course, custodial mental hospitals.[17]

In Gary Wamsley's study of the Selective Service system in mid-1960, he paid particular attention to the doctrine of decentralization—the grass-roots involvement of little groups of neighbors.[18] This gave enormous legitimacy to an enterprise that had been contested by riots and violence throughout our nation's history. It also buried the decision-making process and the decision rules in the homely ambience of volunteer citizens doing their best at what was, inevitably, a distasteful job. In reality, Wamsley shows, the system was highly centralized in its basic tenets, giving only trivial leeway (and considerable anxiety and bewilderment in the process) to the local boards. These boards were highly homogeneous—they consisted mainly of older veterans of past wars who glorified their experience, were active Legionnaires, and were overwhelmingly middle-class in character—while the draftees were lower class. Those lower-class individuals who appealed their cases to the board were lectured on the virtues of military life and often went away feeling, as did the board, that military life was best for them after all; middle-class youths found more routine methods of escape.

---

[17]For prisons, see Donald R. Cressey, "Achievement of an Unstated Organizational Goal: An Observation on Prisons," *Pacific Sociological Review* 1 (1958): 43–49; and Gresham M. Sykes, *The Society of Captives: A Study of a Maximum Security Prison* (Princeton, N.J.: Princeton University Press, 1971). For reform schools, see Mayer N. Zald, "The Correctional Institution for Juvenile Offenders: An Analysis of Organizational 'Character'," *Social Problems* 8, no. 1 (Summer 1960): 57–67; and David Street, Robert Vinter, and Charles Perrow, *Organizations for Treatment* (New York: The Free Press, 1966). For mental hospitals, see the review of the literature in Charles Perrow, "Hospitals: Technology, Goals, and Structure," in *Handbook of Organizations*, chapter 22, ed. James March (Chicago: Rand McNally & Company, 1965), pp. 910–971. For a basic work, and one of the most perceptive, on the "underlife" of institutions, see Erving Goffman, *Asylums* (New York: Doubleday & Company, 1961).

[18]Gary L. Wamsley, *Selective Service and a Changing America* (Columbus, Ohio: Charles E. Merrill Publishing Company, 1969); James W. Davis, Jr., and Kenneth M. Dolbeare, *Little Groups of Neighbors: The Selective Service System* (Chicago: Markham Publishing Company, 1968).

Philippe Nonet's detailed historical study of the activities of the California Industrial Accident Commission during the first half of this century illustrates the fate of idealism (representing the interests of workers who have been injured on the job) when it has to contend with powerful organizations—the insurance carriers and the employees on the one hand, and the large unions on the other hand.[19] Between the two of them, the unorganized worker became unprotected, and the commission's policy of industrial justice and welfare gave way to narrow legalism and professional self-protection.

These examples suggest some of the "exposé" character of this body of literature. The major message is that the organization has sold out its goals in order to survive or grow. The values that should have been institutionalized have been undermined by organizational processes. The grandfather of this approach was Robert Michels, who formulated the "iron law of oligarchy," which suggested that a few leaders will inevitably dominate even supposedly democratic political organizations and will put their interest in preserving the organization and their leadership of it ahead of the interests of the members.[20]

But exposé of this sort is not a necessary aspect of the institutional school; there is also guarded optimism about the beneficent effects of natural processes. Morris Janowitz, for example, shows how the military in the late 1950s was increasingly coming under civilian control; increasingly (though not greatly) concerned with economic and political strategies rather than hydrogen wars; increasingly sophisticated and committed to democratic policies and civilian control.[21] The social base from which it recruited officers had been the southern middle class. Recruitment into the officer corps was now geographically more widespread (thus minimizing the tradition of violence that characterizes the South), and more and more officers had technical training in places other than military academies. The routes to the top were now through innovative and novel assignments and activities (foreign advisory posts, weapons analysis) rather than heroic postures in wartime. Sophisticated political liaison men were counseling restraint. The complexity of the weapons systems gave power to what might be called, after Galbraith,[22] a military "technostructure" rather than to right-wing

[19]Philippe Nonet, *Administrative Justice: Advocacy and Change in Government Agencies* (New York: Russell Sage Foundation, 1969).

[20]Robert Michels, *Political Parties* (New York: The Free Press, 1966), originally published in 1915.

[21]Morris Janowitz, *The Professional Soldier* (New York: The Free Press, 1960).

[22]John Kenneth Galbraith, *The New Industrial State*, 2nd ed. (Boston: Houghton Mifflin Company, 1971).

generals. Thus, without deliberate planning or even conscious awareness, broad social forces were changing the character of the military establishment. (That all these changes need not mean more civilian control or less emphasis upon atomic destruction is clear in retrospect. The military built a bridge with powerful industrial and economic interests, intensified the political role of the military abroad, made its domestic surveillance machinery and domestic intervention more effective, deepened its ties with the more conservative elements of Congress, and, with the CIA, exercised considerable power over President Kennedy with regard to the Bay of Pigs invasion and over Presidents Kennedy, Johnson, and Nixon with regard to Vietnam and Southeast Asia.[23])

CONTRIBUTIONS

The emphasis upon actual organizations with histories and functions in society, and existing in a variety of sectors that we all know of, makes the institutional school's output the most fascinating of any in organizational analysis. After the arid and dense forest of two-variable propositions in the first part of March and Simon,[24] the inventories of hypotheses about leadership,[25] and the axiomatic edifice of Jerald Hage,[26] it is a pleasure to read about a real organization confronting real problems in real time and space. But what does this school contribute to organizational theory beyond a few concepts such as co-optation and precarious goals?

The institutional school's main contribution, I feel, lies in three areas. First, the emphasis upon the organization as a whole forces upon us a conception of the variety of organizations. Not a hopeless variety such that every organization is unique (which it is, of course, in the ultimate sense, even as every man is unique), but a sense that there are basic characteristics of organizations that must be taken

---

[23]Several books have appeared recently documenting these changes. See, for example, Richard Barnet, *The Economy of Death* (New York: Atheneum House, Inc., 1969); Seymour Melman, *Pentagon Capitalism: The Political Economy of War* (New York: McGraw-Hill Book Company, 1970); and Gabriel Kolko, *The Roots of American Foreign Policy* (Boston: The Beacon Press, 1970).

[24]James G. March and Herbert A. Simon, *Organizations* (New York: John Wiley & Sons, Inc., 1958).

[25]Philip B. Applewhite, *Organizational Behavior* (Englewood Cliffs, N.J.: Prentice-Hall, Inc., 1965).

[26]Jerald T. Hage, "An Axiomatic Theory of Organizations," *Administrative Science Quarterly* 10, no. 3 (December 1965): 289–320. See also the comment by Allen Barton and Patricia Ferman, *Administrative Science Quarterly* 11, no. 1 (June 1966), and the reply by Jerald T. Hage in the same issue.

into account, and these can lead, though they have not as yet, to a classification scheme for specific purposes. For example, some organizations are highly dependent upon the goodwill of powerful elites, others have considerable autonomy, and still others exist in a vacuum of autonomy without power. The Community Chest and the San Jose Junior College are dependent; no analysis of leadership style, technology, or Weberian bureaucracy can neglect this. Large business and industrial organizations are largely autonomous, and for that reason leadership processes are presumably different, technology has more leeway, and bureaucratization is essential for efficiency. Prisons, mental hospitals, and many small welfare agencies[27] exist to show that *something* is being done about some problems, but few care just what it is or how effective it is; those who control the organization's resources (legislators, religious boards, etc.) care only that the "something" should not involve scandals and should not cost too much. Here again, the environment for leadership, technology, and structure will be different, and inventories, elegant formal theories,[28] and so on may miss the point. For this nascent emphasis, we can thank the institutional school; it keeps reminding us how widely organizations differ and generates broad bases to classify them. (One such base—the distinction between organizations and institutions—will be discussed shortly.)

Second, the institutional theory points to the real possibility that at least some organizations do take on a life of their own, irrespective of the desires of those presumably in control. All organizations do so to some extent, presumably, but for some this is the dominant fact. The matter has not been explored empirically at all, nor has it even been the subject of much speculation (beyond Selznick's distinction between organizations and institutions). But, clearly, important consequences for theory, operationalizations, and the conception of organizations in society will stem from a scholar's disposition to treat organization as primarily tools, or as primarily things-in-themselves. It makes a difference, for example, if the Department of Defense is seen as a tool of powerful economic elites in our society, protecting their foreign investments, financing their research and development, providing plants and machinery, absorbing surplus productivity, and protecting inefficient organizations such as Lockheed or the Penn-Central railroad when they are in trouble, or whether it is seen as a gigantic Leviathan, consuming resources to satisfy its own appetite, setting foreign policies in its

---

[27]John Maniha and Charles Perrow, "The Reluctant Organization and the Aggressive Environment," *Administrative Science Quarterly* 10, no. 2 (September 1965): 238–257.

[28]Peter Blau, "A Formal Theory of Differentiation in Organizations," *American Sociological Review* 35, no. 2 (April 1970): 201–218.

own commanding interest in growth and power, and pursuing a war long after the business elites had wearied of it. The first view is more or less held by Gabriel Kolko in his book *The Roots of American Foreign Policy;* the second is closer to Seymour Melman's view in his book *Pentagon Capitalism: The Political Economy of War.*[29] The fear of the Pentagon is present in both cases, of course, but if one were to try to control this colossus, which is bigger in financial terms than all but a few countries of the world, it would make considerable difference which view was held. The institutional school argues persuasively for the possibility of the latter view, seeing organizations as taking on a life of their own.

The major area of contribution of the institutional school must surely be the emphasis upon the environment. No other model of organizations has taken the environment into account as much as the institutional model. Of course, Weber saw organizational forms as deeply rooted in the social structure, and as part of society, organizations could not help but be so rooted. The progressive rationalization of life, the supremacy of rational-legal authority over traditional authority was the consequence of capitalism and its bureaucratic organizations, of the state bureaucracy, and of the bureaucratic political, educational, and voluntary associations.[30]

But the institutional school has detailed, for specific organizations and their recent history, the close interaction of organizations and their environments. Some, such as the WCTU or the Townsend organization, are fading daguerreotypes of a bygone age; others, such as the YMCA or the sects analyzed by S. D. Clark,[31] change and flourish with the times. Most are constantly adopting and improvising to keep afloat and to find goals and values that are consistent with their basic dependencies—sources of financial support, legitimacy, personnel, and technologies. No clear "theory" has emerged from this effort, just as no clear theory has emerged which distinguishes types of organizations; it may be some time before we have further clarification.

---

[29]Gabriel Kolko, *Roots of American Foreign Policy* and Seymour Melman, *Pentagon Capitalism.* Melman's empirical evidence is far stronger than Kolko's hasty essay. Melman's position is announced at the outset: The Defense Department's "main characteristics are institutionally specific and therefore substantially independent of its chief of the moment. The effects of its operations are independent of the intention of its architects, and may even have been unforeseen by them." Pp. 1–2.

[30]Another "grand theorist," Joseph Schumpeter, dealt with many of the same themes as Weber, and his *Capitalism, Socialism and Democracy* (New York: Harper & Row, Inc., 1950) is still exciting reading today. The most brilliant essay on organizations and environment is Arthur Stinchcombe, "Social Structure and Environment," in *Handbook of Organizations,* pp. 142–193.

[31]S. D. Clark, *The Church and Sect in Canada* (Toronto: University of Toronto Press, 1948), pp. 381–429.

But what kind of theories would emerge? What are the underlying assumptions that would guide them? How would they help us to see how organizations shape our lives and our world, set our priorities, define our sense of what is possible and what is desirable? In this respect, I think, the area of institutional analysis reflects in part what is worst about sociology. It is still tied to the enfeebling assumptions of structural-functional theory and is unlikely to squarely face up to the fact of organizational power in an organization society. To analyze this school in these terms, we must turn to its most important innovator and persuasive spokesman, Philip Selznick.

ORGANIZATIONS AND INSTITUTIONS

Basic to Selznick's view of organizations is the distinction between the rational, means-oriented, efficiency-guided process of administration and the value-laden, adaptive, responsive process of institutionalization.[32] Some organizations are merely organizations—rational tools in which there is little personal investment and which can be cast aside without regret. Others become institutionalized. They take on a distinctive character; they become prized in and of themselves, not merely for the goods or services they grind out. People build their lives around them, identify with them, become dependent upon them. The process of institutionalization is the process of organic growth, wherein the organization adapts to the strivings of internal groups and the values of the external society. Selznick says that the administrative leader becomes a statesman when he uses his creative abilities to recognize and guide this process.

The distinction is an attractive one. We can all recognize organizations that have become valued for their own sakes and whose disappearance or even drastic change would have more effect upon members and the public than would a loss of jobs. Universities are seen in this light when they are under attack; the Marine Corps has such a halo surrounding it; the disappearance of a newspaper is treated in this fashion; even local businesses become prized as familiar, stable resources and depositories of community values. Furthermore, the process of institutionalization is a

---

[32]In original form, it is a contrast of the "economy" of an organization and its institutional aspects. See Selznick, "Foundations of a Theory of Organizations." In *Leadership in Administration* it is a contrast of the degree of institutionalization. Those with less precise goals, for example, are more open to institutionalization (*Leadership*, pp. 5–6, 16.)

familiar theme of sociology, and the insights of the structural-functional school are tailored to its analysis. Finally, the image of a mechanical, engineered organization, impersonal and disposable, is an unattractive one.[33]

But the distinction needs to be questioned. Selznick puts forth a more complex view of types of organizations. Besides the distinction between the organization and the institution, he implicitly distinguishes the inflexible, dedicated, unswerving organization, deriving its goals from its participants, from the flexible, adaptive, outward-looking organization—the one impregnated with the values of the community. This is not a repeat of the earlier distinction, for institutions, too, can be inflexible. One of the major tasks of the institutional leader is to weld the members of the organization into a "committed polity," with a high sense of identity, purpose, and commitment. This would seem to imply an inflexible organization, drawing heavily upon the internal strivings of its groups and maximizing its "distinctive competencies." On the other hand, the flexible, outward-looking organization need not be responsive to real needs, but only to vagrant pressures. It can be opportunistic, drifting, and experiencing a failure of leadership and clear purpose. We might chart this elaboration as follows:

	Organization	*Institution*
Nonflexible, internal source of values	The tool view; a rational, engineered instrument, with technicians directing it	The committed polity, with clear identity and purpose, serving the selfish strivings of its participants
Flexible, external source of values	The drift view; opportunism without goal-directed leadership	Adaptability, responsiveness, impregnated with community values

The tension between the two varieties of institutionalization, commitment and responsiveness, is never resolved and barely admitted.[34]

The matter of commitment to the organization also deserves discussion. Selznick notes in his most recent book that some theorists

---

[33]The distinction is not merely a product of the middle 1950s, the decade of a search for order and stability after a cataclysmic depression and a horrendous world war. The liberal values it reflects show again in Selznick's *Law, Society and Industrial Justice,* p. 44ff, where the mechanical application is again contrasted with organic and adaptive forms. See also his rejoinder to the criticisms of Sheldon Wolin in Amitai Etzioni, ed., *A Sociological Reader on Complex Organizations* (New York: Holt, Rinehart & Winston, Inc., 1969), pp. 149–154.

[34]See, for example, Selznick's *Leadership in Administration,* p. 18.

see dangers in members giving full commitment to the organization, for then the organization subjects them to too much control. As Selznick puts it, they view "the organization as a necessary evil to be approached warily and embraced without ardor."[35] While he recognizes the advantages of limited commitment, he is more concerned that limited commitment often means too little recognition of the rights of participants in organizations—a central theme of his volume. He asks: "Can individual rights in associations be fully protected without some concept of meaningful membership?" Presumably, a wary, limited commitment does not justify protection of one's rights; it resembles the tool view of organizations as limited-purpose rational instruments, while full commitment is the source of protection and is to be found in institutions. One might justly argue, however, that rights need protection independent of the type of organization or commitment. If we can only have rights by which we embrace the values and goals of the organization, these rights may have little meaning.

Selznick takes the matter further still. Explicating a desideratum of the pluralist doctrine—a doctrine that easily justifies the goals of all organizations—he says: "Through significant membership in corporate groups the individual's relation to the larger commonwealth can be extended and enriched."[36] This is true enough—if those groups are in his interests and controlled by him. Just as full commitment poses no dangers for those in control, so do they enrich their relationship to the larger society. But these advantages are limited to the few at the top. The top management of General Electric (GE), the American Medical Association (AMA), and the University of California no doubt extend and enrich their relationships through these groups, and their commitment can be full. But does the average employee of General Electric extend and enrich his relationship to the larger commonwealth through working for GE? Does the doctor who favors broader health coverage or better care for those in the ghetto enrich himself through membership in the AMA? He will receive a higher income as a result of the AMA's restrictive trade practices and control of the rate of entry of new doctors, but he will hardly derive an extended relationship to the larger community in the sense that Selznick clearly has in mind— nor will the student at Berkeley (or the assistant professor) protesting war-related research or the 1968 plans to channel students into the physical sciences and professions and out of the humanities and social sciences.[37] A limited commitment, necessary to provide, for

---

[35]Selznick, *Law, Society and Industrial Justice*, p. 43.

[36]Ibid., p. 43.

[37]According to a document on the "academic master plan" formulated by the University and protested by some student groups.

the worker, a livelihood, for the doctor, guaranteed access to hospitals and malpractice insurance, and, for the student, certification for employment through the attainment of a college degree, would seem to be sufficient in all cases. Selznick is far more critical of organizations and the way they subvert values than is Barnard, but he comes close to Barnard's view that man finds himself and his society through organizations.

More serious, however, than the discrepancies between two different types of institutions and the elitist view of commitment is the question of the source of the values to be realized by the organization. For the engineered tool view, that source is presumably the values of the master of the organization. For the opportunistic organization, it is the ebb and flow of opportunities for short-run gain within the organization, where groups vie for power, and outside of it, in the marketplace of ideas and consumer preferences. We may legitimately fear or decry both of these, the engineered and the opportunistic models. But what about the institution?

For both types of institutions, there is nothing to guarantee accountability or responsibility. The committed polity attempts to impose its view upon the world; the right-wing John Birch Society or the Minutemen would qualify, as would the more self-conscious branches of the military establishment, as well as the radical Left. Granted, perhaps, that these excesses, if they be that, will always be with us, what about the adaptive, responsive institutions that concern Selznick the most?

The Moral Ambiguity of Functionalism

It is here that the moral ambiguity of the functionalist position is most exposed. The Crown-Zellerbach Corporation, with its distinguished leadership (one chairman was ambassador to Italy; the firm is noted for philanthropic activities in San Francisco, etc.), "adapted" to the community values of Bogalusa, Louisiana, for years, even as the federal government was taking legal action to force the company to integrate its facilities.[38] It was responsive to local community values and strivings—those of the minority white community—with disastrous consequences for the rest of the community—the black and poor majority. U.S. Steel performed a similar rite of institutionalization in Birmingham for years when it ignored job segregation, racial unrest and injustice until the disruption of production following the riots, along with some national criticism, forced it to take slow,

---

[38]Vera Rony, "Bogalusa: The Economics of Tragedy," *Dissent* (May-June 1966): 234–242.

hesitant steps to "adapt" to another part of the community.[39] The organization can choose; there is no "community" value, there is only the conflict of group interests. Selznick's own analysis of the TVA makes this clear. But there his conclusion is *not* that there was effective leadership selecting certain interests to align with in order to achieve its ends. Instead, he sees a "failure of leadership" and the melancholy fate of idealism and abstract goals in organizations. His remedy in *Leadership in Administration* is equally disturbing· "Creative men are needed . . . who know how to transform a neutral body of men into a committed polity. These men are called leaders; their profession is politics."[40] This makes a virtue of the danger. Creative men did shape the TVA to their own politics. He does not applaud the results (he says elsewhere that much institutionalization can be pathological), but he does not attribute it to leadership, but to its failure. This suggests that when we get results we approve of, this is leadership; when we do not, it is a process of goal displacement.

Michels' insight, thus, has blinded us all. He showed how men of goodwill with liberal values become transformed, through institutional processes that sociologists are so adept at studying, into men who compromise their original goals and those of the organizations they head in the interests of preserving their own position as leaders. According to Michels, they do it unwittingly, without conscious malice, and inevitably. True enough; this does occur. But it is also possible that we cannot freely assume goodwill on the part of leaders. What some sociologists like to see as "goal displacement"[41] may refer only to goals never entertained by the leaders. The outputs of the organization may be just what they planned.

Consider another example, again from a liberal, concerned sociologist who wishes to stem some of the evil found in an organizational society. In Wilensky's lively and informative volume, *Organizational Intelligence*, the grim array of examples of the abuse of organizational power in all types of organizations is attributed to the failure of intelligence (information).[42] Wilensky indicates that if in-

---

[39]See the description of this case in Clarence C. Walton, *Corporate Social Responsibilities* (Belmont, Calif.: Wadsworth Publishing Company, Inc., 1967), pp. 156–172.

[40]Selznick, *Leadership in Administration*, p. 61.

[41]See Chapter Two of David Sills, *The Volunteers* (New York: The Free Press, 1957) for an excellent discussion of goal displacement. For a categorization of goals that would be more meaningful for the kind of analysis I am suggesting here, see Charles Perrow, "Organizational Goals," *International Encyclopedia of the Social Sciences*, rev. ed. vol. 11 (New York: The Macmillan Company, 1968), pp. 305–311.

[42]Harold L. Wilensky, *Organizational Intelligence* (New York: Basic Books, Inc., 1969). For a more extensive discussion of the point to be made below see Charles Perrow, "Review of Organizational Intelligence," *Trans-action* 6 (January 1969): 60–62.

formation were of better quality, not distorted by the bureaucratic hierarchy, if it quickly reached the proper people, and if it were evaluated fearlessly regardless of career implications and interpersonal dependencies, our organizations would function much more in keeping with their announced goals—and much more effectively.
In many cases, one can agree; people in organizations do a great many wrong things and a great many ineffective things, and there are structural sources of these imperfections. But what is striking is the number of cases where it does not seem to be a failure of intelligence that was at stake. The information was available; it was simply not in the interests of the leaders to use it. Changing the structure, reducing the levels of hierarchy, eliminating the "pathologies" of bureaucracy would mean little if the goals, perspectives, or prejudices of the elite were not changed. To change these might mean to change the whole structure of society and the goals of all the organizations that support that structure.[43]

Take the case of the military, in particular the Air Force. After World War II an extensive study of the effects of strategic bombing in Germany indicated that its costs, in pilots and equipment, far outweighed its military effects, which were surprisingly nominal. Yet in the Korean War, the military bombed North Korea even more heavily than they had bombed Germany. Once again, a study by the Air Force disclosed the poverty of the policy. The message was not heeded. By mid-1970 we had dropped 50 percent more tons of explosives upon the tiny, underdeveloped area of North and South Vietnam than we had used in both the European and Pacific theaters combined during World War II, and had lost thousands of Air Force personnel and planes. This time, in addition to the demonstrated ineffectiveness of this saturation bombing, we were also aware of the disastrous ecological effects of turning large areas of the countryside into a pock-marked landscape where insects and diseases could breed and where the ecological balance could not

---

[43]This poses the dilemma of those who would work within the system and those who would not. Presumably, for Selznick, Wilensky, and most other concerned sociologists, an assumption is made that "goodwill" is available to be tapped, and if we inform leaders and policy makers, or the students who will have the power in the future, of the way in which they go wrong, they will correct their ways. I have written a book which in part is guided by this assumption and which I consider to be an elaboration and extension of Selznick's *Leadership* book. See Charles Perrow, *Organizational Analysis: A Sociological View* (Belmont, Calif.: Wadsworth Publishing Company, Inc., 1970). An alternate view is that the present structure of society allows only minor, remedial adjustments, those which would reduce some of the strains without disturbing the whole. Those who contribute to this effort only preserve the system even as they liberalize parts of it. For a discussion of this more radical view, see Charles Perrow, *The Radical Attack on Business* (New York: Harcourt Brace Jovanovich, Inc., 1972).

be maintained. In late 1970 and early 1971 we bombed sections of supply trails in Laos with more intensity than any other area of land had ever been bombed, still without producing the desired effect of interdicting supplies. A ground invasion of the area was necessary.

The problem in all these cases does not appear to be lack of information about the failure of strategic bombing and its high costs. There was plenty of information available, including, but not limited to, two systematic, extensive studies commissioned by the Air Force itself. The problem appears to be that it was in the interests of the Air Force and the military in general to pursue this kind of effort, regardless of its irrelevance to the stated goals of quickly bringing various enemy nations to their knees. No correction of organizational malfunctions would be likely to change these interests. As a matter of fact, according to Melman's analysis, the restructuring of the military in the interests of efficiency that took place under Defense Secretary Robert McNamara—an operation organizational theorists presumably would applaud—led to its enormous growth and power and to the distortion of societal goals of peace and freedom.[44]

This is not to say that leaders are all-powerful; there are many constraints on their ability to freely use the organization as a tool. We have considered some of these constraints in previous chapters: the necessity to treat labor as a resource which is more productive if handled well and paid well; tenure provisions for management; limits upon arbitrary authority; technological constraints; internal goal conflict; and, most important of all, cognitive limits on rationality—which entail such things as limited search and lack of innovation. To these we must now add, following the institutional school, more pervasive aspects of tradition and history than the decision-making model envisions: unplanned adaptations; the failure of leaders to have and set clear goals; and internal group strivings. Surely this limits the tool view of organizations; organizations are not simply resources to be utilized at will. But it does not suggest that for all, or even most organizations, that their leaders are not in a position to transform a neutral body of men into a polity committed to what the leaders believe to be important, rather than to what the individual members and the plurality of groups in the environment think of as important. Organizations are imperfect tools, but the powerful ones appear to do well enough for their masters. Selznick is right; leadership is decisive. Our quarrel with him is the implication that leadership is decisive in realizing the goals of the members and the environment, rather than the goals of the leaders.

---

[44]Melman, *Pentagon Capitalism*.

Trivial Organizations

The work of Wilensky, Selznick, Janowitz, and some others, despite the flaws, has at least paid attention to important organizations in our society. Most of the literature in the institutional school, including my own, has dealt with relatively trivial organizations. There are the freaks, like the Townsend movement or the WCTU; the accessible welfare institutions such as general hospitals or the blind agencies; the obvious "social problem" institutions such as mental hospitals, prisons, and reform schools, whose impact upon a tiny minority of incarcerated individuals is frightening but trivial compared to the dominant economic institutions of our society. Occasionally, a note of organizational dominance creeps in, or is given some sustained analysis, as when the Community Chest is seen as an occupying army, or when the Communist party manipulates voluntary associations, or when a federal narcotics agency is seen as making a menace out of marijuana in the interests of growth and power.[45] But these are exceptions.

There are many reasons for the focus upon relatively inconsequential organizations. There are only a small number of researchers doing institutional analysis, as contrasted to the large number involved in the factory studies of the human relations movement. There are problems of access to the powerful, dominant organizations in our society; their sheer size poses one formidable problem. Government and foundation funding plays a key role. The institutions that cope with the deformed products of our society are more visible as social problems than those organizations that contribute to the deformity, and symptoms are safer to treat than causes.

Finally, this focus on trivial, symptomatic organizations is also probably due to a characteristic of the profession as a whole. Sociologists are interested in values, but they have traditionally studied values in cameo settings—the family, small group, small town—or in the organizations that blatantly distort our values, such as prisons or asylums. Academic inquiries do not differ that much from the commercial, nonacademic forms of social inquiry. Television specials will focus upon such symptomatic problems of society as racial discrimination, poverty, violence, insanity, and addicts and such isolated groups as migratory workers or the Indians. But TV usually ignores the mass media itself, big business, the military-industrial ties, the propertied elite, the self-serving powerful professional associations. Just so with organizational sociologists.

---

[45]Seeley, Junker, and Jones, *Community Chest;* Selznick, *The Organizational Weapon;* and Donald Dickson, "Bureaucracy and Morality," *Social Problems* 16, no. 2 (Fall 1968): 129–142.

They have neglected, if not avoided, those institutions that create and manipulate our values, despite their preoccupation with values. The corporations which select and package our very view of what is happening—the mass-media institutions such as CBS, the Associated Press, the newspaper chains, the *New York Times*—are almost totally neglected. Their absence until the middle 1970s in the inventory of sociological studies of organizations was conspicuous.

Oddly enough, there is a large body of valuable data on the powerful governmental and economic organizations in our society, including the mass media, but it is scarcely mined by organizational theorists. I am referring to the massive amount of information to be found in the records of committee hearings of congressional groups and in the reports of governmental regulatory agencies and government agencies in general. It is public information. It would not take an agency-funded research grant, extensive field work, or elaborate questionnaires to mine these data.

Organizations and Society

Among the many reasons given above for the failure to go beyond trivial organizations, we should also include the most significant failure of all of organizational theory: the failure to see *society* as adaptive to *organizations*. A view of organizations as protean in their ability to shape society would direct us to the study of the powerful organizations and to the public data gathered by governmental agencies and congressional committees.

It is here that we see the gravest defect of the institutional school in particular, for it has been the one most concerned with the environment. *That school's view of organizations and society fails to connect the two.* Parts of the "environment" are seen as affecting organizations, but the organization is not seen as defining, creating, and shaping its environment. We live in an "organizational society," the institutionalists routinely announce, but the significant environment of organizations is not "society"; they do not realize that it is other organizations, and generally other organizations that share the same interests, definitions of reality, and power. Society is adaptive to organizations, to the large, powerful organizations controlled by a few, often overlapping, leaders. To see these organizations as adaptive to a "turbulent," dynamic, ever changing environment is to indulge in fantasy. The environment of most powerful organizations is well controlled by them, quite stable, and made up of other organizations with similar interests, or ones they control.[46] Standard Oil and Shell may compete at the intersection of two highways, but they do not compete in the numerous areas where

---

[46]I have argued this point in more detail in Charles Perrow, "Is Business Really Changing?" *Organization Dynamics*, (Summer 1974): 31-44.

their interests are critical, such as foreign policy, tax laws, import quotas, government funding of research and development, highway expansion, internal combustion engines, pollution restrictions, and so on. Nor do they have a particularly turbulent relationship to other powerful organizations such as the auto companies, the highway construction firms, the Department of Defense, the Department of Transportation, the State Department, the major financial institutions.

Why would the logic of the relationship between organizations and their environment be turned around so persistently? There are technical and conceptual reasons, no doubt. But one important reason is probably the heritage of the functionalist tradition in organizational analysis. A highly oversimplified parable will illustrate, though hardly verify, the point. Imagine an Indian tribe in the Southwest, before the advent of the white man. It lives peacefully and peaceably, bestowing its honors upon those who can promise rain, solve disputes, and provide an oral tradition which links the past with the present. A disturbance occurs; a new tribe enters the area and starts to fight our tribe. Over the years of protracted defense and combat, the honors go to those who are most warlike. They become the chiefs and dictate the pattern of culture. They succeed in driving out or subjecting the offending intruders. But now the position of the warriors is threatened; without war there will be no honors for the warrior. So the warriors expand their surveillance of the environment until they come across other tribes, which they challenge and fight. Their power is secured. In time, the once peaceful group becomes an expanding, subjugating, warlike tribe, seeking ever new territories and spoils to support the military superstructure. The other tribes, perforce, must adapt similarly or be conquered.

By the time the functionalist studies the tribe, its social structure is "functional"; the military should dominate. The environment is hostile, their lands are challenged. The military is needed to police the areas and to fight off offending and aggressive tribes, which always seem to materialize. Defense is a basic need of all communities; this one is doing a highly effective job at it. Power follows function and is legitimized. The society, like the organization, has adapted. But what has happened, of course, is that those with power made sure that their skills would be the primary requisites for the community. They have shaped the environment, not the other way around. As Joseph Schumpeter noted, speaking of the war machines of ancient times, "Created by the wars that required it, the machine now created the wars it required."[47]

---

[47]Joseph H. Schumpeter, *Imperialism and Social Classes* (Cleveland: Meridian Books, 1955), p. 25.

So it may be with organizations in the modern state. Janowitz's predictions about the military, noted early in this chapter, may still bear fruit at some future time, but right now it seems to matter little that the military was shaped by the changing class structure, new technologies, and ideologies that brought professionals into command. The military has been, many believe, able to create, define, and shape our foreign environment and promote its own goals. It is feared that it is also doing so with our internal environment.

When we look at the matter from this perspective, I think we have additional grounds to question the explanation of goal displacement, natural processes, drift, and so on when we take our liberal values and the exposé tradition into the study of organizations. The goals of the agencies for the blind may be displaced but those of the American Medical Association seem very much intact—even though they do change gradually. The large defense contractors are not likely to drift toward refusing to produce weapons; the large banks are not likely to give up their critical role in our economy and our foreign policy. Chase Manhattan is not likely, for example, to pull out of racially segregated South Africa, and it was not drift that put it there. The AMA annually spends millions to stave off national health insurance, but not to attend to health needs of the poor in a country that has a higher infant mortality rate than most other industrialized countries. The contenders for top leadership positions in our large voluntary and economic organizations are those who share the dominant perspectives of the organization's elites—or they would not be contenders. There are exceptions, of course, but those exceptions stand out for this reason.

It is precisely because the dominant organizations or institutions of our society have *not* experienced goal displacement and have been able to institutionalize on their own terms, to create the environments they desire, shape the existing ones, and define which sections of it they will deal with, that the failure to link organizations such as these with society is so alarming. It is from the muckrakers, journalists, congressional committees, historians, and, occasionally, the economists and political scientists that we learn about the ways in which organizations shape our environment, not, ironically, from the organizational sociologists. The WCTU may drift, but General Motors does not.

In fact, we need not count the WCTU as an exception. A close analysis of those research findings cited at the beginning of this chapter, indicating the exposé character of this school, suggests that for many of the organizations involved the problem was that they *were* tools in the hands of their leaders; that Mr. Townsend found it profitable to shift from political reform to patent medicine; that the Selective Service system was dominated by General Hershey and reflected *his* values and those of the people who appear to have controlled him; that a set of leaders dominated the policies of the WCTU; that the affairs of San Jose State College were firmly in the hands of the leaders of other organizations in the "administrative web" that Clark describes so well; that it is the decisions of the heads of the many agencies for the blind to ignore the old, handicapped, and minority-group members who are also blind. We need not doubt that power was exercised from the top in these organizations, and we may doubt that either internal group strivings or a sense of the mission of the organization as a whole was responsible for these policies.

In an earlier chapter, I argued that we have more to fear from organizations than their negative effect upon the spontaneity and self-realization of their members; I would now add that we have more to fear from organizations than the displacement of goals we attribute to them. The assumptions we have made about the nature of organizations—whether as cooperative systems or natural systems—have made the task of linking organizations and society in this fashion difficult. A tool view, based upon a neo-Weberian view of structure modified by the insights of the institutional school, but not posing the latter's functionalist questions, would serve us better.

SUMMARY

In sum, then, the institutional school has served organizational theory well in several respects. The natural systems view, stressing the organic entity, is an analogue to some of the themes of March and Simon. Their notion of organizational vocabularies and the stabilizing force of custom, well-worn communication lines, and so on resembles the institutional view of basic identity, or character, and the "conservative" nature of institutions that resist fortuitous change. The exposé tradition has highlighted the dangers we can expect from even well-meaning organizations in their search for stability and growth and their resistance to character restructuring. It also highlights the "underlife" of the organization, the latent functions and unplanned aspects of complex systems. Above all, the descriptive and historical nature of this school gives us an essential "feel" for how organizations operate, something dramatically absent from the March and Simon volume, for example.

More important than these contributions, however, is what this school presses upon us. For one thing, there is the inescapable variety of organizations, a variety that the technological school cannot hope to reflect in its three- or fourfold categorizations. The institutional school has not sought to capture and discipline this variety in a fashion that would serve research and conceptualization as yet, but it provides the leads. Second, institutional theory throws up to those who would use a neo-Weberian model the possibility that organizations do develop an inner logic and direction of their own that is not the result of those who appear to control them. We have challenged this view, but the nagging question remains: When we identify General Hershey or whoever as the "leader," are we merely picking out a person cast up by "the organization" to do its work? I think the evidence is that this is not generally the case, but as yet the question has not been posed with sufficient clarity to even say what evidence is relevant, let alone what kinds of organizations fit which model. But it is a very important question, and the answer may limit the applicability of the neo-Weberian model.

Of the third contribution there is no doubt that it is essential. This school, almost alone among those we have considered, has taken the environment seriously and tried to understand the organization's relationship to it. No neat conceptual schemes have emerged; it is a vastly more complex problem than understanding the internal workings of organizations. But again, I have argued that the school has led us astray. It has seen the organization as adaptive to and dependent upon the environment. It has not considered the other possibility, which, for the important organizations in our society, is at least equally possible: that the environment has to adapt to the organization. The major aspect of the environment of organizations is other organizations; the citizen and the "community" fall between the stools.

We outlined some other deficiencies. We questioned the importance of the organizations which this school has been wont to study; the question-begging distinction between organizations and institutions, and the school's idea of commitment to the organization; the easy faith that the large and powerful organizations will select liberal values, rather than self-serving values, to be infused with, or, worse, will create self-serving values in their environment. And we argued that this was an expression of the posture of structural-functionalism that pervades sociology today.

Finally, we examined the more direct challenge to our own evolving position that organizations are tools in the hands of masters, and we concluded that it appears that the masters are in substantial command in most organizations, even the weak and trivial (though interesting) ones this school has been most prone to study.

We could have hoped for more, then, from the institutional school. It appears to have been a product of its times—reflecting the disillusionment with radical change in the late 1930s and the 1940s, when the leading spokesmen came to fruition, and the empty, quiet

1950s, when their students were trained. It is also a product of the guiding perspective of sociology itself since the 1930s—"value-free" functionalism, the pluralist doctrine, and the emphasis upon norms, values, and culture at the expense of power and the material aspects of existence. Hopefully, new winds will stir in this most sociological of all schools of organizational theory, and the tradition of patient inquiry, case studies, historical perspectives, the environment, natural processes, unplanned adaptations, and values can be wedded to a tool view of organizations that gives the devil his full due. Referring to bureaucracy, Selznick once warned against the tendency to gaze at the devil with fascinated eyes, but we should also be warned against the tendency to call for the transformation of men into committed polities in organizations where centralized power and unobtrusive means of manipulation and control are necessities.

It is perhaps ironic that those who appear to understand the devil best—theorists such as Herbert Simon and James March—are the least concerned in their writings with liberal values, goals, and responsiveness, while those most concerned with these things are the least likely to recognize the devil in his consummate disguises. It is more than ironic; it is a melancholy conclusion in a social landscape strewn with the wastes of our organizations.

6

The Environment

If one can think of waves of theory, the post-World War II period was dominated by human relations theory until the mid-1960s. Contingency theory (the "technological school") was gathering strength and clarity in the early 1960s and hit with solid force in 1967 with three similar formulations by James Thompson, Paul Lawrence and Jay Lorsch, and my own piece.[1] These stimulated a wave of theorizing and research which is now rapidly being absorbed. It has left its mark, as did the human relations tradition, but it has lost its handsome crest of frothy promise. Task, or technology, prove to be important variables, but not of the overriding importance we first claimed for them. The new wave-gathering force appears to be the environment.

It was always there in organizational theory, from Weber on. Indeed, the contingency theory of Lawrence and Lorsch was formulated in such a way that the environment set varied tasks for different organizations and units of organizations. Formulation of interorganizational relations was set forth in the early 1960s.[2] The institutional school, as we have seen, has always emphasized the environment—but not self-consciously so—and did not concep-

---

[1]James Thompson, *Organizations in Action* (New York: McGraw-Hill, Inc., 1967); Paul R. Lawrence and Jay W. Lorsch, *Organization and Environment* (Cambridge, Mass.: Harvard University Press, 1967); Charles Perrow, "A Framework for Comparative Organizational Analysis," *American Sociological Review* 32, no. 2 (April 1967): 194–208.

[2]Sol Levine and Paul E. White, "Exchange as a Conceptual Framework for the Study of Interorganizational Relationships," *Administrative Science Quarterly* 5 (March 1961): 583–610; Eugene Litwak and Lydia F. Hylton, "Interorganizational Analysis: A Hypothesis on Co-ordinating Agencies," *Administrative Science Quarterly* 6, no. 4 (March 1962): 395–420; Herman Turk and Myron J. Lefkowitz, "Toward a Theory of Representation Between Groups," *Social Forces* 40 (May 1962): 337–341.

tualize it in any distinct way. The new concern with the environment is trying to do just this, conceptualize it, or tell us how to think about it, and that will be the concern of this chapter.

First, we will start with some work on the recording industry and the pharmaceutical industry, to indicate how an organizational analysis helps us see the issue of bias and cultural control, but even more important, the relationship between organizations and the industry they are in, and between the industry and the rest of society. I will also rejoice in this section that there is now good work on large and powerful organizations, rather than just the trivial ones.

Then we will examine the recent notion of "networks" carefully by seeing what difference it can make if one uses an interorganizational framework rather than an organizational one. It seems quite likely that many of our hard-won conclusions about organizations as such will have to be upset once we look at the network they are involved in. To explore this, I will use a fabricated but realistic extended case study of a network of hospitals and political power.

The notion of networks in particular, and organization environment relations in general, is still fluid. Competing paradigms appear to be emerging. In the third part of the chapter I will examine one impressive contender—a revitalized population-ecology model—and suggest that our discipline of organizational analysis still goes astray every time it gets a chance. I will try to rein it in at this early stage of development. Then I will have a short comment on the new neo-Marxist and ethnomethodological tendencies that are just emerging. I will be brief because the approach is quite new and this is not the place to do more than let the reader know what the important citations seem to be and what promise it might have. It certainly shows that whether we are going astray or heading to where the action really is, the field is unquestionably lively—livelier than I imagined when I finished the first edition of this book in 1971.

PART ONE: THE INDUSTRY

A Question of Bias

We will back into the environment gently by first looking at a problem that clearly can have its source within the organization, and then examine its source in the environment. This is the problem of bias in the selection of cultural products to be produced. Certain people play roles of the creative artist—the reporter, the musician, the movie director, the actor—and they come up against the demands of the organization, or even the political or artistic prejudices of the top executives. It is a familiar focus in organizational studies because it examines individual roles. It is similar to studies of the role of the foreman and his cross pressures as he tries to serve the men under him and the organization over him; or of the scientist supposedly suffering under the lash of company profit objectives when he just wants to do good science; or the departmental manager trying to make his department look good while at the same time subordinating its interests to the interests of the company as a whole.

In the case of the "cultural industry" (vaguely defined here as involving the media as well as literature, art, music, drama, etc.), these role conflicts are reportedly severe and they always entail issues of bias in the selection of cultural products. Surveys and studies have shown that reporters are more liberal in their views than are the owners of the paper, and thus a subtle censorship is at work because they know that certain kinds of stories will not be selected for publication, and certain kinds of information or observations will not be retained in the story as they write it, so they write what they know will be accepted. The editor does not have to tell them that the publishers want stories reflecting a more conservative view; it becomes apparent. Producers of TV programs often would prefer to handle more controversial and even liberal material but end up following the current bland fads because of the censorship of network owners and sponsors. Musicians are forced to play music that the club owner thinks the patrons like; after hours they play the kind they feel reflects their creative urges. Most movie actors cannot choose their own scripts or directors; directors cannot stop the producers from ordering a change in endings (usually calling for an upbeat one) or editing the film to suit their tastes. Rock groups are told to emphasize certain kinds of sounds or lyrics even if they feel these are mere fads.

These are important problems, but if the inquiry ends with the artist-producer interaction, or stays within the organization, we make the presumption that the system is closed and we may be misled. If we assume the system is open to outside influences, we will look at the conditions under which the owners or producers or whatever operate, generally the conditions of the industry as a whole and its market, and alternative explanations are possible. (Paul Hirsch, in a seminal piece on industrial sociology, advocates such a move from the organization to the industry, giving some examples of the difference it makes.[3])

Can the owners or producers shape the cultural product of the

---

[3]Paul M. Hirsch, "Organizational Analysis and Industrial Sociology: An Instance of Cultural Lag," *The American Sociologist* 10, no. 1 (February 1975): 3–10.

artist against the will of the artist? Of course they can, and it happens regularly. But when is it likely to happen, and how, and why, and how frequently? Is it a characteristic of the kind of individuals who control the organization, or the setting in which the organization operates regardless of the owners or top management?

When a freelance journalist, Seymour Hersh, submitted reports to the *New York Times* and other newspapers on the My Lai massacre in Vietnam at the height of our military involvement, the reports were rejected.[4] It would appear to be a clear case of censorship since the reports showed the U.S. military in an appalling light, and the reports would have eroded the legitimacy of a long, costly war effort. Such information, even if true, could hardly be welcomed by the media, which is a part of the national power structure and depends upon the military and the White House for information and freedom from harassment.

An alternative interpretation, however, is simply that where stories are controversial, the media needs strong guarantees regarding the reliability of the reporter and his or her story. Hersh was not, at that time, on the staff of the *Times* and so there was good reason for the *Times* to be cautious.

Both interpretations could be true—it could be politically motivated suppression or it might be organizational caution. But the second seems to have the edge because after the accounts were accredited (they were not dismissed out of hand), the story was published. Indeed, the nightly television news was carrying bits and pieces of the U.S. military behavior which suggested such massacres could occur, and the Pentagon was complaining of the "biased" coverage by the television networks. Finally, Hersh was hired as a staff investigative reporter by the *Times* after his stories were verified. (The popular book: *All the President's Men* by Carl Bernstein and Bob Woodward provides interesting examples of the norms the press uses for verifying stories, the costs of mistakes, and the drudgery, errors, and lucky breaks associated with this type of media production.[5])

This example does not prove that censorship does not occur; it quite obviously does, as does blacklisting, witch hunts, deliberate distortions, and so on. The book, *The First Casualty*,[6] details the

---

[4]I am following the illustration of Paul Hirsch here: Paul Hirsch, "Occupational, Organizational and Institutional Models in Communication Research," in Paul M. Hirsch, Peter V. Miller, and F. Gerald Kline, *Strategies for Communication Research* (Beverly Hills, Calif.: Sage Publications, 1977).

[5]Carl Bernstein and Bob Woodward, *All the President's Men* (New York: Simon & Schuster, Inc., 1974).

[6]Phillip Knightley, *The First Casualty: From the Crimes to Vietnam: The War Correspondent as Hero, Propagandist, and Myth Maker.* (New York: Harcourt Brace Jovanovich, Inc., 1976).

censorship and distortions practiced in recent wars by governments, publishers, and reporters themselves. Indeed, in many socialist countries and in all dictatorships no such thing as a free market for news exists, by design and by explicit policy. But where such a free market is claimed, as it endlessly is in the United States ("All the news that's fit to print" says the *New York Times*), it is worth inquiring whether bias is intended by the masters of these organizations, or is the result of organizational and industrial contexts.

The charge of bias, favoritism, suppression of innovation, and so on often occurs in the cultural industry for the simple reason that potential suppliers and supplies exist in vast numbers, but very few of them are selected. When this occurs it is very easy to allow ideological bias to enter, and more important, it is easy to believe it enters even if it doesn't. Newsworthy events far outnumber the space available for presenting them; aspiring rock stars or movie stars or authors or painters are legion, the number who get a hearing is tiny. Among reputable scholarly publishers, about 96 percent of the manuscripts received are rejected; possibly only 10 percent of those received are given any serious attention.[7] Scholarly journals regularly reject 90 percent or more of the papers sent to them. Even after the small percentage of popular music groups are recorded and offered for sale, less than a quarter of the single records produced are ever played on radio stations (the only marketing mechanism that is effective). The newspaper editor rejects perhaps 90 percent of the stories that come in over the two wire services, Associated Press and United Press International. Film scripts are offered to producers in great numbers, and even after being produced a fair number of films never get distributed. Such massive rejection rates encourage the operation of ideological and cultural biases, and invite attributions of biases even when they are not present.

But what are the bases of bias? If the profit motive is dominant, and radical ideas are selling, how many owners and producers are willing to forego the profits that pushing radical ideas would bring for ideological ends? Some will, of course. But on the other hand, how many of the presumably few left-leaning owners, producers, and sponsors are willing to buck the market trend if radical ideas are not selling, and try to introduce controversial ideological material? Very, very few, one suspects. The source of what, from one political or cultural perspective, can be seen as a conservative bias may reside in the financial characteristics of the industry.

---

[7]Walter Powell, personal communication. See his "Control and Conflict in the Publishing Industry," unpublished manuscript, State University of New York at Stony Brook, December 1977; and Lewis A. Coser, "Publishers as Gatekeepers of Ideas," *The Annals, American Academy of Social Science* 421 (September 1975): 12-22.

For example, producers of television programs and shows cover a fairly wide ideological perspective, but the resulting product does not reflect it. The selection process operating is fairly subtle. Erik Barnouw notes that television network executives and sponsors do not have to exercise overt censorship.[8] Producers present a variety of programs for network executives and sponsors to choose from; the latter indicate by their selection what they think will sell. A program with high ratings may not be continued because the sponsor determines (through the Nielsen rating system) that though it is watched by a large number of people, these people are middle-aged or older and do not spend much money on the consumer products the sponsor is selling. The program is dropped in favor of one which is watched by fewer people, but by people who buy a lot of the sponsor's trash. The "creative people"—writers, actors, producers—get the message and offer up programs that seem to draw a segment of the population that is "economically active" with regard to low-priced, mass-produced (the young, often the very young). Public television might seem to be free of this, but it isn't. Its government grants cover only a minority of its costs; it must seek the rest from sponsors such as Exxon or Gulf. This gives these corporations the power to select among the programs offered—or to choose none at all. Producers for public television programs then tailor their offerings in the same way as for commercial television. Exxon is marketing its image, and the market, as they perceive it, will play a large role in determining the ideological and cultural content. No "censorship" is operating, only unobtrusive controls.

Ideally, for corporations, profits and ideology will work hand in hand. The largest profits would come from producing cultural products whose ideology most supports the private profit system, the class system, sexism, racism, or whatever is in their interests. It is said to be a characteristic of monopoly capitalism that it is just such a system which can maximize long-range profits for a ruling class through long-range ideological control. But it is not an easy task; unsuspecting things intrude, the system is very complex and can briefly get out of hand. There may be a flowering of protest songs, novels which challenge the system, cultural heroes who are anti-establishment, and so on. The history of popular music illustrates the point well. Large profits could be made while the content of the music was safe for the system. But because of some unrelated technological innovations, suppressed tastes were allowed to come to the fore, the companies that dominated the industry lost control of it, and only now are they regaining profitable control and once again apparently trying to shape the cultural product. They are not

---

[8]Erik Barnouw, *The Sponsor: Notes on a Modern Potentate* (New York: Oxford University Press, 1978).

that concerned about radical lyrics or life-styles; the threat to the system is trivial, and if radical lyrics will sell, they will be sold. But they would presumably prefer the interpersonal focus of The Eagles to the social problem lyrics of Bob Dylan. The following account of this history of an industry draws upon the excellent work of Richard Peterson, David Berger, and Paul Hirsch.[9] Its implication for the study of organizations goes far beyond the question of bias as I shall note at the end of it.

THE POPULAR MUSIC INDUSTRY

The Giants Fall

From the days of Tin Pan Alley (the 1920s) up through the era of swing music (to about 1955), a fortuitous combination of maximizing profits and minimizing system dissent seems to have existed. The music world was dominated by four firms. The domination was achieved by vertical integration: the firms owned the artists through long-term contracts, and hired producers who gathered the ancillary talent, produced the record, and packaged the result. They also owned the manufacturing facilities and controlled the distribution system. Most hits came out of the musical comedy films and shows, which the giants controlled; they processed the records and distributed them. There were some points of uncertainty; record sales depend upon "air time"—repeated playing over radio stations. Not all radio stations were controlled by the giants, so they resorted to bribery ("payola," it was called) to induce disc jockeys to feature their records. (It has been suggested that independents trying to break in used organized crime to threaten stations.) If an independent company (or a big competitor) came up with a hit tune, it was "covered" by the majors—they had their own artists record it, cashing in on the tune's popularity. The majors also controlled the distribution of the films that featured popular songs, further rationalizing the system. As a result, the four largest firms ac-

---

[9]Paul M. Hirsch, *The Structure of the Popular Music Industry* (Ann Arbor: University of Michigan Survey Research Center, 1969); P. M. Hirsch, "Processing Fads and Fashions: An Organization-Set Analysis of Cultural Industry Systems," *American Journal of Sociology* 77, no. 4 (January 1972): 639–659; P. M. Hirsch, "Organizational Effectiveness and the Institutional Environment," *Administrative Science Quarterly* 20, no. 4 (September 1975): 327–344; Richard A. Peterson and David G. Berger, "Entrepreneurship in Organizations: Evidence from the Popular Music Industry," *Administrative Science Quarterly* 16, no. 1 (March 1971): 97–106; R. A. Peterson and D. G. Berger, "Cycles in Symbol Production: The Case of Popular Music," *American Sociological Review* 40, no. 2 (April 1975): 158–173.

counted for 78 percent of the sales of single records from 1948 to 1955; the eight largest for 96 percent.

The system was probably very efficient and economical for the companies. In the period from 1948 to 1955, sales growth was not large, but it was acceptable. Costs were controlled because most people involved were on contracts, and in a rationalized system there was not much competition that would drive up the costs of paying artists, producers, etc. Finally, there seemed to be no doubt that the public was satisfied with Doris Day, Vaughn Monroe, The Ink Spots, and Frank Sinatra, all singing of moon and June. As Peterson and Berger note, two studies both found that "over 80 percent of all songs fit into a conventionalized love cycle where sexual references are allegorical and social problems are unknown."[10] Most of American industry reflects these characteristics: substantial oligopoly (production concentrated in a few firms), vertical integration, routine production, and little innovativeness except in marginal aspects such as packaging or novelty.

Then three changes took place, all of them, ironically, brought about by the industry itself. First, the long-playing record made record production very cheap. It actually appeared in 1948, but the impact was slow. Second, with the advent of television, advertising income from radio stations dropped alarmingly (38 percent from 1948 to 1952), and the majors abandoned network programming on radio and transferred it to TV. This made stations autonomous and they could be purchased cheaply by local entrepreneurs. Third, the development of the cheap transistor radio resulted in a 30 percent increase in radio set production from 1955 to 1960, and a 27 percent increase in the number of AM radio stations.

The low cost of producing records affected the input side; the low cost of radio broadcasting (cheap stations, many new listeners) affected the output side. The majors lost control of each to new independent firms which made vertical integration and homogeneous products—the ingredients of success for monopoly capitalism—impossible for a time.

First, there had to be a profound change in programming for the stations. As Peterson and Berger note, though the idea was simple, it took a full decade to perfect. The audience was gradually no longer defined as a mass audience, but as a number of discrete groups with different tastes. Each station picked its particular brand of recorded music and played it all day. But where did all these different tastes come from? Presumably, they were there all the time, but latent; they had never had the chance to develop because the recording and broadcast segments of the industry were con-

---

[10]Peterson and Berger, "Cycles," p. 163.

trolled by the majors and devoted to the standard fare. The varied tastes were being met on an extremely local level through live performance of jazz, rhythm and blues, country and western, gospel, trade union songs, and urban folk songs. When recorded, which was infrequent, they appeared on small esoteric labels that were sold only in a local area, were hard to get, and never played on the radio. (They also broke easily and wore out quickly, as any fan of jazz or gospel, sharpening cactus needles every three plays in the late 1930s and early 1940s, will testify.)

With inexpensive recording and pressing techniques, and disc jockeys hungry for novel sounds that would build up a loyal audience, the boom was on. Between 1955 and 1959 the number of records in the weekly top ten increased from 57 per year to 75; the number of cover records dropped to zero; the number of new performers represented each week doubled, and record sales soared. The number of labels and the number of firms tripled. The four firms' concentration ratio went down from 78 to 44 percent of the business (and to 26.5 percent by 1963). While the sales and profits of the majors continued to climb—they benefitted from the freeing of suppressed tastes also—they did not climb nearly as much as those of the industry as a whole, and certainly not like those of the new independent groups. Here was something to worry about, and worry they did. After ignoring the new sounds as fads, they then condemned them. Frank Sinatra, with not only his records to protect, but his investments in the industry, called rock-n-roll "phony and false, and sung, written, and played for the most part by cretinous goons."[11] (Ironically, Sinatra was a teenage idol himself earlier and then later linked to Mafia "goons" in a Congressional inquiry.)

The Giants Adapt Their Organizations

Before we examine the way the giants fought their way back to create some degree of profitable order for themselves, let us examine how the industry functioned when vertical integration and taste-makers such as Mitch Miller no longer dominated. Following contingency theory predictions, when faced with a high degree of uncertainty about what would sell, and an inability to immediately shape and define the market, firms had to forego the economies of vertical integration and centralization, and decentralize and contract out for services. Even prior to 1955 there was uncertainty about when tunes or performances would become hits, but since all the tunes and performers were more or less similar, having a small stable of both tunes and performers would suffice. The tunes and

---

[11]Ibid., p. 165.

performers were similar because of the tight control over talent and marketing. After 1955 (an arbitrary year—1954 to 1956 would be more appropriate) tunes and performers multiplied; some of the majors decided to wait the "fad" out, others were not able to move fast enough to expand their stables; many new performers only lasted a year or so; and hit tunes no longer lasted months, but only weeks.

The response, by both the majors and the new independents (some of whom, like Motown, soon became majors) was to segment the organization and separate the functions. We will consider three functions: producing the master disc or tape (bringing together the performers, songwriters, recording technicians, and so on); manufacturing the records; and promoting and selling them. Manufacturing is the most routine, and it can be cut off from the other functions quite easily. If an organization gets a hit and its own manufacturing division cannot handle the instant demand, it is easy to contract out to independent stamping plants. These plants can survive because the appearance of hits is more or less steady, so several firms will use them. A small producing firm need not even invest in manufacturing facilities at all; this reduces the cost of entry into the business. (For the majors, however, contracting out means that another organization makes the profit on manufacturing rather than the major so they try to avoid the use of independents, but in the process they drive the price of manufacturing down, thus aiding the independents.)

The promotion and sales division is changed under the new conditions; more uncertainty and spatial dispersion is introduced. Before there were oligopoly outlets, a firm could make a movie and also make the records of the songs in the movie and sell them in their stores, or records would be promoted over national network shows such as the Jack Benny Hour or Make Believe Ballroom. Under the new market conditions, it must motivate and control many agents around the country who are responsible for pushing the records with disc jockeys and stocking many more independent record stores. This results in a flat organization (many people at the lowest level) with little interdependence among the geographically separated promoters and salesmen. It is "loosely coupled" internally, because there are local hits which are independent of other hits.

The producing division is the most "tightly coupled," and absorbs most of the turbulence of the environment, protecting the other divisions as much as possible by being only moderately coupled to sales and promotion, and hardly coupled at all to manufacturing. The production people are expected to create a succession of hit records, and for this teams of specialists form and re-form around each group of artists and each recording session. There are talent scouts scouring the clubs "armed with intuition, empathy, and durable eardrums" as one commentator puts it,[12] and the producer himself does a lot of this. Then there are recording engineers and other studio specialists, background musicians brought in for one record, the artist or group itself, their agent who is there to protect their interests and promote them, record jacket designers and writers, and above all the producer who brings the whole team together. He must have a sense of what the particular segment of the public wants, rapport, sincerity, and other interpersonal skills that will bring out the best in the artists and technicians, ideas for packaging, and angles for the promotion division.

Prior to the deconcentration of the industry and market, the producer was on a long-term contract and his decisions were carefully reviewed by upper management; indeed, much of the work was comparatively routine because songwriters and artists were under contract and stable relationships were formed. Under the new conditions, the producer emerges as the most powerful member of the whole input-throughput-output process. How then does the organization control these people? First, performance can be exceptionally well monitored; the fate of a record is known within a matter of weeks. If the producer does not have a succession of hits, his decisions are scrutinized, his latitude reduced, and contracts must be countersigned by a vice-president. Second, the organization seeks to minimize the risks entailed in giving one person so much power by increasing the number of entrepreneurial decisions; the firm has many producers turning out many records, but needs to invest comparatively little in each one. The market is flooded with records. In 1967, Columbia Records produced an average of one new album a day, and ten new single 45 rpm records each week. The vast majority of these will never be played on the air, but some of them have to be played and a few will be hits. The profits on a hit are enormous because production costs are so low. The total cost of production, manufacturing, and promotion is often under $50,000; Columbia Records' sales exceed $200,000,000. Thus, a producer can be given a great deal of discretion because of the small investment in each decision. This is quite different from, say, making a pilot film for a TV series. There, top management is involved in each step, and the product is test marketed. The costs are much greater, so the discretion is less.

Note that the costs of this turbulence are not significantly borne by the record company; they are pushed onto the producing phase where they are absorbed by producers on very short contracts; jit-

---

[12]Peterson and Berger, "Entrepreneurship," p. 99.

tery aspiring artists, most of whom make no money at all for their recording efforts unless they are selected, and whose records have only about a one-to-four chance of bringing them any royalties; the disc jockeys trying to both guess and guide the public tastes; and by those that rent out studios, supply backup musicians, wait for stamping contracts, and so on. Everyone is betting on the big thing, so there are always bettors willing to absorb the costs of turbulence. It is an extreme form of craft production as described by Arthur Stinchcombe in his seminal article on the environment and organizations.[13]

Thus we have a dramatic example of how organizations adapt to changes in their environments. The notions of contingency theory give analytic power to the work of Hirsch and especially Peterson and Berger, and I have added some of the more recent notions of coupling. But were we to stop here we would have a model of the environment shaping the organization starting about 1955. Before that, the organization more or less controlled the environment. But the organization seeks to control its environment, not to be controlled by it. In the 1970s the majors again managed to shape and control the environment to meet their needs, though they have as yet not been as successful as they were between 1920 and 1955.

The Giants Recover

After the critical period from about 1956 to 1960, when tastes were unfrozen, competition was intense, and demand soared, consolidation appeared. The number of firms stabilized at about forty. New corporate entries appeared, such as MGM and Warner Brothers, sensing, one supposes, the opportunity that vastly expanding sales indicated. Some independents grew large. The eight firm concentration ratio also stabilized (though not yet the four firm ratio). The market became sluggish, however, as the early stars died, were forced into retirement because of legal problems, or in the notable case of Elvis Presley, were drafted by an impinging environment. Near the end of this period the majors decided that the new sounds were not a fad and began to buy up the contracts of established artists and were finally successful in picking and promoting new ones, notably The Beach Boys and Bob Dylan. A new generation (e.g., The Beatles) appeared from 1964 to 1969 and sales again soared.

But now the concentration ratios soared also. From 1962 to 1973

---

[13]Arthur L. Stinchcombe, "Bureaucratic and Craft Administration of Production: A Comparative Study," *Administrative Science Quarterly* 4 (September 1959): 168–187.

the four firm ratio went from 25 to 51 percent; the eight firm ratio from 46 to 81 percent, almost back to the pre-1955 levels. The number of different firms having hits declined from forty-six to only sixteen. Six of the eight giants were diversified conglomerates, some of which led in the earlier period; one was a new independent, the other a product of mergers.

How did they do it? The major companies asserted "increasing central control over the creative process"[14] through deliberate creation and extensive promotion of new groups, long-range contracts for groups and reduced autonomy for producers. In addition, legal and illegal promotion costs (drug payola to disc jockeys, for example) rose in the competitive race and now went beyond the resources of small independents. Finally, the majors "have also moved to regain a controlling position in record distribution by buying chains of retail stores."[15] The diversity is still greater than it had been in the past, and may remain high, but it is ominous that the majors have all the segments covered. As an executive said, "Columbia Records will have a major entry into whatever new area is broached by the vagaries of public tastes." But for a concentrated industry, the "vagaries of public tastes" are not economical; it is preferable to stabilize them and consolidate them. This would be possible through further control over the creative process and marketing. The next decade will tell.

Some Conclusions

We started our history of the popular music industry with the question of bias. Do industrial elites exercise bias in selecting what we shall see or hear, or do they merely respond to public tastes? In this instance, the mindless formats for popular music before 1955 primarily served the economic interests of the majors—a variety of tastes would mean loss of economic control to some extent and loss of efficient production. Any concern with tastes per se was probably quite secondary. If homogeneity is once again established, it will still probably be for economic reasons, not because punk rock or disco (or whatever it is that is in vogue by the time you read this book) is ideologically preferred by the majors. So ideological biases probably played a trivial role in this case; but that does not mean that public tastes played the major role. Some public tastes were probably suppressed for a long time and, of course, tastes can be

---

[14]Peterson and Berger, "Cycles," p. 170.
[15]Ibid., p. 170.

manufactured as well through repetition and availability of a limited range of products. Economic considerations appear to have been foremost, and an industry analysis makes this clear.

This example of an industry in a changing environment allows us to sort out a number of additional observations that are more important for organizational analysis:

* Organizations do "adjust" to environmental changes, such as technological developments and product substitution (TV for radio), but the drive is to control and manipulate the environment.

* The turbulence can be created by their own efforts to rationalize and introduce new innovations (TV, LP records, transistor radios). As Pogo might say: "We have met the environment and he is us."

* New technological developments do not determine cultural outcomes. For example, mass markets and cultural homogeneity are not due to the invention of the radio, or records, or TV; all three are compatible with diversified, segmented markets that reflect diverse cultural styles and interests. But the way new technologies are used by powerful firms can create massification.[16]

* The most salient environment for the majors is other majors; despite competition between them, they collectively evolve strategies to eliminate or absorb threatening minors.

* The public is poorly served in the process. If we have to hope for the accidental conjunction of three major technological changes (LP records, TV, and transistor radios) to have a diversity of tastes served, we are in deep trouble as a public. Many consumer goods industries are highly concentrated, and innovations are marginal or cosmetic improvements on standard goods, not a diversity that would offer substantial choices. (As with junk foods, such as snacks, sugared cereals, and nitrates in meats, some innovations are not even improvements, but poisons.)

* The costs of turbulence and change, when it occurs, are "externalized" to dependent parts of the industry, and thus are borne by artists, producers, and other creative people, or satellite firms that provide standby facilities. The majors did not show any decline in profits during the turbulence; the costs could be passed on. (Just as the costs of a fiasco such as the Ford Motor Company's Edsel did not cause a drop in Ford's dividends; the cost was borne by workers through a drop in employment.)

Because the popular music industry could not utilize the state for protection, it was subject to disturbances from new technologies which inadvertently nourished suppressed tastes.

---

[16]Hirsch, "Organizational Effectiveness."

THE PHARMACEUTICAL INDUSTRY

Hirsch[17] points out that had the record industry been as successful as the pharmaceutical industry in securing state (that is, Federal Government) entitlements of various sorts, it could have protected itself much better and not have been subject to strong competition from new companies. The popular music industry tried; it lobbied for legislation that would have given a firm an exclusive license for recording and promoting a new song. They argued they were entitled to a royalty any time a record was played, but were unsuccessful. Radio stations, naturally, fought this attempt, since they had an essentially free product to use on the air.

In contrast, the pharmaceutical industry was strikingly successful despite similarities in organizational structure. The two industries were quite similar in organizational terms, Hirsch notes. Both had mechanized and simple production technologies. Both used external "gatekeepers" (physicians and disc jockeys) to introduce and advertise their product. Profits overwhelmingly came from the sale of new products. Both were dependent upon technological inventions, and had grown much faster than the average industry since 1945. The big threat to the major pharmaceutical companies was the manufacture of drugs under generic names by small competitors. So they formed a trade association that within eight years got legislation in 38 states prohibiting the substitution of chemically equivalent drugs at about one quarter the price for the brand name drug. This way captive markets could be preserved and the costs of entry into the industry became very high. They were not subject to the kind of competition that the majors in the record industry were after 1955.

Next, the major firms brought pressure upon the U.S. Patent Office to change its interpretation of the law that no "naturally occurring" substances could be patented, in particular, antibiotics. The prices of antibiotics had fallen drastically in the 1940s and early 1950s as new firms started producing them. In 1955 penicillin, for example, cost only 6 percent of what it had cost in 1945. The firms were successful, and they patented everything in sight (in eight years, 6,107 new prescription drugs and 2,000 variations on antibiotics). Unpatented antibiotics yielded a profit of about 20 percent, patented ones a profit of 75 percent or more.

Finally, the major drug companies bought off one of the major gatekeepers, the American Medical Association. The AMA had strict requirements regarding advertising drugs in its twelve journals in the 1940s, including one that required advertising by generic

---

[17]Ibid.

name, rather than brand name, except for the original producer. It published an annual handbook on drugs for physicians. After pressure and the lure of high advertising revenues, all this changed. The manufacturers now wrote the book advising doctors on drugs and the AMA book was discontinued; any drug could be listed by brand name; and the AMA's Council on Drugs was replaced by a committee with more lenient standards. Between 1953 and 1960, AMA income from advertising tripled. (Hirsch documents an unusual degree of job mobility between the AMA and the pharmaceutical trade association, and AMA lobbying support for the industry when it battled the weak FDA.) The record companies used payola as an equivalent device, but of course it was an illegal tactic, while those of the pharmaceutical industry were legal.

Thus, to our list of observations about the environment we could add the following: The power of the state to regulate and disburse entitlements is probably the single most important means of controlling an environment. This is notwithstanding the fact that the state can also block attempts to control environments, as with antitrust laws, limits on deceptive advertising, protection of unions and regulations on pensions, workmen's compensation, and so on. It is to the role of the state in capitalist societies that much of the exciting work on organizational environments is turning. A major debate at present is whether the state is primarily a "tool" of the capitalist class, an umpire reconciling the diverse interests and conflicts of the capitalist class in order to preserve its hegemony, or an independent entity with organizational needs of its own, thus serving as a broker between the capitalist class and other classes, and meeting its own needs for growth and power in the process.[18] The logic of this book would tentatively suggest the latter, viewing as we do organizations (including government agencies) as resources for many groups, but it is an area we are not prepared to explore here.

The Non-Trivial Organization

Fortunately, the new interest in the environment comes at a time when there is also a new interest in organizations other than hospitals and social agencies, or the efficiency of factories or groups of salesmen. The modern world is also made up of banks, investment houses, pharmaceutical companies, brokerage firms, television networks, newspapers, record companies, not to mention conglomerates and multinational firms. All of them are receiving attention in the 1970s as organizations (rather than as incidental settings to test

---

[18]See the thoughtful article by John Mollenkopf, "Theories of the State and Power Structure Research," *The Insurgent Sociologist* 5, no. 3 (Spring 1975): 245–264.

theories of internal structure or process), and much of the attention involves the interactions of these organizations in industries and networks. Indeed, Immanuel Wallerstein has challenged us with a stimulating treatise on the emergence of world capitalism which deliberately eschews a national focus in favor of an international one, an analysis parallel in some respects to what we shall offer when we discuss networks in the second part of this chapter. The individual unit, nation, or organization, must be understood in terms of the network it exists in.[19] Interlocking directorates among the 500 largest industrials and the largest banks and retail firms are being studied in explicit network terms.[20] Journalists of high quality are aiding us.

Robert Caro has analyzed the career of the czar of city building, Robert Moses, in a massive work of great sociological interest.[21] Two other journalists (or investigative reporters as they are now called), Jack Newfield and Paul DuBrul, explore the interdependencies of major financial institutions, industry, and political corruption that brought about the crisis in New York City in a stunning work that sheds a glaring light upon the paucity of most organizational and interorganizational analysis.[22] Graham Allison of Harvard uses an implicit organizational set model to analyze the frightening Cuban Missile Crisis of 1962, in one of the few scholarly books that asks the question: "What difference does it make if one use a rational organizational model, a bureaucratic power one, or a political actor one?"[23] The notion of analyzing an industry rather than one or two

[19]Immanuel Wallerstein, *The Modern World-System: Capitalist Agriculture and the Origins of the European World-Economy in the Sixteenth Century* (New York: Academic Press, Inc., 1974).

[20]Peter Mariolis, "Interlocking Directorates and Control of Corporations," *Social Science Quarterly* 56 (December 1975): 425–439; Thomas Koenig, Robert Gogel, and John Sonquist, "Theories of the Significance of Corporate Interlocking Directorates," *American Journal of Economics and Sociology* (1978); "Interlocking Directorates as a Social Network," *American Journal of Economics and Sociology* (1978); Koenig and Sonquist: "Studying Interrelations Between Corporations Through Interlocking Directorates" in Tom Burns and William Buckley, eds. *Power and Hierarchical Control* (New York: Sage Publications, 1977); Beth Mintz, Peter Freitag, Carol Hendricks, and Michael Schwartz, "Problems of Proof in Elite Research," *Social Problems* 23, no. 3 (February 1976): 314–324; Peter J. Freitag, "The Cabinet and Big Business," *Social Problems* 23 (December 1975); Beth Mintz, "The President's Cabinet, 1897–1972," *Insurgent Sociologist* (Spring 1975); Peter Mariolis, "Bank and Financial Control Among Large U. S. Corporations," Ph.D. Dissertation, SUNY at Stony Brook, 1978; Beth Mintz, "Who Controls the Corporations: A Study of Interlocking Directorates," Ph.D. Dissertation, SUNY at Stony Brook, 1978.

[21]Robert Caro, *The Power Broker: Robert Moses and the Fall of New York* (New York: Random House, Inc., 1975).

[22]Jack Newfield and Paul DuBrul, *The Abuse of Power: The Permanent Government and the Fall of New York* (New York: Viking Press, Inc., 1977).

[23]Graham T. Allison, *Essence of Decision: Explaining the Cuban Missile Crises* (Boston: Little, Brown & Co., 1971).

organizations within it—commonplace with economists but virtually absent from the organizational literature—is strongly urged by Paul Hirsch in a seminal piece,[24] and we have followed up on it in our examination of popular music and the drug industry. Mayer Zald has raised the crucial question of how society seeks to control organizations.[25] Amitai Etzioni adopts an organizational framework in much of his discussion of what might lead to a just and active society,[26] as does Michel Crozier in his criticism of contemporary France.[27]

It is clear that the large, powerful organizations of our society are now under scrutiny by at least a few analysts (aided by journalists of high quality) and they are being considered in network or environmental terms. The field is alive and well.

PART TWO: THE NETWORK

Initially the environment was anything "out there" of interest to the researcher. Progressively we have begun to catalogue things that we should look for out there. The first step was the analysis of two or three interacting organizations, initially labeled interorganizational analysis, with the emphasis upon the effect of the other organizations on the "focal" organization—the one we were primarily interested in. Then the idea of a set of organizations came into the literature, with some implicit criteria for what organizations should be considered in the set.[28] From there we went to the idea of networks of organizations, focusing upon the properties of the networks rather than any one organization in it. (The work we have just considered, on industries, is not explicitly a network analysis, since it doesn't deal with the interaction of specific organizations. It is a specification of a part of the environment.) While still primitive, and possibly distorted by heavy borrowing from the biological sciences, the concept of networks is the most exciting development in this new preoccupation with the environment. We shall deal with it in several ways in this part of the chapter.

Think of conceptualizing the environment as a nested box problem; inside each box is a smaller box whose dimensions are constrained by the larger box. Each box is independent to some

---

[24]Paul Hirsch, "Organizational Analysis and Industrial Sociology."

[25]Mayer N. Zald, "On the Social Control of Industries," *Social Forces* (in press).

[26]Amitai Etzioni, *The Active Society* (New York: The Free Press, 1968).

[27]Michel Crozier, *The Stalled Society* (New York: Penguin Books, Inc., 1974).

[28]William M. Evan, "The Organization-Set: Toward a Theory of Interorganizational Relations," in J. D. Thompson, ed. *Approaches to Organizational Design* (Pittsburgh: University of Pittsburgh Press, 1966), pp. 175-191.

extent of the large boxes (and the smaller ones within it), and can be analyzed as such. But it is also quite dependent upon the shape of those within and without it. Extended to social organization in general, we get the familiar hierarchy of forms, with the familiar problems of infinite regress and infinite progress. The group is made up of individuals, but the individuals are made up of organs, and these of cells—that is the regress. But the group may exist in a department, the department in a division, the division in an organization, the organization in an industry, the industry in a region, the region in a nation, and so on up to the solar system.

Galaxies and cells aside, we do not know where to either begin or stop. Can you analyze the division without analyzing the organization it exists in or the departments within the division? Worse yet, we are a part of this hierarchy, so our thinking about it is conditioned by our presence within it. The general rule that most social scientists follow is that whatever "level" is selected as the unit of analysis—say the group—we had better make at least a cursory examination of the levels above it (department) and below it (the individuals). Here is where our basic assumptions or, to put it less favorably, our stereotypes come into play. We may think ourselves to be reasonably open-minded about the nature of groups, and trying to discover this nature, but if we see individuals as basically rational, materialistic beings, that will foreclose much inquiry. Similarly, if we believe that groups exist within departments that are striving to be efficient (rather than striving to maximize comforts or not particularly striving for anything), that also will shape our inquiry. We would not think of looking for some things and would amplify others. Some of the most bitter disputes about organizational analysis turn upon basic preconceptions, especially those concerning the "nature of man." These preconceptions can foreclose open inquiry.[29]

Moving from organizational to interorganizational analysis to sets and then to networks does not signify any particular progress on this problem. Conflicting views of basic social processes or the nature of man are mainly carried over to the extended hierarchy. For example, do networks develop or only change; is change generally orderly or disorderly; are network ties rational or nonrational? But at least we are now in a better position to conceptualize levels above that of the organization, and to uncover and expose to inquiry some assumptions about basic social processes. Perhaps the greatest return will come from flexibility on these issues. For example, recent

---

[29]This is the force of Chris Argyris' denunciation of Peter Blau, James Thompson, myself, and others in his *The Applicability of Organizational Sociology* (New York: Cambridge University Press, 1974).

work in cognitive processes, discussed at the end of Chapter 2, has led me to emphasize accident, random choice, and poorly ordered preferences much more than I did in the past, but without assuming that most of life is like that. This should enable me to recognize these processes when they do occur, but not bend every occurrence to either fit them or exclude them.

LEVELS OF ANALYSIS

Below I list some basic issues that must be dealt with, no matter what the level of analysis is. To some extent these may be empirical problems, to be solved by looking at actual data and behavior. Change may be orderly for some systems but disorderly for other systems, for example, and research might determine that. Or some organizations (or small groups, or world capitalism) might be seen as basically goal-directed entities controlled by a dominant group or person; whereas other organizations or some parts of world capitalism may be seen as collections of resources that all kinds of groups, rather than a controlling elite, try to latch on to and use for their own ends.

However, I believe that we are rarely as open as that; we are not prepared to invoke cultural other-regarding norms in some cases and economic, self-regarding ones in others. Instead we tend to favor the data that suggest one or the other. We lean toward the data and problems that would suggest that change is orderly (or

---

TABLE 1   BASIC ISSUES FOR ALL LEVELS

Is the system goal-directed, or does its direction merely emerge as the product of multiple interests and uses?

Is rationality, intended rationality, or nonrationality emphasized in analysis?

Rationality aside, how much emphasis is placed upon random, nonpurposive, and accidental behavior?

Is change seen as orderly or disorderly, continuous or discontinuous, progressive, cyclical, or random?

Is the unit seen as independent or dependent upon levels above and below it?

Is the basic form of interaction of units cooperation, conflict, or superficial contact and adjustment?

Are the subunits of the level tightly or loosely coupled?

Is behavior governed by cultural norms and values, or by economic and self-regarding ones?

Are norms and values stable, or fluctuating with the situation, or are there even such things as norms and values?

Is behavior a function of conditioning, learning, sentiments, norms, or traditions?

FIGURE 1   THE GREAT CHAIN OF BEING

Levels	Some topics

INDIVIDUAL

GROUP

DEPARTMENT

DIVISION

ORGANIZATION

INTERORGANIZATION   Competition; cooperation; contacts; exchanges; dominance

ORGANIZATIONAL SET   Set size; boundary personnel; heterogeneity; stability

FIGURE 1 (continued)

Levels	Some topics
NETWORKS See Figure 2	Tight or loose coupling; strength of ties; regulatory functions; scope and diversity of organizations in network; network persistence; power centers
INDUSTRY	Norms; internal controls; concentration and monopoly; growth and decline; modern; traditional
REGION	Regional dependencies; expanding and declining regions; federal policies; specialization
NATIONAL (U.S.)	Conglomerates; interlocking directorates; role of government (the "state") in capitalism
WORLD	Multinationals; dominant and dependent countries; extractive or manufacturing economies; world capitalism versus socialist sectors

disorderly), or tend to ask the kind of questions that would "prove" that organizations are more or less rational instruments on the other hand, or that they are congeries of utilizable resources. Over time, the analyst tends toward one or the other position on this list, or only slowly changes his way of seeing things. You might read the "Basic Issues" list now (p. 219) to try to see to what extent you would lean toward one or the other of the alternatives.

Figure 1 lays out the familiar hierarchy of social actors, from the individual to the world system, but we have now inserted the recently conceptualized levels of interorganizational analysis and networks. I indicate some of the major topics of the more general and unfamiliar levels, and how we represent some of the levels in diagrams.

Figure 2 presents an example of what a network diagram might look like, with the length of the lines indicating closeness of the organizations. It is a very simple conception, since it does not indicate the kind of information, resources, dependencies, influences, and so on that move through the channels, nor their direction, and it leaves out the whole funding complex of governmental subsidies, tax breaks, "third party" fund sources such as insurance companies

FIGURE 2   IMAGINARY CITY HEALTH NETWORK

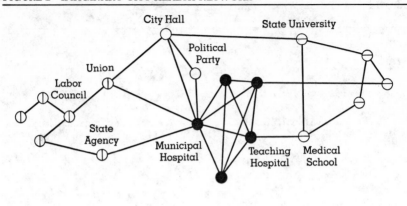

Legend:

○ Political (allocative) groups
⦵ Regulatory and special-interest groups
● Hospitals
⊖ Support groups:
  Medical school
  Nursing school
  University
  Private research foundation
  Government research agency

and medicine. Yet, simple as it is, it has some revealing characteristics.

A SIMPLE NETWORK

Let us assume that Figure 2 deals with part of a health system. The five hospitals (solid dots) would be said to be *tightly coupled;* a "disturbance" or change in any one of them would have rapid ramifications for all the others. Each is linked to the others directly; there are eight links, the maximum number possible. The five organizations on the right (support groups), however, are only *loosely coupled;* they all deal with training or research, but they are not very interdependent. The six organizations on the left can hardly be said to be coupled at all; only two of the six have more than one tie into this network (they may be tightly coupled to other networks not considered here). These are, let us say, regulatory and special interest groups.

An action by an organization in this group (i.e., the auditors in a state agency) that affects the municipal hospital run by the city will have consequences for all the organizations in the hospital cluster. It may be the only way for the state auditors to affect the standards and practices of the private and voluntary hospitals, since only in some areas can they control these directly. The results of a state requirement that patients be offered drugs by their generic name rather than by their brand name, to reduce costs to patients and cut profits to dominant drug companies, could set up a chain of interactive influences in all the hospitals which might spill over into other billing practices. This is what we mean by a tightly coupled network; change is fast and the interactive effects may be unpredictable.[30]

The effect of this change on the major medical school in the area would be considerably "dampened," however, since it is linked only to the voluntary hospital that is the main teaching hospital for the medical school. The medical school is not likely to respond to directives from the state agency which primarily affect the municipal hospital, though some effects will be felt. Nor are the other organizations on the right-hand side likely to be affected. They are linked to one another and to the medical school, but not closely.

The city hall has the furthest reach of any of the organizations, even though it is not closely tied (in terms of distance of line) to any but the dominant political party. It can reach into the supportive network on the right, and the regulatory and interest group network on the left, and reach the hospital network both directly and through the political party. No other organization has this degree of reach and centrality. The number of ties it has into the health system (all groups except the political party and the city hall itself) is small— only three. The municipal hospital has six. But city hall can reach further. Once we know something about the six ties of the hospital, the diagram suggests that the municipal hospital is at the center of the network only by reason of its dependency and its use by other organizations; its centrality does not necessarily mean dominance.

Though the medical school and the teaching hospital are crucial for the support cluster and the hospital cluster, since they provide the sole important link between the two, they are isolated from the political, the regulatory, and the special interest organizations. (The diagram is oversimplified in this and in other ways; a self-respecting medical school would not have to go through the state university to reach city hall, since medicine is too powerful for that in most cities. A more complex diagram would note a more complex relationship.)

None of the organizations on the left are depicted as particularly

---

[30]Karl Weick, "Educational Organizations as Loosely Coupled Systems," *Administrative Science Quarterly* 21 (March 1976): 1–19.

important, even though they include the hospital council, the labor council, a union that has some municipal hospital employees in it, the welfare department, state regulatory agencies, and perhaps the Community Chest. The labor council has four links but they don't go anywhere in this network.

The diagram does not suggest that an organization on the edge of the network can only reach, say, city hall on health matters by literally going through one or two or three other organizations. Of course direct ties exist, and they are used for routine and symbolic purposes. What are depicted here, though, are ties that indicate strong influence or power, and the direction may go both ways. For example, if the state university wished to improve the quality of care in the municipal hospital, it might have little clout if it went directly and preached to them. However, if it activated city hall and the dominant political party (which probably allocates positions in the hospital on the basis of patronage), it could exert leverage. Furthermore, if it had the medical school, which is nominally a part of the university but really quite separate, bring pressure to bear on the teaching hospital, which in turn relieves a fair bit of the overcrowding in the municipal hospital by taking away the valuable clinical cases for teaching purposes, a good bit might be done. It is unlikely that the university would care in the normal run of things. But suppose its own internal network of interdependencies—student interests, faculty members connected with the social sciences, and some liberal associations—made it important to take a posture of public service and drain off some student discontent with a special sequence of field courses with social and political content. It could be done.

There are a number of points to be made about this exercise in simple network analysis. First, even though all organizations may be quite aware of each other, and do routine business with each other on occasion, everything does not affect everything else. The number of possible ties in this (simple) network is immense, but most of them would mean little. The popular research techniques of watching mail flows, counting telephone contacts, or giving checklists to executives could be very misleading. Parts of the network are buffered from changes in other parts because there is no link that is powerful. Some powerful links are not all that obvious (the political ones, in this case). A weak tie may provide a strong link, paradoxically, in network analysis, though there is no good illustration in my example.[31] Some "central" organizations, in this case the municipal hospital, may be central only as a resource for other groups but otherwise may be quite dependent. The hospital supplies jobs for

---

[31]Mark Granovetter, "The Strength of Weak Ties," *American Journal of Sociology* 78 (May 1973): 1360–1380.

the party and the city hall; teaching cases for the teaching hospital and thus the medical school; relieves the other private, voluntary hospital from having to care for poor and undesirable patients; supplies members for the union; and gives state agencies leverage on the other hospitals. It is a very useful organization, quite apart from its manifest functions of caring for the poor.

Second, the analysis suggests different degrees of density in different parts of the network. While everything is not tied to everything else, one part of the network is highly interactive, another one only somewhat so, and the third—the regulatory and special interest groups—hardly interactive at all. Of course, the investigator chooses how to measure the degree of interaction between any two organizations, so it is she who constructs the network to show the density of various parts. This takes more than a count of phone calls or logging of mail; it takes political judgment and detailed case histories. But network analysis allows that kind of information and judgment to be utilized, laid out, and made subject to criticism from others.

Third, the emphasis, the unit of analysis, is the network itself, not the particular organizations in it. Our conceptual vocabulary is not yet developed enough to label this network in any revealing way (moderately complex; multi-density; triadic; or whatever), but it has properties of its own which would distinguish it from other networks. Even if our interest is primarily in one organization, the next level up—network—is crucial, as I indicated in my remarks about Figure 1. The state agency becomes more understandable as an organization in itself if we know that it is cut off from the patronage system, loosely tied to organized labor, loosely tied to most hospitals and tightly tied to the municipal hospital, and cut off from all support groups. In another city or state, a similar agency might be tightly linked to the dominant political party and the patronage system, to the medical school and other support groups including the university, thus its power might be considerable. We can best understand a particular organization, if that is our interest, if we understand the network it has to play in.

Furthermore, we could use network analysis to examine changes over time. The Federal Government has become more active in health polities; it supplies more and more of the funds for construction, equipment, and patient costs, so it can require health organizations to do things in order to keep the funding. Thus, over time, it can increase the density of parts of the network, perhaps by adding organizations such as "Health Maintenance Organizations," and decrease the importance of other organizations (perhaps organized labor, or the local medical society). Charting networks over time would show these shifts.

Network analysis is obviously not limited to health organizations. An industry such as steel might be analyzed in these terms. To convert our rudimentary diagram, consider the center cluster as the primary producers, the right-hand cluster as the industrial customers, with the medical school being a major auto manufacturer whose actions will affect the appliance industry and others in the cluster. The city hall, the central one despite its apparent isolation, is analogous to the central banks, and the left-hand cluster the supportive infrastructure and government. Laumann and Pappi[32] have attempted such analysis in a small German town and an industrial city in the Midwest using techniques that allow the graphic representation of social distance. The technique is complicated and still somewhat controversial, and as yet, the findings are not much different from what conventional analysis might predict with much less effort. Still, it is a pioneering effort and organizational theorists should consider it seriously.[33]

A HEALTH SYSTEM ANALYZED

To illustrate the development over time of increasingly sophisticated views of the environment, I will again use an example from the health field and review the fictional history of research on "Westwood Hospital." While fictional, it draws upon the experiences of researchers, illustrates how far we have come, and demonstrates the importance of network analysis. Let us say Westwood is a private voluntary hospital in Regional City serving largely a middle- and upper-class clientele. A study made in the early 1960s would have focused upon the internal structure and leadership, with some vague reference to the environment. In the late 1960s it would have been an interorganizational study, focusing upon Westwood, but now examining the major organizations it had contact with. This shift from an organizational to interorganizational framework would have considerable impact. For example, in the early 1960s, one might have made an intensive analysis of the characteristics of key medical officers—the Chief of Staff, Chief of Surgery, and so on. The

---

[32]Edward O. Laumann and Franz U. Pappi, "New Directions in the Study of Community Elites," *American Sociological Review* 38, no. 2 (April 1973): 212–230; E. O. Laumann, Lois M. Verbrugge, and F. U. Pappi, "A Casual Modelling Approach to the Study of a Community Elite's Influence Structure," *American Sociological Review* 39, no. 2 (April 1974): 162–174; and E. O. Laumann, *Networks of Collective Action* (New York: Academic Press, Inc., 1976).

[33]A scheme which inspired my illustration, and is more useful for organizational analysis than Laumann's, is presented by Howard Aldrich, "Organization Sets, Action Sets, and Networks: Making the Most of Simplicity," unpublished manuscript, Cornell University, 1976.

administrator of the hospital and the president of the board of trustees would have commented upon the kind of person they desired,
and the matter would be fully "explained"—they selected the best
women and men. But in the late 1960s it would be noted that
Westwood was a teaching hospital for the major medical school in
the area, State University Medical School. This meant that medical
school professors and students used the patients in Westwood as
teaching material. The school would have a major interest in who
was Chief of Staff or Chief of Surgery at the hospital. It could easily
turn out that appointments to such key offices were really dictated
by the Dean of the State Medical School, and the judgments of the
trustees and the administrator counted for little. After the fact, the
latter would justify the selection on the basis of vague qualities (such
as leadership, outstanding internist, able to cooperate effectively
with the medical school), but they actually would have had little
choice.

A second example: The administrator of the hospital may have
wanted to cut back on the outpatient department because it cost so
much and attracted too many poor patients. But these patients were
useful teaching cases, so the Medical School dean would have discussed the matter with a trustee of Westwood one day at the country
club, and that would take care of it; no cut would be made. Interviewed by an organizational researcher in 1962 as to why the outpatient department was maintained, the administrator probably
said "public service" to the researcher, but "the power structure" to
himself. Interviewed by a researcher in 1968, who had taken the
trouble to do some interviews at the medical school first (thus using
an interorganizational framework), the question he asked could
have been phrased: "How important is it to the trustees to keep the
affiliation with the medical school—for example, is this why you
have such a large outpatient department?" The answer would have
been: "Of course, that tie means a lot to them, and while the department gives me problems, it also helps the hospital to have all
those interns and residents around doing the work the private
physicians are too busy to do." A public service is provided, but now
it appears that this was a side benefit, not the major purpose. The
difference is substantial. A rational, official goal perspective is replaced by a political perspective that sees the organization as having multiple functions, one of which may be, but not necessarily to
any great extent, public service.

By 1973, there could be a further shift in conceptualization. A
researcher might not even have Westwood in mind as the focal
point of his research. In the course of trying to understand how the
medical "system" works in Regional City, he would interview
executives at the four major hospitals, the medical society, the

medical school, a few rehabilitation agencies, the Community Chest, and the Hospital Council. The questions would probably be simple ones—how much contact does each have with the others; who initiates the contact; what is the principal business transacted (e.g., sharing resources, sending or receiving patients, providing information, coordinating development plans, etc.)? Unfortunately, we would probably not be privy to the insight that Westwood and the medical school have a symbiotic relationship, wherein each feeds on the other, and that this keeps the tradition of free or low-cost care to the poor alive. Counting contacts will not disclose that. But nevertheless the researcher would find that Presbyterian Hospital is at the center of the system, of which Westwood is a part, directing information and requests to the other hospitals and sitting on more community boards than any other. He would be able to note that Westwood seeks information from Presbyterian before acting and presents requests for expansion or a larger slice of the Community Chest budget to committees whose chairpersons are closely tied to Presbyterian.

Now Westwood again looks different. It is a fairly dependent part of the whole. What the 1962 researcher saw as a titanic battle between the medical staff, administrator, and the trustees concerning the form of expansion, could now be seen as a very narrow issue, the terms of which were set by Presbyterian and, say, the medical school. Westwood could decide to do either A or B, but they were not allowed to consider D, E, F, and G, any one of which might have been much better for them and perhaps avoided the internal conflict that the choice of either A or B created.

By 1980, hopefully, another researcher will be able to put Westwood into a still larger context. For example, she might find that the medical system in Regional City is made up of clusters of highly interactive organizations and interests, but the clusters themselves are only loosely connected to each other, such that major Federal policies have strong effects upon some clusters but weak ones upon others, and that Federal policies in turn are shaped by national interests that are formed out of numerous cities such as Regional City. (The rising involvement of the government makes an interorganizational or network viewpoint more necessary now, but it would have been just as appropriate in the 1950s and, of course, has always been appropriate for modern business and industry.)

To be more specific about the link between Federal policies and local networks, suppose we find that Westwood is about to expand greatly with highly specialized facilities and expensive new wings, using a mixture of Federal, State, and City tax dollars, Community Chest funds, and private donations. The sign, one might have said, of a healthy expanding organization, drawing resources from its environment and providing services in return. There is a dynamic administrator at the head, and his relations with the trustees and the medical staff are excellent.

A network analysis might reason differently. Suppose we simplify things greatly and say there are two aspects of government aid to medical care. One system is concerned with medical research, innovative techniques, and upgrading hospital standards. Another system is concerned with the distribution of medical services, matters such as excess beds in some areas, excess operating equipment that is rarely used, and the access of the poor to medical care. Each system has its own network of public and private organizations, but the two systems are only loosely joined to each other; there are different agencies, different politicians, and different commercial groups in each cluster. (The two clusters share a basic set of beliefs about health matters, however. Neither would advocate socialized medicine, for example.)

The first system is a tightly coupled network itself. There are many points of interaction where information, advice, help, and resources are shared and traded. It includes the powerful medical equipment industry and the medical supply industry (two of the most profitable industries on record for over two decades, along with the pharmaceutical industry). These actively promote research, innovation, new equipment, and more beds in more hospitals. It also includes the organized medical profession, the heads of the large metropolitan medical centers where most of the research is done and the high quality care is provided, and the insurance industry. One indicator of a tightly coupled network is the extent that people can move freely among the organizations. Though it has not as yet been documented, there are strong suggestions[34] that people move freely among: (a) government health agencies; (b) the American Medical Association; (c) the equipment, supply, and drug companies; (d) the major medical centers; and (e) the major insurance firms such as Blue Cross or Prudential.

Let us say a "disturbance" occurs in this sector. A Congressman wants to show that he is for something that is noncontroversial, so he hits upon health research as an issue, builds a powerful committee, and gets bills through that literally flood the agencies with money. In a tightly coupled network the effect is immediately felt. Regional City political leaders are part of the Congressman's party; they have additional links to members of the network through prep schools, elite vacation spots, memberships in "discriminating clubs," and so on. They are making plans even before the new government pro-

---

[34]Barbara and John Ehrenreich, *The American Health Empire: Power, Profits, Politics* (New York: Vintage Books, Random House, Inc., 1971).

grams are announced. One is to upgrade hospital standards by providing funds for expensive new equipment and expensive new services (all rarely used).

Now Presbyterian Hospital is the natural candidate to receive this largess, but it is quite glutted with expensive gadgets, and it lacks space for expansion. The blacks in the adjoining area have protested expansion plans. The matter will be taken care of in time, for the banks in Regional City have been persuaded to "red line" the area (refuse to lend money to those in poor areas who want to improve their properties or put up new buildings); the police are withdrawing and concentrating in the adjacent middle-class area. Soon it can be declared a disaster area and the hospital will acquire condemned land for new buildings, parking, housing for nurses, and so on. But that will take time. So Westwood Hospital is the logical choice to receive the funds. But there are problems. The medical school wants more control over appointments to its staff, and middle-income people want easier access to beds. Both of these can be accommodated with some effort. But some segments of the local power structure insist that lower-income people in Westwood's area should continue to have access to it. It is a middle-class hospital, but takes in a sizable proportion of lower-class people too, largely but not exclusively for teaching purposes.

Meanwhile, in another part of the Federal bureaucracy, there are other developments. This "distribution" system is less tightly coupled than the "resource" system described above, so things are slow in moving, and the various groups have only partially shared interests. There are liberal politicians, liberal groups such as the National Council of Churches and the NAACP, liberal foundations, and, in uneasy alliance, some consumer-oriented health groups ranging from moderate to radical. The general concern is more equitable access to health facilities for low-income people and the very poor. But there is also a concern with the extraordinary growth in cost of the health system, and attendant wastage.

In particular, Regional City is declared as an overbedded city—an excess of beds per population—by a key Federal agency. The consequences could be severe; Westwood could not expand, and some hospitals with low standards could be closed. Liberal groups nationally and in Regional City are fighting to prevent the closing of poorly financed, poorly run, poorly cleaned, poorly staffed, overcrowded old hospitals in the declining central city areas, because the poor cannot get into the outlying ones. Enough beds have been built in the suburbs to produce an overbedded situation, but in the central city there is overcrowding. In Regional City the target of the Federal agency is Good Samaritan Hospital—a firetrap with largely foreign-trained physicians, a high turnover of nurses and technicians, chronic shortage of sheets and bandages, beds in the halls, ancient operating equipment, and largely uninteresting teaching cases.

In Regional City a link is finally found between the two systems, the resource expanding one and the beleaguered distribution system, and an accommodation is worked out. The administrator of Presbyterian Hospital and the administrator of Good Samaritan Hospital have a little chat after an inconclusive meeting of the Regional City Coordinating Council for Medical Care. Until now, they had never conversed because they moved in two very different systems; until now, the Coordinating Council had rarely done much and this was the first time the chief administrator of Presbyterian had not sent an assistant but came himself.

The accommodation involves a number of informal agreements. First, Good Samaritan will be allowed to conduct a fund-raising drive that will be independent of the Community Chest campaign. This is an unusual event and normally the Chest would have prevented it, but the head of the Chest is also a key trustee of Presbyterian and a judge belonging to the dominant political party. Presbyterian and Westwood will both give the drive full support and ask their large donors to contribute part of their annual tax-saving contributions to Good Samaritan. Second, the city will be persuaded to condemn some property next to Good Samaritan, move out the low-income tenants from two stable apartment houses, and let the hospital take them over for expansion. Third, Federal antipoverty funds, channeled through the state and the city, will be used to finance the expansion of Good Samaritan, as long as the liberals will not protest the use of antipoverty funds to also help in the expansion of Westwood Hospital.

Finally, the city ambulance service, which has traditionally been run from Good Samaritan because of its central location, and staffed by them, will be taken over by Westwood. Why? Because this service allocates emergency cases to the major hospitals and can be designed to ship the interesting cases to Presbyterian and Westwood for teaching purposes and to justify the new exotic facilities, and the uninteresting ones to other hospitals, in particular, shipping the unattractive or disruptive ones to Good Samaritan. Many emergency patients designate the hospital they wish to go to, but the ambulance crews have some latitude and they will be attentive to their new superiors. The switch is justified on the grounds that Good Samaritan loses money on the ambulance service since the city reimbursement rates are so low. It is true, but hospital operating costs in an era of prepayment for the nonpoor are of little concern to middle-class hospitals, so Westwood won't suffer.

The results of the compromise are extensive. Poverty money

that had been tied up by political controversy and charges of mismanagement and corruption can now be allocated to both the poor
and the rich hospitals. Neither of the good hospitals will be flooded
with undesirable patients, but will receive a sufficient stream of
good teaching cases to supply that need, increase occupancy
somewhat, and justify expansion of beds and facilities. The poor
hospital will receive resources and some relief from its crushing
burden of poor patients. There is even vague talk of a geriatric
hospital that could be attached to Good Samaritan to segregate the
dying poor (Westwood and Presbyterian have the bed space to
handle the dying nonpoor). Both the resource and the distribution
systems are satisfied, since there will be Federal money for more
facilities, and yet a poor hospital slated for closing will be revived.
The overbedding problem is intensified, unfortunately, but it is
primarily a bed distribution problem and there is no easy solution
for that (as with the problem of the maldistribution of physicians).

At the proper time, if the systems were well managed and well
coordinated in just this one instance, it would be convenient to have
the local spokesman for the poor clamor for an expansion and improvement of the only hospital the poor can be assured of getting
into, whereupon the conservative mayor would show his responsiveness and leadership by announcing plans for the expansion of
Good Samaritan. Meanwhile, Westwood officials call a press con-
ference and discuss the new challenges of medical technology and
how they will meet them. Most trustees of Westwood, not privy to our
network analysis, are thrilled by the leadership their hospital is
showing.

A naive researcher operating out of an organizational analysis
framework, or even an organization set one, would not be likely to
even connect the two events—the expansion of Westwood and
Good Samaritan. She could cite the latter case as an example of the
creative use of antipoverty funds, the responsiveness of local officials given the newfound power of the blacks, and the generosity of
large donors. If she were studying Westwood, she might discuss
how an organization adjusts to the turbulent environment of
technological change, or how dynamic, farsighted leadership
makes a difference for organizations, or how an organization's
"problems" can be solved if administrators, trustees, and medical
leaders sit down and plan and work together. All of these are possible; such things do happen. But in this semifictitious composite case,
none of them did in fact occur. Westwood was a rather dependent
part of a system in which it had nonobvious links to both Presbyterian and Good Samaritan; it was allowed to act and it was given a
script; the script reflected a struggle at the Federal level; and the

best and the worst hospitals in the city made the actual compromise that created Westwood's script.

The analysis just presented bears a stronger resemblance to sophisticated muckraking journalism than it does to conventional organizational analysis.[35] This is not surprising. Our preoccupation, as the previous chapters of this book demonstrate, has been with *the* organization. The political reporter is concerned with how organizations can be used in political and social struggle. She casts a larger net; when we do the picture changes.

To summarize this lesson: Only a network analysis, and one that reaches up into the national system, can properly describe what happened to one of the organizations, or even that organization in its "set." Dynamics at the organizational level or at the set level would be seriously misinterpreted without this larger understanding. It was particularly important to know how tightly or loosely connected the systems were; the dependencies of the organizations; the circumstances in which very weak links (the Coordinating Council) could prove to be crucial; and the rationalizations and justifications that masked the actual process. When we can perform actual analysis such as this one we will have moved organizational analysis a very long way from its present status.

The Network and the Background

But even this semifictitious example still carries the trace of conceptual baggage that should be closely examined. I described two general positions in the national context of health care—an expansionary one with emphasis upon new technologies, research, and high standards of care (for elite hospitals), and a distributive one concerned with the poor, with the application of present knowledge to the segregated sectors of society lacking in decent care, and the

---

[35]The example of the ambulance firm in this account was inspired by an unpublished manuscript by Murray Milner of the University of Virginia (and supported by a series of news articles in the *New York Times* in early 1978 dealing with "patient snatching" by the city ambulance system). For two excellent recent medical studies that verge on a network analysis see Robert Alford, *Health Care Politics* (Chicago: University of Chicago Press, 1977); and Kenneth McNeil and Edmond Minihan, "Regulation of Medical Devices and Organizational Behavior in Hospitals," *Administrative Science Quarterly* 22, no. 3 (September 1977): 475–490. The health field has probably moved the furthest in an interorganizational direction, indeed, the topic originated there. But the specific organization-environment studies have not been particularly imaginative. Though not concerned with interorganizational matters per se, the best insights still come from the several outstanding works of David Mechanic and Eliot Friedson.

maldistribution of beds and physicians. What is not revealed is the extent to which the two systems share the same values, and the extent to which both would reject socialized medicine, or even a massive reduction in emphasis upon new technologies and research, and a massive increase in preventive facilities, public health measures, and occupational and environmental standards. Outside of the truly radical literature on health care, there is a common "ground" against which we see the "figure."[36] A network analysis presents a figure, which is largely visible because of the background which it is set off from; dissolve that background and the figure is no longer so visible. The nature of the background highlights the figure, and thus suggests what we should examine. It should be the task of the sociologist to examine the background as well.

At the end of this chapter, I will tersely suggest how neo-Marxist thought is moving in such a direction, but it is still too early to draw much from it for a work such as this. But there is one piece of research that does move in this direction. It is not all that new—the research was conducted from 1968 to 1970 and published in 1974. But none of the several new extensive network studies that I know of being conducted from 1976 to 1978 makes any attempt to consider the ground as well as the figure. In most of our work on networks, our conceptual and ideological baggage, developed in the context of solving managerial problems within organizations, has merely been put on a new train and opened up again at a new destination without having been enriched or changed by the journey. Network analysis should permit us to challenge our previous understandings, and this one piece of research makes a tentative step in that direction. The book in question is by Roland Warren, Steven Rose, and Ann Bergunder, and titled *The Structure of Urban Reform.*[37]

Warren and his associates examined the operation of the Model Cities Program, part of the Great Society Program of President Lyndon Johnson, and designed to introduce new community action agencies into urban areas, to stimulate coordination among all agencies concerned with social problems, and to promote innovative responses to these problems.

The problems had been documented extensively since the early 1960s when the civil rights movement, the peace movement, and the student movement heightened our awareness of poverty, decay, discrimination, and helplessness in a rich and bountiful society. One part of the analysis was that existing social agencies were too

---

[36]This point and the analogy were suggested by John Meyer.

[37]Roland Warren, Stephen Rose, and Ann Bergunder, *The Structure of Urban Reform* (Lexington, Mass.: Lexington Books, 1974).

entrenched in traditional ways of doing things; their actions, in addition, were not coordinated even though the problems demanded coordinated attack; and, finally, there were unattended problems and areas of life that would need new agencies. The Model Cities Program was designed to rectify the situation.

The prevailing conception at the time (and continuing today in most quarters) was that attempts to deal with poverty and decay were chaotic because of the hundreds of organizations each going their own way, refusing to cooperate with one another, fighting each other for money, areas of influence, and even clients. Executives were so distracted by the chaos and interactions that they had little time to plan or direct their own agencies. Model Cities programs were introduced to produce cooperation and coordination through centralized planning and through large chunks of new money.

Warren had been thinking and writing about community agencies for a long time, and he was gradually beginning to question these very plausible conceptions of how it was with the community. He and his associates conducted a fairly intensive study of six key agencies in each of nine representative cities during the stormy years of 1968–70. Rather than assuming what the situation was and then looking for new solutions, they asked:

1. How much actual interaction was there between the agencies in this supposedly dense network of interactive relations? Very little, it turned out to the surprise of most of us. Agencies mostly went their own way.

2. Well, what about the contest over "domains" and competition for funds? Very little actually occurred; where it did it was not because an organization saw an opportunity and moved aggressively to occupy the "niche" of another, but because they occasionally bumped into each other without looking and had to sort the problem out.

3. What, then, about the lack of coordination? Little was needed; there was an overall consensus as to who should do what, a division of labor or of sectors, and new formal coordination mechanisms did not increase the efficiency of the agencies. As others have pointed out, coordination has costs associated with it, as well as presumed benefits, and there may be substantial gains with redundant, uncoordinated activity and substantial costs with coordination which eliminates backup facilities.[38]

---

[38]Martin Landau, "Redundancy, Rationality, and the Problem of Duplication and Overlap," *Public Administration Review* 29, no. 4 (July/August 1969). Robert Morris and Ilana Hirsch-Lescohier, "Service Integration: To What Problems is it the Presumed Solution?" in Rosemary C. Sarri and Yeheskel Hasenfeld, eds. *The Management of Human Services* (New York: Columbia University Press, 1978).

4. But with new coordinating agencies and new funds, was there not an increase in innovative attacks on problems? If there was, it was exceedingly small, since the agencies averaged only five to six minor innovations per year, and one moderate innovation; there were virtually no major ones (defined as involving a shift from emphasizing individual deviance or deficiency as the cause of urban problems to an emphasis upon the dysfunctions of the institutional structure such as lack of jobs, discrimination, exploitation, and so on). They note that others who have reviewed the history of the Model Cities program have come to similar conclusions regarding the lack of innovation.[39]

What, then, can we make of it all? Rather than a picture of a disorganized, crowded interorganizational field with great competition for scarce funds and other resources, the research teams came away from their two years of continuous field observations in nine cities with evidence of a high degree of organization, with stable patterned relationships that had little contest or conflict, very little contact or interdependence, and almost no change. Why? Because the agencies shared a common "institutionalized thought structure."[40] This is the "ground" that, once seen, altered the nature of the network or "figure" that would be set off. Warren et al. stress the similarity of this thought structure not only within each of the cities, but among the cities, even though they differed widely in other ways. The thought structure holds that American society, though hardly perfect, is essentially sound in its institutional composition. Problems are transitory or the result of temporary malfunctions, or reside in the character of the individuals. Furthermore, "any group of people who share the same interests and concerns can organize and bring their interests to the attention of appropriate governmental bodies,"[41] and if they don't, it's their own fault. (This is the sociological doctrine of "pluralism," which has come under increasing attack in the last decade.) Furthermore, if problems still remain, there is a constant process of organizational reform and comprehensive planning and coordination taking place which will rectify them if people are tolerant and patient.

Guided by such assumptions, there is little need for interaction, or even conflict among the agencies. When new agencies come in, there is some disturbance but plenty of room to accommodate the newcomer and its money. Agencies agreed on the nature of the clients, the basic soundness of the system, and the ameliorative steps that should be taken. When more radical philosophies were

---

[39]Warren, Rose, and Bergunder, p. 90.
[40]Ibid., pp. 19–25.
[41]Ibid., p. 21.

occasionally espoused, they were quickly made to conform to the institutionalized thought structure.

Warren, Rose, and Bergunder explicitly do not argue that lazy administrators or greedy politicians or callous, indifferent agencies lay behind the ineffectiveness of the programs. (This would be the emphasis of both run-of-the-mill muckrakers, and of those liberal indigents that persist in using a strictly organizational perspective, focusing upon leadership.) The interorganizational field was not even deliberately structured to protect the interests of the individual agencies; given the institutionalized thought structure, their interests were bound to be protected. To them, the problems were temporary, or they resided in the deficient character of those with the problems. It is customary in some quarters, the authors say, to criticize the agencies for promoting their own needs rather than those of the poor, yet given the prevailing assumptions about the problem and the structure of relationships among agencies that is consistent with these, agency needs are bound to take precedence. If one steps out of line, it is necessary to force it back into line or the whole web of understandings and relationships will be disrupted.[42] Finally, the web is neither as dense nor as complex as we generally think; there is surprisingly little interaction, conflict, or need for accommodation. As they repeatedly insist, focusing upon one organization, or a pair of organizations, would be quite misleading; only when the network is examined is the single organization placed in the proper perspective.

PART THREE: LOOSE ENDS

It is fitting that a book which sees a revitalization of organizational theory should end up with several loose ends. These are: the population-ecology model which may be destined to become the dominant one in formal theories of organization-environment relations in sociology; a new appreciation of historical analysis; a growing emphasis upon ethnomethodology; and a major turn toward neo-Marxist forms of analysis. I have grave qualms about the first, but it is intellectually substantial and must be considered. Despite the diversity of the other three, I think they may yet form a coherent new tradition, though it is far too early to tell.

The Population-Ecology Model

The human ecology, population-ecology, or the sociological formulation of natural selection theory has been around for several

---

[42]Ibid., p. 34.

decades in sociology, but only in the last couple of years has it found its niche in organizational theory.[43] It has lodged there, I think, because once we began considering the environment seriously, we were tempted to think of the environment as a more or less unanalyzed thing that could *act*. The language of this school of thought is decisively anthropomorphic: environments act, organizations respond; environments select some organizations for extinction, and allow others to survive. This is the meaning of natural selection—it is "in nature" or "natural" for some organizations to be "selected out" or "negatively selected" (killed) and others to be "selected in" or "positively selected" by the environment.

• There must be natural laws behind this, the theorists reason, which will explain the types of organizations we have. Indeed, such laws are being discovered for the survival of types of fish in lakes, or fruit flies in a laboratory environment, or prehistoric tribes of people faced with the onset of an ice age. They have been used to explain the succession of racial or ethnic groups in areas of Chicago. Why not explain populations of organizations in the same way? Organizations can be said to exist in an ecological setting, just as the pond is an ecological setting for fish. Independent of any of the individuals in these organizations or individuals directing them, they may be subject to laws governing the competition for resources; they may have the ability to adapt to changes in the pond, to retain adaptive forms or programs within them; and to grow complex as the pond grows complex. Principles formulated for general systems theory, such as the law of requisite variety, are adapted: Organization structure should be only as complex as the complexity existing in the environment. To be less complex reduces adaptability; to be more complex signifies waste.

This raises an old problem which has dogged sociology: Because groups and society resemble the natural world in many respects, we tend to interpret things as being "in nature" or natural, or, in our favorite formulation, as "functional." Sociology is a liberal profession, so it is not inclined to extend the mantle of natural to all things; differences in income or on scores on standardized tests between blacks and whites are not considered as in nature, but as manmade through a process of discrimination. But in less touchy areas, we are inclined to say that if a pattern of behavior exists, or if it has existed for a long time, it must serve some societal purpose or have a function; it is the task of the sociologist to discern that func-

---

[43]The most influential statement at present on the ecological view of organizations is by Michael T. Hannan and John Freeman, "The Population Ecology of Organizations," *American Journal of Sociology* 82, no. 5 (March 1977): 929–966. Howard

tion. On the other hand, there have always been critics of this approach who see the social world as manmade; indeed, as largely made by an identifiable minority of men and women. Patterns of behavior can have functions, not for "society," but for specific individuals or parts of society such as classes. The pattern of behavior may be quite dysfunctional for other parts, generally for the weaker, dependent, conquered, or enslaved parts. Slavery was certainly a functional pattern of behavior for landowners in the South, but not for the slaves. Thus, the critic of the functionalist position is likely to insist upon identifying specific groups and avoiding abstractions such as "society" or "man." Similarly, in my criticism of the ecological view of organizations I will insist upon identifying specific aspects of the environment and asking whose interests are served. The natural selection approach, by speaking only of the environment, neglects these considerations.

Often attached to the functionalist and the ecological perspective is an evolutionary one. Those patterns of activity that serve a group or society best will be reinforced and maintained, those that don't will disappear and the end result is the evolution of a form of activity that provides the best service. Society evolves in the direction of more efficient ways of meeting needs, even though an occasional way may provoke unwanted consequences which society then has to cope with. Sometimes it is added that society evolves toward creating ever higher needs, such as self-fulfillment for individuals rather than just survival. These views have ancient roots in social thought. In recent generations, partly in response to the Social Darwinism we encountered in Chapter 2, they were in some disfavor. But, "conservative" Darwinism was replaced by a "reform" Darwinism; the latter sees progress as under human control rather than the result of survival of the fittest. This progress is not absolute, but relative to our evolving intentions.[44] Even this view had its problems, so today, those who look for evolutionary patterns are quick to disclaim any imputation of value in their scheme. What is new is not necessarily better; one can have evolution without "teleology" (the notion that there is some ideal toward which all things strive). But it is hard to avoid the association of ecological adaptation in human societies with the notion of evolution toward higher forms,

---

Aldrich is finishing a volume on organizations and environments that adopts this view as its model (and I am grateful to him for a chance to examine it in draft form and borrow liberally from it). John Kasarda and Charles Bidwell also have a book in draft form which I have examined in part that explicitly uses this model. Since these are some of the brightest theorists around, it is clearly an important development. To my knowledge, it has not as yet been criticized as such.

[44]Mathew Zachariah, "The Impact of Darwin's Theory of Evolution on Theories of Society," *Social Studies* 62, no. 2 (February 1971): 69–76.

better fits, more efficiency, and so on. Talcott Parsons, who has been exploring evolutionary ideas, has recently been criticized on these grounds,[45] and in the scant organizational material in this framework I find the same problem.

The ecological model identifies three stages in a process of social change.[46] First is the occurrence of *variations* in behavior. They may be intended or unintended, it doesn't matter. In organizations, a production crew might gradually vary their techniques, or a shortage of gasoline might lead to a variation in truck delivery practices. Second, natural *selection* occurs as some variations are eliminated because they are undesirable, and others are reinforced because they work. Third, there is a *retention* mechanism which allows those "positively selected variations" to be retained or reproduced. Since nothing ever stands still, either for those in the organization or for its environment, over the long run positively selected variations that become stable activities will be subject to variation in time. The new delivery system may be "selected out" as still another system gets positively selected and built into the structure or behavior of the organization. In the grander scheme of things, the development of a bureaucratic model of organizations was a result of variations in practices, with the firms that tried bureaucracy being successful, thus positively selected. The practice was retained through imitation, takeover of inefficient firms, and imposing the new structure through management textbooks and eventually through state power by insisting that to receive the many benefits of incorporation, subsidies, and legal protection, the organization has to adapt certain accounting procedures, have an identified head, keep records, etc. Meanwhile, the environment changes for some firms, debureaucratization takes place in those dealing with nonroutine tasks, and new decentralized ones appear. This differentiates organizations into types and creates new variations, selection, and retention processes.

Let us examine variation first. As with the ecologists and biologists, natural selection theorists in organizations are fond of citing the huge number of organizations in any society and the rapid rate of change—births, deaths, takeovers. In 1957, for example, 398,000 new businesses were created in the United States, and

---

[45]See the excellent discussion of evolutionary theory in Mark Granovetter, "The Idea of 'Advancement' in Theories of Social Evolution," Department of Sociology, SUNY at Stony Brook, 1978.

[46]Donald Campbell, "Variation and Selection Retention in Socio-Cultural Evolution," *General Systems* 16 (1969): 69–85; Walter Buckley, *Sociology and Modern Systems Theory* (Englewood Cliffs, N.J.: Prentice-Hall, Inc., 1967); Amos Hawley, *Human Ecology: A Theory of Community Structure* (New York: Ronald Press, 1950).

about the same number were transferred to new owners, and almost as many failed outright in the year.[47] This generates a great deal of variation, allowing selection and retention, and leading to better fits with the environment. If only 50 firms were created, 50 transferred, and 48 died, there would be less chance for the proper "niche" to be found in the environment—the "environment" would have less to select from when it selected positively or negatively.

But the vast majority of the business firms in the United States are extremely tiny. Sixty-eight percent of them had sales of under $25,000; two percent of them accounted for 76 percent of the sales. The figures in assets are even more striking: 61 percent of all corporate assets were controlled by one tenth of one percent of firms in 1972.[48] So the great variation provided by many different units is a variation among trivial organizations who are, in addition, operating at the sufferance of the few large ones. This suggests the model is not appropriate for enacted organizations.

But the theorists note that the large organizations also experience variation, selection, and retention *within* them. Here there is a change from the natural model. In contrast to natural organisms, such as fish or amoeba, artificial ones have the capacity to change extensively through structural alteration, thus avoiding extinction. When fish learned to walk, if that is what they did, it took place over centuries; when J. P. Morgan learned to buy up several steel plants and form U. S. Steel Corporation in order to dominate the market, he did it in a matter of years. The evolution of a divisionalized structure at General Motors took decades, but that is a mere mite in terms of natural evolution. The structure was adapted by those industries where it was appropriate, but not by others, illustrating the variability in environments. Organic evolution, then, entails the survival or extinction of entire units; social evolution includes this—all those failing small businesses—but also the structural change of units. (Whether this addition violates the theories borrowed from biology and ecology is not clear.)

But, one can argue, the merger process at the end of the nineteenth century when Morgan formed U. S. Steel and the centralization of power that Alfred Sloan of General Motors brought off in the 1930s were not necessarily adaptations to a changing environment. They *created* a new environment, and other organizations (and communities, families, and individuals) had to do the adapting. In fact, Gabriel Kolko[49] demonstrates that the mergers of the

---

[47]Howard E. Aldrich, *Organizations and Environments* (Englewood Cliffs, N.J.: Prentice-Hall, Inc., 1979).

[48]Ibid.

[49]Gabriel Kolko, *Triumph of Conservatism* (New York: The Free Press, 1977).

nineteenth century were quite uneconomical for the first ten or so years, and were brought about largely for stock manipulation. Someone benefitted, of course, or they would not have gone to all that trouble, but it was not society, the communities, or even the industry. Given the new form, ways were found to make it work, but that is quite contrary to the model's logic. Much the same analysis could be made of Sloan's structural changes; society had to adapt to the consequences of it.[50]

"Why are there so many kinds of animals?" asks a famous essay in ecology; "Why are there so many kinds of organizations?" echoes Hannan and Freeman.[51] But this question highlights the difference; in most areas of economic power—railroads, auto manufacturing, oil production and marketing, steel production—there are very few organizations, and they are of the same kind. There are three major U. S. auto manufacturers, and while organizational theorists could pour over the differences among them (if they bothered to study them), in species terms they are very similar. In the social world, then, a different kind of logic seems to be working. There is not much variation among units; a few giant organizations dominate the many small ones; the giant ones rarely die (there is little negative selection); and in the public sector, efficiency and adaptation are not effective criteria—we simply do not let schools and garbage collectors go out of business. If there is little variation, and little negative selection, then, what is the value of the theory?

One has the same problems when dealing with internal variation and selection. Here, the organization is the environment for the groups within it. Now, of course, there is change within organizations. For example, some people are fired, groups are disbanded, practices are changed, new technologies are introduced. I have been negatively selected myself on occasion, and have selected out others; most of us will have our turns. Which statement was the most illuminating for steelworkers to make when they were laid off in massive numbers in 1977? "I was fired today by the environment"; or, "In its shortsighted concern with profits the major steel companies in the United States refused to modernize their plants, and take cognizance of worldwide overproduction of steel during several years of stagnation of the world economy, so they had the workers and the single-industry communities bear the cost of their mismanagement, dramatizing the cost in the media. This brought pressure upon the Federal Government to institute a variety of

---

[50]Charles Perrow, "Is Business Really Changing?" *Organizational Dynamics* (Summer 1974): 31–44; Emma Rothschild, *Paradise Lost: The Decline of the Auto-Industrial Age* (New York: Random House, Inc., 1973).

[51]Hannan and Freeman, p. 939.

'welfare' programs for the industry that will further subsidize inefficient management and plants through tax breaks and import restrictions. This solution makes the workers more tractable and dis-
places the burden of ineffective management to the taxpayers in
general."

The second statement sees the "environment" in terms of
specific groups and interests, political and economic power, choices
and decisions that are manmade and could have easily been different. The first statement—I was fired today by the environment—
suggests that vague natural forces were working in that direction. It
is almost as if God does the negative and positive selecting.

Or take the law of requisite variety—organizations will be as
complex as their environment. In some cases, it makes some sense;
as corporations grew, the unions had to grow in complexity, dif-
ferentiating and specializing to cope with their antagonists (though
they are far less differentiated and specialized than the corporations
they deal with). In other cases, it makes more sense to see organizations as creating their environment and displacing the costs of operation onto the environment. The differentiation and specialization of
industrial tasks that took place at the end of the nineteenth century,
we have argued, were means of labor control and wage reduction.
There was no "environment" out there with a complexity that had to
be matched. The policies changed the environment, which had to
react with social legislation, industrial conflict, and community disruption, but the reaction was not in terms of a law of requisite
variety.

Thus, the new model of organization-environment relations
tends to be a mystifying one, removing much of the power, conflict,
disruption, and social class variables from the analysis of social
processes. It neglects the fact that our world is made in large part by
particular men and women with particular interests, and instead
searches for ecological laws which transcend the hubbub that
sociology should attend to. It will have a promising future, I fear,
because it is allied with the prestigious natural sciences,[52] is amen-
able to the statistical tools we have developed and the emphasis
upon large surveys, and is, in a curious way, comforting.

---

[52]Rather it is allied with a superficial reading of these sciences; for example, the
basic tenet that a turbulent environment favors complex structures, taken almost for
granted by this school and echoed in contingency theory, is not a basic tenet of
ecology and biology. Under turbulent conditions *simple* structures may survive best;
only if there are rather unique and strong selection pressures (such as might be found
in human communities where symbols and power play such dominant roles) is the
correlation between stability and complexity likely to appear. See the brief note on
this in Granovetter, op. cit., and his reference to the work of Robert May, *Stability and
Complexity in Model Ecosystems* (Princeton, N.J.: Princeton University Press, 1973).
See also Stephen Gould, "A Threat to Darwinism," *Natural History* 89, no. 4 (1975): 9.

Historical Analysis and Ethno-Marxism

Despite the seductions of the natural selection model, despite the continued preoccupation with the variable of size and administrative ratio,[53] despite the false promises of contingency theory, and despite the continued neglect of the most powerful organizations in our society, there is a great deal of room for enthusiasm for someone of my persuasions in the field. I have indicated excitement over the continuing development of network analysis, the emphasis upon nonrational models, and the development of more subtle notions of control. In addition, let me briefly note some of the recent work in historical analysis and a tradition that might be loosely called, to the annoyance of all involved, "ethno-Marxism."

The first of these new directions is a revitalization of the institutional school, but in political and historical terms that emphasize not adaption to norms or values of the community, but seeing organizations as finding ways to gather in resources, to legitimize themselves with mantles of myth and ceremony, and to cope with external controls imposed by governments or dominant monopolies.[54] The argument runs as follows, drawing upon John Meyer and Marshall Meyer in particular: Organizations become increasingly insulated from technical work and the criteria of technical efficiency. For example, large organizations do some sort of business with the Federal Government, even if it is only to pay taxes. This allows the government to insist upon specific accountancy procedures, civil service rules in some cases, employment policies, environmental impact policies, and upon creating internal specialized units such as planning bodies and quality control units. Much of this attempt at regulation is symbolic and ceremonial, but conformity guarantees existence for the organization even to the point of special loans and tax advantages to keep the organization from failing. Technical

---

[53]See a good discussion of this work in Richard Hall, *Organizations, Structure and Process*, rev. ed. (Englewood Cliffs, N.J.: Prentice-Hall, Inc., 1977), pp. 104–119.

[54]The two key people in this work appear to be Marshall Meyer and John Meyer (no relation). Rather than cite their many works, here are the latest: Marshall Meyer and M. Craig Brown, "The Process of Bureaucratization," *American Journal of Sociology* 83, no. 2 (September 1977): 364–385; John Meyer and Brian Rowan, "Institutionalized Organizations: Formal Structure as Myth and Ceremony," *American Journal of Sociology* 83, no. 2 (September 1977). Though not notable for an emphasis upon history, the work of Jeffrey Pfeffer and Gerald Salancik has a compatible emphasis upon resources and political processes, and indeed, the work of Michael Hannan and John Freeman shows affinities (despite my skepticism about their evolutionary framework). A useful place to review some of the previously published articles and some new ones of what has been called the West Coast Mafia, is in a book the above and several colleagues have put out: Marshall Meyer and Associates, *Environment and Organizations: Theoretical and Empirical Perspectives* (San Francisco: Jossey-Bass, Inc., 1978).

criteria and output standards decline in importance. In addition, the economy is becoming more centralized, so monopolistic and oligopolistic positions are more common, ensuring survival and de-emphasizing traditional "efficiency" and rationality.

As I see it, correlations between size and structure, studies of administrative ratios, searches for the optimum span of control, and generalizations about the rise of powerful middle management technostructures and experts are misleading. New offices are added, not because they promote efficiency in the service of official goals, but because the government demands them to assure that quite different goals will be attended to, ones the organization must be forced to handle. Recent expansions of employees in the personnel function, for example, are directly related to the problems of reporting on, and complying to, matters that Congress has decided were grossly neglected—occupational health and safety, pension reforms, and equal employment opportunities and affirmative action. The growth of financial offices within private (and public) organizations is not necessarily the result of some internal logic of differentiation as size increases, nor of contingency theory, but because of the demands of various levels of government (and perhaps the growing power of financial institutions in monopoly capitalism). Large-scale cross-sectional comparative studies (the dominant research design of the late 1960s and early 1970s) are likely to simply miss the point and mislead us.

Public service organizations such as schools, hospitals, and armies are under little constraint to achieve "official" goals, since their outputs are hard to measure and their real value lies in the multitude of usages that groups outside them and within them can put them to.[55] Meanwhile, organizational theorists go on creating more and more subtle measures of "efficiency" for goals that are merely weak constraints on their behavior.[56] We push the rhetoric of rationality in our theories while it declines in actual social life. According to John Meyer: "Much current research on organizations (see typical articles in the *Administrative Science Quarterly*) is in fact a celebration of the myths of rationality or a discovery of new devices for giving these myths vitality in organizational domains

---

[55]Charles Perrow, "Demystifying Organizations" in Rosemary C. Sarri and Yeheskel Hasenfeld, eds. *The Management of Human Services* (New York: Columbia University Press, 1978).

[56]Charles Perrow, "Three Types of Effectiveness Studies," in Paul S. Goodman, Johannes M. Pennings, and Associates, *New Perspectives on Organizational Effectiveness* (San Francisco: Jossey-Bass Inc., 1977), pp. 96–105; John Meyer, "Strategies for Further Research: Varieties of Environmental Variation," in Marshall Meyer and Associates, op. cit., Chapter 14.

where they have grown opaque."[57] Meyer prefers to define the problem in terms of the environment, in general terms. Thus: "The organizational effects and effectiveness which really operate in social life to regulate organizational survival are matters of political agreement and social definition negotiated between organizations and their environments."[58] I would prefer to dissolve as far as possible the boundary between an organization and its inclusive environment, and speak in terms of groups within and without the organization using it for their own purposes; I would see organizations as socially constructed, supported, and subsidized resources for a wide variety of often contradictory purposes, which includes the likelihood that groups within the organization create, select, and define the environment—i.e., the various groups and piles of resources outside of the organization. Thus, I see it as more of an interactive and more of a fragmented process, including large opportunities for accident and short-run opportunism. But whether the environment is considered in general terms or specified, the main effect remains the same. To again quote John Meyer:[59]

> We construct, with increasing elaborateness, models of organizational structure and organizational action, which reflect a world that is dying: the world of the autonomous organization surrounded by free labor, capital and commodity markets, using determinate technologies to produce outputs of known properties and market-determined value. We adapt these models by incorporating in them more and more forms of uncertainty; giving them quite complex mathematical structures. And we ignore the obvious fact that postindustrial society creates vast new forms of certainty, which organizations may obtain by the mere process of conformity to environmental specifications. Organization theorists sit in universities—highly stabilized and ritualized structures that are much more dependent on ceremonial and political congruence with their environments than on any aspect of technical efficiency—and imagine that the world outside is still that of a 19th Century factory. As with other outmoded forms of social life in complex societies, rational models of organization and action may make their last stand in the ideologies of academics in ivory towers.

As yet this neo-institutional school of thought—if there is enough unity there to designate it as a school—is still separate from the other major development I see, the ethno-Marxist approach. I use the prefix "ethno" to catch the flavor of ethnography, ethnomethodology, phenomenology, and symbolic interaction which characterized some of the efforts. This is an emphasis upon the daily construction and reproduction of basic social patterns by all actors in the system. There are studies of the meaning of rules, the negoti-

---

[57]Meyer, "Strategies for Further Research," p. 364.
[58]Ibid., p. 365.
[59]Ibid., p. 363.

ation of power relations, of retrospective accountings, unobtrusive controls, and so on. Organizations must be continually reproduced or recreated through the actions of concrete individuals. When examined closely, what appears to be quite rational (the division of labor, hierarchy, rules, specialization) in terms of technical efficiency, comes to have many other meanings, such as maintenance of class relations, deskilling, legitimizing myths, obfuscating ceremonies, and the production of ideologies. The interpretation of daily life can be in social-psychological terms, but when an ethnology is practiced by those with a Marxist view, the interpretation is in terms of categories such as power, conflict, contradictions, crises, dialectics, and class; thus the Marxist part of ethno-Marxism. The label highlights a focus upon actual concrete daily behavior which was always present in Marx, but not always present in Marxism. Today, it is often conveyed by the term "praxis," meaning action or activity or practice.

The ethno-Marxist approach challenges conventional organization theory on almost every score. The matter is both too complicated to go into here, and too poorly worked out. We are discussing work that is only now appearing. One very good, though uneven, attempt to bring much of this together is a special issue of *The Sociological Quarterly*, edited by J. Kenneth Benson. I strongly recommend Benson's introductory article for an overview, as well as his article on a dialectical view of organizations.[60] It is possible that were this new edition of *Complex Organizations* being prepared in 1984 rather than 1978, it would require a new chapter that would bring together the new institutional viewpoint and the ethno-Marxist one, placing the iconoclastic work of James March and Karl Weick—the ambiguity of decisions and organizations as running backwards, as discussed in Chapter 4—in this larger context. Thus, the baleful call at the end of the original edition for bringing together the institutional and the neo-Weberian models can be replaced by a more optimistic one, wherein history, plus new developments in psychology and phenomenology and neo-Marxism may all find their place.

---

[60]J. Kenneth Benson, "Innovation and Crisis in Organizational Analysis," *The Sociological Quarterly* 18 (Winter 1977): 3–16. The entire issue will be reprinted by Sage Publications under the title *Organizational Analysis: Critique and Innovation*. For the dialectical view with ethno overtones see J. Kenneth Benson, "Organizations: A Dialectical View," *Administrative Science Quarterly* 22, no. 1 (March 1977): 1–21. See also the equally basic challenge to the existing paradigm in McNeil's discussion of the legacy of Weber in Kenneth McNeil, "Understanding Organizational Power: Building on the Weberian Legacy," *Administrative Science Quarterly* 23, no. 1 (March 1978): 65–90; and Erik Olin Wright's influential piece, "To Control or Smash Bureaucracy: Weber and Lenin on Politics, the State and Bureaucracy," *Berkeley Journal of Sociology* 19 (1975): 69–108. See also Wright's book, *Class Crisis and the State* (New York: Schocken Books, Inc., 1978).

Bibliography

Adams, Walter. "Competition, Monopoly, and Planning." In *American Society Inc.*, Maurice Zeitlin, ed. Chicago: Markham Publishing Co., 1970, pp. 241–248.

Aldrich, Howard. *Organizations and Environments.* Englewood Cliffs, N.J.: Prentice-Hall, Inc., 1979.

————. "Technology and Organizational Structure: A Reexamination of the Findings of the Aston Group." *Administrative Science Quarterly* 17, no. 1 (March 1972): 26–43.

Alexander, Tom. "Computers Can't Solve Everything." *Fortune* (October 1969), pp. 126–129.

Alford, Robert. *Health Care Politics.* Chicago: University of Chicago Press, 1977.

Allison, Graham T. *Essence of Decision: Explaining the Cuban Missile Crisis.* Boston: Little, Brown & Co., 1971.

Applewhite, Philip B. *Organizational Behavior.* Englewood Cliffs, N.J.: Prentice-Hall, Inc., 1965.

Argyle, Michael. "The Relay Assembly Test Room in Retrospect." *Occupational Psychology* 27 (1953): 98–103.

Argyris, Chris. *The Applicability of Organizational Sociology.* New York: Cambridge University Press, 1974.

————. *Interpersonal Competence and Organizational Effectiveness.* Homewood, Ill.: The Dorsey Press, 1962.

Bandura, Albert. *Social Learning Theory.* New York: General Learning Press, 1971.

Baritz, Loren. *The Servants of Power.* Westport, Conn.: Greenwood Press, Inc., 1974.

Barnard, Chester, *The Functions of the Executive.* Cambridge, Mass.: Harvard University Press, 1968.

————. *Organization and Management.* Cambridge, Mass.: Harvard University Press, 1948.

Barnet, Richard. *Economy of Death*. New York: Atheneum House, Inc., 1969.

Barnouw, Erik. *The Sponsor: Notes on a Modern Potentate*. New York: Oxford University Press, 1978.

Barton, Allen and Ferman, Patricia. "Comments on Hage's 'An Axiomatic Theory of Organizations.'" *Administrative Science Quarterly* 11, no. 1 (June 1966).

Becker, Howard S., ed. *The Other Side: Perspectives of Deviance*. New York: The Free Press, 1964.

————. *Outsiders: Studies in the Sociology of Deviance*. New York: The Free Press, 1963, pp. 147–163.

Bell, Gerald. "Determinants of Span of Control." *American Journal of Sociology* 73, no. 1 (July 1967): 90–101.

Bendix, Reinhard. "Bureaucracy." *International Encyclopedia of the Social Sciences*. New York: The Free Press, 1977.

————. *Work and Authority in Industry*. New York: John Wiley & Sons, Inc., 1956.

Bennis, Warren G. *Changing Organizations*. New York: McGraw-Hill Book Co., 1966.

————. "A Funny Thing Happened on the Way to the Future." *American Psychologist* 25 (June 1970): 595–608.

————. "Post-Bureaucratic Leadership." *Trans-action* 6 (July/August 1969): 44–51ff.

————, and Slater, Philip. *The Temporary Society*. New York: Harper & Row, Inc., 1968.

Benson, J. Kenneth. "Innovation and Crisis in Organizational Analysis." *The Sociological Quarterly* 18 (Winter 1977): 3–16.

————. "Organizations: A Dialectical View." *Administrative Science Quarterly* 22, no. 1 (March 1977): 1–21.

Blau, Peter M. *The Dynamics of Bureaucracy*, 2nd rev. ed. Chicago: University of Chicago Press, 1973.

————. "A Formal Theory of Differentiation in Organizations." *American Sociological Review* 35, no. 2 (April 1970): 201–218.

————. "The Hierarchy of Authority in Organizations." *American Journal of Sociology* 73 (January 1968): 453–457.

————, and Scott, W. Richard. *Formal Organizations*. San Francisco: Chandler Publishing Co., 1962.

Bowers, David G. and Seashore, Stanley E. "Predicting Organizational Effectiveness with a Four-Factor Theory of Leadership." *Administrative Science Quarterly* 11, no. 2 (September 1966): 238–263.

Braverman, Harry. *Labor and Monopoly Capital*. New York: Monthly Review Press, 1975.

Brayfield, Arthur H., and Crockett, Walter H. "Employee Attitudes and Employee Performance." *Psychological Bulletin* 52, no. 5 (1955): 396–424.

Brown, Wilfred. *Exploration in Management*. New York: John Wiley & Sons, Inc., 1960.

Bucher, Rue. "Social Process and Power in a Medical School." In *Power in Organizations*, Mayer Zald, ed. Nashville, Tenn.: Vanderbilt University Press, 1970, pp. 3–48.

Buckley, Walter. *Sociology and Modern Systems Theory*. Englewood Cliffs, N.J.: Prentice-Hall, Inc., 1967.

Burns, T. and Stalker, G. M. *The Management of Innovation*. New York: Barnes & Noble, 1961.

Campbell, Donald. "Variation and Selection Retention in Socio-Cultural Evolution." *General Systems* 16 (1969): 69–85.

Campbell, John P. and Dunnette, Marvin D. "Effectiveness of T-Group Experiences in Managerial Training and Development." *Psychological Bulletin* 70, no. 2 (August 1968): 73–104.

Carey, Alex. "The Hawthorne Studies: A Radical Criticism." *American Sociological Review* 32, no. 3 (June 1967): 416.

Caro, Robert. *The Power Broker: Robert Moses and the Fall of New York*. New York: Random House, Inc., 1975.

Chandler, Alfred D. *Strategy and Structure*. Cambridge, Mass.: M.I.T. Press, 1969.

Child, John. "Organizational Structure, Environment, and Performance: The Role of Strategic Choice." *Sociology* 6, no. 1 (January 1972): 1–22.

————. "Predicting and Understanding Organization Structure." *Administrative Science Quarterly* 18, no. 2 (June 1973): 168–185.

Clark, Burton. *Adult Education in Transition*. Berkeley: University of California Press, 1956.

————. *The Open Door Challenge: A Case Study*. New York: McGraw-Hill Book Co., 1960.

Clark, S. D. *The Church and Sect in Canada*. Toronto: University of Toronto Press, 1948.

Clawson, Daniel. "Class Struggle and the Rise of Bureaucracy." Ph.D. Dissertation, State University of New York at Stony Brook, 1978.

Coch, L. and French, J. R. P., Jr. "Overcoming Resistance to Change." *Human Relations* 1, no. 4 (1948): 512–532.

Cohen, Michael D., March, James C., and Olsen, Johan P. "A Garbage Can Model of Organizational Choice." *Administrative Science Quarterly* 17, no. 1 (March 1972): 1–25.

Coser, Lewis. *Greedy Institutions*. New York: The Free Press, 1974.

————. "Publishers as Gatekeepers of Ideas." *The Annals, American Academy of Social Science* 421 (September 1975): 12–22.

Cressey, Donald R. "Achievement of an Unstated Organizational Goal: An Observation on Prisons." *Pacific Sociological Review* 1 (1958): 43–49.

Crozier, Michel. *The Stalled Society*. New York: Penguin Books, Inc., 1974.

Cummings, L. L., and Scott, W. E. *Readings in Organizational Behavior and Human Performance*, rev. ed. Homewood, Ill.: The Dorsey Press, 1973.

Cyert, Richard M. and March, James G. *A Behavioral Theory of the Firm*. Englewood Cliffs, N.J.: Prentice-Hall, Inc., 1963.

Dale, Ernest. *The Great Organizers*. New York: McGraw-Hill Book Co., 1971.

Dalton, Melville, *Men Who Manage.* New York: John Wiley & Sons, Inc., 1959.

Danielian, N. R. *AT&T, The Story of Industrial Conquest.* New York: The Vanguard Press, 1939.

David, Nuel Pharr. *Lawrence and Oppenheimer.* New York: Simon & Schuster, Inc., 1968.

Davis, James W. and Dolbeare, Kenneth M. *Little Groups of Neighbors: The Selective Service System.* Chicago: Markham Publishing Co., 1968.

Demerath, N. J. and Peterson, Richard A., eds. *Systems, Change, and Conflict.* New York: The Free Press, 1967.

Deutscher, Irwin. *What We Say/What We Do.* Glenview, Ill.: Scott, Foresman & Co., 1973.

Domhoff, G. William. *The Higher Circles.* New York: Random House, Inc., 1971.

————. *Who Rules America?* Englewood Cliffs, N.J.: Prentice-Hall, Inc., 1967.

Dornbush, Sanford and Scott, W. Richard. *Evaluation and the Exercise of Authority.* San Francisco: Jossey-Bass, Inc., 1975.

Drucker, Peter. *Concept of the Corporation.* New York: John Day Co., 1972.

Dubin, Robert. "Supervision and Productivity." In *Leadership and Productivity,* Robert Dubin, George C. Homans, Floyd C. Mann, and Delbert C. Miller, eds. San Francisco: Chandler Publishing Co., 1965.

Dunnette, Marvin, Campbell, John, and Argyris, Chris. "A Symposium: Laboratory Training." *Industrial Relations* 8, no. 1 (October 1968), 1–46.

Durkheim, Émile. *Division of Labor in Society.* New York: The Free Press, 1947.

Ehrenrich, Barbara, and Ehrenrich, John. *The American Health Empire: Power, Profits, and Politics.* New York: Vintage Books, Random House, Inc., 1971.

Emery, F. E. and Trist, E. L. "The Causal Texture of Organizational Environments." In *Readings in Organization Theory—A Behavioral Approach.* Walter A. Hill and Douglas Egan, eds. Boston: Allyn and Bacon, 1966, pp. 435–447.

Etzioni, Amitai. *The Active Society.* New York: The Free Press, 1968.

————. *A Comparative Analysis of Complex Organizations,* rev. ed. New York: The Free Press, 1975.

————, ed. *Complex Organizations: A Sociological Reader.* New York: Holt, Rinehart & Winston, Inc., 1962.

————. *A Sociological Reader on Complex Organizations,* 2nd ed. New York: Holt, Rinehart & Winston, Inc., 1969.

Evan, William M. "The Organization-Set: Toward a Theory of Interorganizational Relations." In J. D. Thompson, ed. *Approaches to Organizational Design.* Pittsburgh: University of Pittsburgh Press, 1966, pp. 175–191.

Federal Trade Commission. *Economic Report on Corporate Mergers*. Staff Report. Washington, D.C.: U.S. Government Printing Office, 1969.

Fiedler, Fred. "Engineer the Job to Fit the Manager." *Harvard Business Review* 43, no. 5 (1965): 115–122.

————. *A Theory of Leadership Effectiveness*. New York: McGraw-Hill Book Company, 1967.

Freidson, Eliot, ed. *The Hospital in Modern Society*. New York: The Free Press, 1963.

Freitag, Peter J. "The Cabinet and Big Business." *Social Problems* 23, no. 2 (December 1975).

Gagnon, John H., and Simon, William. *Sexual Conduct: The Social Sources of Human Sexuality*. Chicago: Aldine Publishing Co., 1973.

Galbraith, John Kenneth. *The New Industrial State*, 2nd ed. Boston: Houghton Mifflin Co., 1971.

Gerth, Hans, and Mills, C. Wright, eds. and trans. *From Max Weber: Essays in Sociology*. New York: Oxford University Press, Inc., 1946.

"GM's Mini: The Very Model of Automation." *Business Week*, August 8, 1970, p. 26.

Goffman, Erving. *Asylums*. New York: Doubleday & Company, 1961.

Goldner, Fred H. "The Division of Labor: Process and Power." In *Power in Organizations*, Mayer Zald, ed. Nashville, Tenn.: Vanderbilt University Press, 1970, pp. 97–144.

————, and Ritti, R. R. "Professionalization as Career Immobility." *American Journal of Sociology* 73 (March 1967): 491.

Goss, Mary E. W. "Patterns of Bureaucracy Among Hospital Staff Physicians." In *The Hospital in Modern Society*, Eliot Freidson, ed. New York: The Free Press, 1963.

Gould, Stephen. "A Threat to Darwinism." *Natural History* 89, no. 4 (1975): 9.

Gouldner, Alvin. *Patterns of Industrial Bureaucracy*. New York: The Free Press, 1954.

Graham, W. K. "Description of Leader Behavior and Evaluation of Leaders as a Function of LPC." *Personnel Psychology* 21 (Winter 1968): 457–464.

Granovetter, Mark. "The Strength of Weak Ties." *American Journal of Sociology* 78 (May 1973): 1360–1380.

————. "The Idea of 'Advancement' in Theories of Social Evolution." Unpublished paper, State University of New York at Stony Brook, 1978.

Guest, Robert. *Organizational Change*. Homewood, Ill.: The Dorsey Press, 1962.

Gusfield, Joseph R. "Social Structure and Moral Reform: A Study of the Women's Christian Temperance Union." *American Journal of Sociology* 61 (1955): 221–232.

Hage, Jerald T. "Rejoinder." *Administrative Science Quarterly* 11, no. 1 (June 1966).

————. "An Axiomatic Theory of Organizations." *Administrative Science Quarterly* 10, no. 3 (December 1965): 289–320.

————, and Aiken, Michael. "Routine Technology, Social Structure, and Organizational Goals." *Administrative Science Quarterly* 14, no. 3 (September 1969): 366–377.

Hall, Richard. *Organizations, Structure, and Process*, rev. ed. Englewood Cliffs, N.J.: Prentice-Hall, Inc., 1977, pp. 104–119.

Hannan, Michael T., and Freeman, John. "The Population Ecology of Organizations." *American Journal of Sociology* 82, no. 5 (March 1977): 929–966.

Hawley, Amos. *Human Ecology: A Theory of Community Structure*. New York: Ronald Press, 1950.

Herzberg, Frederick. *Work and the Nature of Man*. New York: T. Y. Crowell Co., 1966.

————, Mausner, B., and Snyderman, B. *The Motivation to Work*, 2nd ed. New York: John Wiley & Sons, Inc., 1959.

Hickson, David, et al. "Operations Technology and Organizational Structure: An Empirical Reappraisal." *Administrative Science Quarterly* 14, no. 3 (September 1969): 378–397.

————, et al. "A Strategic Contingencies Theory of Intra-Organizational Power." *Administrative Science Quarterly* 16, no. 2 (June 1971): 216–229.

Hill, Walter A., and Egan, Douglas, eds. *Readings in Organizational Theory—A Behavioral Approach*. Boston: Allyn & Bacon, Inc., 1966.

Hirsch, Paul M. "Occupational, Organizational, and Institutional Models in Communication Research." In *Strategies for Communication Research*, P. M. Hirsch et al., eds. Beverly Hills, Calif.: Sage Publications, 1977.

————. "Organizational Analysis and Industrial Sociology: An Instance of Cultural Lag." *The American Sociologist* 10, no. 1 (February 1975): 3–10.

————. "Organizational Effectiveness and the Institutional Environment." *Administrative Science Quarterly* 20, no. 4 (September 1975): 327–344.

————. "Processing Fads and Fashions: An Organization-Set Analysis of Cultural Industry Systems." *American Journal of Sociology* 77, no. 4 (January 1972): 639–659.

————. *The Structure of the Popular Music Industry*. Ann Arbor, Mich.: University of Michigan Survey Research Center, 1969.

Homans, George. *The Human Group*. New York: Harcourt Brace Jovanovich, Inc., 1950.

Hopkins, Terence K. "Bureaucratic Authority: The Convergence of Weber and Barnard." In *Complex Organizations*, Amitai Etzioni, ed. New York: Holt, Rinehart & Winston, Inc., 1962, pp. 159–167.

House, Robert J., and Wigdor, Lawrence A. "Herzberg's Dual-Factor Theory of Job Satisfaction and Motivation: A Review of the Evidence and a Criticism." *Personnel Psychology* 20 (1967): 369–389.

Hulin, Charles L., and Blood, Milton R. "Job Enlargement, Individual

Differences, and Worker Responses." *Psychological Bulletin* 69, no. 1 (1968): 41–55.

Jaco, E. G., ed. *Patients, Physicians, and Illness: Source Book in Behavioral Science and Medicine*, 2nd ed. New York: The Free Press, 1972.

Janowitz, Morris. *The Professional Soldier*. New York: The Free Press, 1960.

Jun, Jong S., and Storm, William B. *Tomorrow's Organizations*. Glenview, Ill.: Scott, Foresman & Co., 1973.

Kahn, Robert L. "Human Relations on the Shop Floor." In *Human Relations and Modern Management*, E. M. Hugh-Jones, ed. Amsterdam, Holland: North-Holland Publishing Co., 1958, pp. 43–74.

Kanter, Rosabeth Moss. *Men and Women of the Corporation*. New York: Basic Books, Inc., 1977.

Kaplan, Norman. "Professional Scientists in Industry." *Social Problems* 13 (1965): 88–97.

Kast, Fremont, and Rosenzweig, James. *Contingency Views of Organization and Management*. Palo Alto: Science Research Associates, 1973.

Katz, Daniel, et al. *Productivity, Supervision, and Morale in an Office Situation*. Detroit, Mich.: Darel Press, Inc., 1950.

————, and Kahn, Robert. *Social Psychology of Organizations*. New York: John Wiley & Sons, Inc., 1966.

Kaysen, Carl. "The Corporation, How Much Power and How Much Scope?" In *The Corporation in Modern Society*, E. S. Mason, ed. Cambridge, Mass.: Harvard University Press, 1960, pp. 85–105.

Knightley, Phillip. *The First Casualty: From the Crimes to Vietnam—The War Correspondent as Hero, Propagandist, and Myth Maker*. New York: Harcourt Brace Jovanovich, Inc., 1976.

Koenig, Thomas, Gogel, Robert, and Sonquist, John. "Interlocking Directorates as a Social Network." *American Journal of Economics and Sociology* (1978).

———— et al. "Theories of the Significance of Corporate Interlocking Directorates." *American Journal of Economics and Sociology* (1978).

————, and Sonquist, John. "Studying Interrelations Between Corporations Through Interlocking Directorates." In *Power and Hierarchical Control*, Tom Burns and William Buckley, eds. New York: Sage Publications, 1977.

Kolko, Gabriel. *The Roots of American Foreign Policy*. Boston: The Beacon Press, 1970.

————. *Triumph of Conservatism*. New York: The Free Press, 1977.

Korman, Abraham K. "'Consideration,' 'Initiating Structure,' and Organizational Criteria—A Review." *Personnel Psychology* 19, no. 4 (1966): 349–361.

Kornhauser, Arthur, and Sharp, A. "Employee Attitudes, Suggestions from a Study in a Factory." *Personnel Journal* 10 (1943): 393–401.

Kornhauser, T., Dubin, R., and Ross, A. *Industrial Conflict*. New York: McGraw-Hill Book Company, 1954.

Krupp, Sherman. *Patterns in Organizational Analysis*. New York: Holt, Rinehart & Winston, Inc., 1961.

Landau, Martin. "Redundancy, Rationality, and the Problem of Duplication and Overlap." *Public Administration Review* 29, no. 4 (July/August 1969).

Landsberger, Henry. *Hawthorne Revisited*. Ithaca, N.Y.: Cornell University Press, 1958.

Laumann, E. O. *Networks of Collective Action*. New York: Academic Press, Inc., 1976.

————, and Pappi, Franz U. "New Directions in the Study of Community Elites." *American Sociological Review* 38, no. 2 (April 1973): 212–230.

————, Verbrugge, Lois M., and Pappi, F. U. "A Casual Modelling Approach to the Study of a Community Elite's Influence Structure." *American Sociological Review* 39, no. 2 (April 1974): 162–174.

Lawler, Edward E., and Porter, Lyman W. "The Effect of Performance on Job Satisfaction." *Industrial Relations* 7, no. 1 (October 1967): 20–28.

Lawrence, Paul, and Lorsch, Jay. *Organization and Environment*. Cambridge, Mass.: Harvard University Press, 1967.

Levine, Sol, and White, Paul E. "Exchange as a Conceptual Framework for the Study of Interorganizational Relationships." *Administrative Science Quarterly* 5 (March 1961): 583–610.

Likert, Rensis. *The Human Organization*. New York: McGraw-Hill Book Company, 1967.

————. *New Patterns of Management*. New York: McGraw-Hill Book Company, 1961.

Litwak, Eugene, and Hylton, Lydia F. "Interorganizational Analysis: A Hypothesis on Co-ordinating Agencies." *Administrative Science Quarterly* 6, no. 4 (March 1962): 337–341.

Lorsch, Jay W. *Product Innovation and Organization*. New York: The Macmillan Company, 1965.

Luthans, Fred, and Kreitner, Robert. *Organizational Behavior Modification*. Glenview, Ill.: Scott, Foresman & Co., 1975.

Lynch, Beverly P. "An Empirical Assessment of Perrow's Technology Construct." *Administrative Science Quarterly* 19, no. 3 (September 1974): 338–356.

Lynd, Robert S. "Review of Leadership in a Free Society." *Political Science Quarterly* 52 (1937): 590–592.

Maniha, John, and Perrow, Charles. "The Reluctant Organization and the Aggressive Environment." *Administrative Science Quarterly* 10, no. 2 (September 1965): 238–257.

Mann, Floyd C. *Leadership and Productivity*. R. Dubin, G. C. Homans, Floyd C. Mann, and D. C. Miller, eds. San Francisco: Chandler Publishing Co., 1965, pp. 68–103.

March, James G. "The Business Firm as a Political Coalition." *Journal of Politics* 24 (1962): 662–678.

————, ed. *The Handbook of Organizations*. Chicago: Rand McNally & Co., 1965.

————, and Olsen, Johan P. *Ambiguity and Choice in Organizations*. Bergen, Norway: Universitetsforlaget, 1976.

_____, and Simon, Herbert A. *Organizations*. New York: John Wiley & Sons, Inc., 1958.

Marglin, Steven. "What Do Bosses Do?" *Review of Radical Political Economics* 6, no. 2 (Summer 1974): 33–60.

Mariolis, Peter. "Bank and Financial Control Among Large U.S. Corporations." Ph.D. Dissertation, State University of New York at Stony Brook, 1978.

_____. "Interlocking Directorates and Control of Corporations." *Social Science Quarterly* 56 (December 1975): 425–439.

Marrow, Alfred J., Bower, David G., and Seashore, Stanley E. *Management by Participation*. New York: Harper & Row, Inc., 1967.

Maslow, Abraham. *Motivation and Personality*, 2nd ed. New York: Harper & Row, Inc., 1970.

_____. *Toward a Psychology of Being*. New York: Van Nostrand Reinhold Co., 1968.

Massie, Joseph. "Management Theory." In *The Handbook of Organizations*, James March, ed. Chicago: Rand McNally & Co., 1965, pp. 387–422.

May, Robert. *Stability and Complexity in Model Ecosystems*. Princeton, N.J.: Princeton University Press, 1973.

Mayo, Elton. *The Social Problems of an Industrial Civilization*. Cambridge, Mass.: Harvard University Press, 1945.

McGregor, Douglas. *The Human Side of Enterprise*. New York: McGraw-Hill Book Company, 1960.

McNeil, Kenneth. "Understanding Organizational Power: Building on the Weberian Legacy." *Administrative Science Quarterly* 23, no. 1 (March 1978): 65–90.

_____, and Minihan, Edmond. "Regulation of Medical Devices and Organizational Behavior in Hospitals." *Administrative Science Quarterly* 22, no. 3 (September 1977): 475–490.

Mechanic, David. "Sources of Power of Lower Participants in Complex Organization." *Administrative Science Quarterly* 7, no. 4 (December 1962): 349–364.

Melman, Seymour. *Pentagon Capitalism: The Political Economy of War*. New York: McGraw-Hill Book Company, 1970.

Messinger, Sheldon L. "Organizational Transformation: A Case Study of Declining Social Movement." *American Sociological Review* 20 (1955): 3–10.

Meyer, John W. and Rowan, Brian. "Institutionalized Organizations: Formal Structure as Myth and Ceremony." *American Journal of Sociology* 83, no. 2 (September 1977): 340–363.

Meyer, Marshall. "Two Authority Structures of Bureaucratic Organizations." *Administrative Science Quarterly* 13 (September 1968): 211–228.

_____, and Associates. *Environment and Organizations: Theoretical and Empirical Perspectives*. San Francisco: Jossey-Bass, Inc., 1978.

_____, and Brown, M. C. "The Process of Bureaucratization." *American Journal of Sociology* 83, no. 2 (September 1977): 364–385.

Michels, Robert. *Political Parties*. New York: The Free Press, 1966.

Miles, Raymond E. "Human Relations or Human Resources." *Harvard Business Review* 43, no. 4 (July/August 1965): 148–155.

Mindlin, Sergio E., and Aldrich, Howard. "Interorganizational Dependence: A Review of the Concepts and Reexamination of the Findings of the Aston Group." *Administrative Science Quarterly* 20, no. 3 (September 1975): 382–392.

Mintz, Beth. "The President's Cabinet, 1897–1972." *The Insurgent Sociologist* 5, no. 3 (Spring 1975).

———. "Who Controls the Corporations: A Study of Interlocking Directorates." Ph.D. Dissertation, State University of New York at Stony Brook, 1978.

———, et al. "Problems of Proof in Elite Research." *Social Problems* 23, no. 3 (February 1976): 314–324.

Mischel, Walter. "Toward a Cognitive Social Learning Reconceptualization of Personality." *Psychological Review* 80, no. 4 (1973): 252–283.

Moeller, Gerald H., and Charters, W. W. "Relations of Bureaucratization to Sense of Power Among Teachers." *Administrative Science Quarterly* 10, no. 4 (March 1966): 457.

Mohr, Lawrence B. "Organizational Technology and Organizational Structure." *Administrative Science Quarterly* 16, no. 4 (December 1971): 444–459.

Mollenkopf, John. "Theories of the State and Power Structure Research." *The Insurgent Sociologist* 5, no. 3 (Spring 1975): 245–264.

Morris, Robert, and Hirsch-Lescohier, Ilana. "Service Integration: To What Problems is it the Presumed Solution?" In *The Management of Human Services*, Rosemary C. Sarri and Yeheskel Hasenfeld, eds. New York: Columbia University Press, 1978.

Newfield, Jack and DuBrul, Paul. *The Abuse of Power: The Permanent Government and the Fall of New York.* New York: The Viking Press, 1977.

Nonet, Philippe. *Administrative Justice: Advocacy and Change in Government Agencies.* New York: Russell Sage Foundation, 1969.

Overton, Peggy, Schneck, Rodney, and Hazlett, C. B. "An Empirical Study of the Technology of Nursing Subunits." *Administrative Science Quarterly* 22, no. 2 (June 1977): 203–219.

Owens, Arthur. "Can the Profit Motive Save Our Hospitals?" *Medical Economics* (March 1970): 77–111.

Palumbo, Dennis J. "Power and Role Specificity in Organization Theory." *Public Administration Review* 29, no. 3 (May/June 1969): 237–248.

Parsons, Talcott. "Introduction." In *Max Weber, Theory of Social and Economic Organization.* Translated and edited by A. M. Henderson and Talcott Parsons. New York: Oxford University Press, 1947, pp. 58–60.

———. *Structure and Process in Modern Societies.* New York: The Free Press, 1960.

Pennings, Johannes M. "Dimensions of Organizational Influence and

Their Effectiveness Correlates." *Administrative Science Quarterly* 21, no. 4 (December 1976): 688–699.

————, and Goodman, Paul S. "Toward a Workable Framework." In *New Perspectives in Organizational Effectiveness*, Paul S. Goodman et al. San Francisco: Jossey-Bass, Inc., 1977, pp. 146–184.

Perrow, Charles. "Demystifying Organizations." In *The Management of Human Services*, Rosemary C. Sarri and Yeheskel Hasenfeld, eds. New York: Columbia University Press, 1978.

————. "Departmental Power and Perspectives in Industrial Firms." In *Power in Organizations*, Mayer Zald, ed. Nashville, Tenn.: Vanderbilt University Press, 1970, pp. 59–70.

————. "The Effect of Technological Change on the Structure of Business Firms." In *Industrial Relations: Contemporary Issues*, B. C. Roberts, ed. London: The Macmillan Company, 1968, pp. 205–219.

————. "A Framework for Comparative Organizational Analysis." *American Sociological Review* 32, no. 2 (April 1967): 194–208.

————. "Goals and Power Structures: A Historical Case Study." In *The Hospital in Modern Society*, Eliot Freidson, ed. New York: The Free Press, 1963.

————. "Goals in Complex Organizations." *American Sociological Review* 26, no. 6 (December 1961): 854–865.

————. "Hospitals: Technology, Structure, and Goals." In *The Handbook of Organizations*, James March, ed. Chicago: Rand McNally & Company, 1965, pp. 910–971.

————. "Is Business Really Changing?" *Organizational Dynamics* (Summer 1974): 31–44.

————. "Members as a Resource in Voluntary Associations." In *Organizations and Clients*, W. Rosengren and M. Lefton, eds. Columbus, Ohio: Charles E. Merrill Publishing Co., 1970, pp. 93–116.

————. *Organizational Analysis: A Sociological View*. Belmont, Calif.: Wadsworth Publishing Co., Inc., 1970.

————. "Organizational Goals." *International Encyclopedia of the Social Sciences*, rev. ed. New York: The Macmillan Company, 1968, pp. 305–311.

————. "Organizational Prestige: Some Functions and Dysfunctions." *American Journal of Sociology* 66, no. 4 (January 1961): 335–341.

————. *The Radical Attack on Business: A Critical Analysis*. New York: Harcourt Brace Jovanovich, Inc., 1972.

————. "Review of Organizational Intelligence." *Trans-action* 6 (January 1969): 60–62.

————. "Three Types of Effectiveness Studies." In P. S. Goodman, J. M. Pennings and Associates, *New Perspectives on Organizational Effectiveness*. San Francisco: Jossey-Bass, Inc., 1977, pp. 96–105.

Perrucci, Robert, and Pilisuk, Marc. "Leaders and Ruling Elites: The Interorganizational Bases of Community Power." Working paper no. 28, Institute for the Study of Social Change, Department of Sociology, Purdue University.

Peterson, Richard, and Berger, David G. "Cycles in Symbol Production: The Case of Popular Music." *American Sociological Review* 40, no. 2 (April 1975): 158–173.

————. "Entrepreneurship in Organizations: Evidence from the Popular Music Industry." *Administrative Science Quarterly* 16, no. 1 (March 1971): 97–106.

Powell, Walter. "Control and Conflict in the Publishing Industry." Unpublished manuscript, State University of New York at Stony Brook, 1977.

"Power to the Coalitions." *Modern Hospital* (April 1970), pp. 39–40d.

Price, James L. "Continuity in Social Research: TVA and the Grass Roots." *Pacific Sociological Review* 1, no. 2 (Fall 1958): 63–68.

Roethlisberger, F. J., and Dickson, William J. *Management and the Worker*. Cambridge, Mass.: Harvard University Press, 1947.

Rogers, David. *110 Livingstone Street*. New York: Random House, Inc., 1968.

Rony, Vera. "Bogalusa: The Economics of Tragedy." *Dissent* (May/June 1966): 234–242.

Rosengren, W., and Lefton, M., eds. *Organizations and Clients*. Columbus, Ohio: Charles E. Merrill Publishing Co., 1970.

Rothschild, Emma. *Paradise Lost: The Decline of the Auto-Industrial Age* New York: Random House, Inc., 1973.

Rushing, W. A. "Hardness of Material as Related to Division of Labor in Manufacturing Industries." *Administrative Science Quarterly* 13, no. 2 (September 1968): 229–245.

Schumpeter, Joseph. *Capitalism, Socialism, and Democracy*. New York: Harper & Row, Inc., 1950.

————. *Imperialism and Social Classes*. Cleveland: Meridian Books, 1955.

Scott, Robert A. "The Selection of Clients by Social Welfare Agencies: The Case of the Blind." *Social Problems* 14, no. 3 (Winter 1967): 248–257.

Seashore, Stanley, and Bowers, David. *Changing the Structure and Functioning of an Organization*. Ann Arbor: Institute for Social Research, University of Michigan, 1963.

————, and Yuchtman, Ephraim. "Factorial Analysis of Organizational Performance." *Administrative Science Quarterly* 12, no. 3 (December 1967): 377–395.

Seeley, John R., Junker, Bulford H., and Jones, R. Wallace, Jr. *Community Chest*. Toronto: University of Toronto Press, 1957.

Selznick, Philip. "An Approach to a Theory of Bureaucracy." *American Sociological Review* 8 (1943): 47–54.

————. "Foundations of a Theory of Organizations." *American Sociological Review* 13 (1948): 25–35.

————. "Rejoinder to Wohlin." In *A Sociological Reader on Complex Organizations*, Amitai Etzioni, ed. New York: Holt, Rinehart & Winston, Inc., 1969, pp. 149–154.

————. *Law, Society, and Industrial Justice*. New York: Russell Sage Foundation, 1969.

————. *Leadership in Administration*. New York: Harper & Row, Inc., 1957.

————. *The Organizational Weapon: A Study of Bolshevik Strategy and Tactics*. New York: McGraw-Hill Book Company, 1952.

————. *TVA and the Grass Roots.* New York: Harper & Row, Inc., 1965.

Silberman, Charles E. "The Truth About Automation." *Fortune* (January 1965), pp. 125–127.

————. "The Comeback of the Blue-Collar Worker." *Fortune* (February 1965), pp. 153–155.

Sills, David. *The Volunteers.* New York: The Free Press, 1957.

Simon, Herbert. *Administrative Behavior,* 3rd ed. New York: The Free Press, 1976.

————. "On the Concept of Organizational Goal." *Administrative Science Quarterly* 9, no. 1 (June 1964): 1–22.

————. *Models of Man.* New York: John Wiley & Sons, Inc., 1956.

Skinner, B. F. *Beyond Freedom and Dignity.* New York: Bantam Books, 1971.

Sloan, Alfred P. *My Years with General Motors.* New York: Doubleday & Co., Inc., 1972.

Smigel, Erwin O. *The Wall Street Lawyer,* rev. ed. Bloomington, Ind.: Indiana University Press, 1970.

Smith, H. L. "Two Lines of Authority: The Hospital's Dilemma." In *Patients, Physicians, and Illness: Source Book in Behavioral Science and Medicine,* 2nd ed. E. G. Jaco, ed. New York: The Free Press, 1972.

Stinchcombe, Arthur L. "Bureaucratic and Craft Administration of Production." *Administrative Science Quarterly* 4 (1959): 168–187.

Stogdill, R. M., and Coons, A. E., eds. *Leader Behavior: Its Description and Measurement.* Columbus, Ohio: Bureau of Business Research, 1957

Stone, Katherine. "The Origins of Job Structures in the Steel Industry." *Radical America* 7, no. 6 (November/December 1973): 19–64.

Storing, Herbert J. "The Science of Administration: Herbert A. Simon." In *Essays on the Scientific Study of Politics,* H. J. Storing, ed. New York: Holt, Rinehart & Winston, Inc., 1962, pp. 63–105.

Strauss, Anselm L., et al. *Psychiatric Ideologies and Institutions.* New York: The Free Press, 1964.

Strauss, George. "Human Relations, 1968 Style." *Industrial Relations* 7, no. 3 (May 1969): 262–276.

————. "Notes on Power Equalization." In *The Social Science of Organizations,* Harold Leavitt, ed. Englewood Cliffs, N.J.: Prentice-Hall, Inc., 1963.

Street, David, Vinter, Robert, and Perrow, Charles. *Organizations for Treatment.* New York: The Free Press, 1966.

Sudnow, David. "Normal Crimes." *Social Problems* 12, no. 3 (Winter 1964): 255–275.

Sykes, A. J. "Economic Interest and the Hawthorne Researches: A Comment." *Human Relations* 18 (1965): 253–263.

Sykes, Gresham M. *The Society of Captives: A Study of a Maximum Security Prison.* Princeton, N.J.: Princeton University Press, 1971.

Tannenbaum, Arnold S. *Control in Organizations.* New York: McGraw-Hill Book Company, 1968.

————, et al. *Hierarchy in Organizations.* San Francisco: Jossey-Bass, Inc., 1974.

Tannenbaum, Robert, Weschler, I. R., and Massarik, F. *Leadership and Organization: A Behavioral Science Approach.* New York: McGraw-Hill Book Company, 1961.

Thompson, James. *Organizations in Action.* New York: McGraw-Hill Book Company, 1967.

Thompson, Victor A. *Modern Organization,* 2nd ed. University, Ala.: University of Alabama Press, 1977.

Turk, Herman, and Lefkowitz, Myron J. "Toward a Theory of Representation Between Groups." *Social Forces* 40 (May 1962): 337–341.

Udy, Stanley H., Jr. "'Bureaucracy' and 'Rationality' in Weber's Organization Theory." *American Sociological Review* 24 (1959): 591–595.

"The University Arsenal." *Look,* August 26, 1969, p. 34.

Vickers, Sir Geoffrey. *Towards a Sociology of Management.* New York: Basic Books, Inc., 1967.

Vitich, Arthur J., and Bensen, Joseph. *Small Town in Mass Society.* Princeton, N.J.: Princeton University Press, 1958.

Vroom, Victor. *Work and Motivation.* New York: John Wiley & Sons, Inc., 1964.

Wallace, Anthony. *Culture and Personality,* 2nd ed. New York: Random House, Inc., 1970.

Wallerstein, Immanuel. *The Modern World-System: Capitalist Agriculture and the Origins of European World-Economy in the Sixteenth Century.* New York: Academic Press, Inc., 1974.

Walton, Clarence C. *Corporate Social Responsibilities.* Belmont, Calif.: Wadsworth Publishing Company, Inc., 1967.

Wamsley, Gary L. *Selective Service and a Changing America.* Columbus, Ohio: Charles E. Merrill Publishing Co., 1969.

Warren, Roland, Rose, Stephen, and Bergunder, Ann. *The Structure of Urban Reform.* Lexington, Mass.: Lexington Books, 1974.

Warwick, Donald P. *A Theory of Public Bureaucracy: Politics, Personality, and Organization in the State Department.* Cambridge, Mass.: Harvard University Press, 1975.

Weber, Max. *Economy and Society,* 4th ed. G. Roth and C. Wittich, eds. Vols. 1 & 3. New York: Irvington Publications, 1968.

————. *The Theory of Social and Economic Organization.* A. M. Henderson and T. Parsons, trans. and eds. New York: Oxford University Press, Inc., 1947.

Weick, Karl. "Educational Organizations as Loosely Coupled Systems." *Administrative Science Quarterly* 21, no. 1 (March 1976): 1–19.

————. *The Social Psychology of Organizing.* Reading, Mass.: Addison-Wesley Co., 1969.

White, R., and Lippett, R. *Autocracy and Democracy.* Westport, Conn.: Greenwood Press, Inc., 1972.

Whitehead, T. N. *Leadership in a Free Society.* Cambridge, Mass.: Harvard University Press, 1936.

Whyte, William F. "Human Relations—a Progress Report." In *Complex Organizations*, Amitai Etzioni, ed. New York: Holt, Rinehart & Winston, Inc., 1962.

_____. *Money and Motivation*. Westport, Conn.: Greenwood Press, Inc., 1977.

Wildavsky, Aaron. *Politics of the Budgetary Process*, 2nd ed. Boston: Little, Brown & Company, 1974.

Wilensky, Harold L. "Human Relations in the Workplace." In Conrad Arensberg et al., *Research in Industrial Human Relations: A Critical Appraisal*. New York: Harper & Row, Inc., 1957.

_____. *Organizational Intelligence: Knowledge and Policy in Government and Industry*. New York: Basic Books, Inc., 1969.

_____. "The Professionalization of Everyone?" *American Journal of Sociology* 70 (September 1964): 137–158.

_____, and Lebeaux, Charles N. *Industrial Society and Social Welfare*, rev. ed. New York: The Free Press, 1965.

Wolin, Sheldon. *Politics and Vision: Continuity and Innovation in Western Political Thought*. Boston: Little, Brown & Company, 1960.

Woodward, Joan, ed. *Industrial Organization: Behavior and Control*. London: Oxford University Press, 1970.

_____. *Industrial Organization: Theory and Practice*. London: Oxford University Press, 1965.

Woodward, Robert, and Bernstein, Carl. *All the President's Men*. New York: Simon & Schuster, Inc., 1974.

Worthy, James C. "Organizational Structure and Employee Morale." *American Sociological Review* 15 (1950): 169–179.

Wright, Erik Olin. *Class Crisis and the State*. Schocken Books, Inc., 1978.

_____. "To Control or Smash Bureaucracy: Weber and Lenin on Politics, the State and Bureaucracy." *Berkeley Journal of Sociology* 19 (1975): 69–108.

Zachariah, Mathew. "The Impact of Darwin's Theory of Evolution on Theories of Society." *Social Studies* 62, no. 2 (February 1971): 69–76.

Zald, Mayer N. "The Correctional Institution for Juvenile Offenders: An Analysis of Organization 'Character.'" *Social Problems* 8, no. 1 (Summer 1960): 57–67.

_____. "Power Balance and Staff Conflict in Correctional Institutions." *Administrative Science Quarterly* 7 (June 1962): 22–49.

_____, ed. *Power in Organizations*. Nashville, Tenn.: Vanderbilt University Press, 1970; entire issue of *Administrative Science Quarterly* 14, no. 4 (December 1969).

_____. "On the Social Control of Industries." *Social Forces* 57, no. 1 (September 1978).

_____, and Ash, Robert. "Social Movement Organizations: Growth, Decay, and Change." *Social Forces* 44, no. 3 (March 1966): 327–341.

_____, and Denton, Patricia. "From Evangelism to General Service: The Transformation of the YMCA." *Administrative Science Quarterly* 8, no. 2 (September 1963): 214–234.

Zeitlin, Maurice. *American Society, Inc.* Chicago: Markham Publishing Co., 1970.

Index